ELIZABETH, SHAKESPEARE AND THE CASTLE

The story of the Kenilworth revels

Ronald Binns

Zoilus Press

First published in Great Britain by Zoilus Press in 2008

A CIP catalogue record for this book is available from the British Library.

ISBN   978-1902878997

Printed by CPI Group, Eastbourne
Typeset by Electrograd

Contents

Preface   1
Acknowledgements   3

1   The castle   5
2   The second visitor   11
3   Elizabeth and Leicester   18
4   'a spy, an atheist and a godless person'   22
5   The first day   35
6   The savage man   44
7   The mermaid and the dolphin   53
8   The masque in the chase   73
9   Crisis   84
10   Sylvanus   91
11   The great hoax   97
12   Woodstock   111
13   A satirist unmasked   117
14   The mysterious *Pastime of the Progress*   125
15   Subterranean textual blues   133
16   Gaudina and Contarenus   149
17   Philip Sidney's revenge   157
18   The Protheus anomaly   167
19   'counterfeit supposes'   175
20   The secret voice of Shakespeare   191
21   Elsinore's ghosts   199
22   'this bare island'   217
23   Zabeta and the others   229

Appendix One: The 19 days   237
Appendix Two: The hunting masque   241
Appendix Three: The huntsman's speech   245
Notes   247
Bibliography   262
Index   268

Illustrations

Leicester's Building	17
The Gascoigne coat of arms	34
A plan of Kenilworth Castle	51
The site of the bay where the mermaid and dolphin floated	71
Leicester's Building	90
The inner courtyard, looking west	96
The Patten coat of arms	109
George Gascoigne: the *Steele Glas* portrait	156
The Gascoigne memorial, Walthamstow	165
The Great Hall, Kenilworth Castle	173
The curtain wall and Leicester's Building	190
The promontory west of Kenilworth Castle	197

(Illustrations 1, 2, 4, 5, 6, 7, 9, 10, 11 and 12 © Ronald Binns)

Preface

The broad outlines of Elizabeth I's visit to Kenilworth Castle in July 1575 are well known. The popular account runs something like this: at Kenilworth that summer the Queen enjoyed the greatest entertainment of her long reign. The visit was a tremendous success. In the glorious surroundings of a fabulous castle beside the greatest artificial lake in England, Elizabeth was entertained by her host, Robert Dudley, Earl of Leicester. Day after day there were masques, speeches, plays, firework displays, dancing, banquets and a range of other amusements, including deer-hunts. It marked the grand climax of the most remarkable of all her royal 'progresses' (or official tours) around England.

This image was perfectly captured by the Victorian lithographer, John Brandard, in a much-reproduced picture which portrays the moment that the Queen first arrived at Kenilworth Castle. Beneath a pale blue sky, Elizabeth rides through a vast crowd of onlookers. A firework explodes like a gigantic white fern above the ancient battlements. The Queen sits side-saddle on her magnificent stallion, banners fluttering behind her, a white, virginal goddess dominating a colourful sea of admirers. Royal authority and dignity are aligned to the tradition and history represented by the castle in the background. The colourful costumes and the glorious weather signify the impending, joyous carnival. This lithograph perfectly expresses a popular image of the long, golden summer of Elizabeth's early reign – a carefree, merry England of gorgeous spectacle, affluence, tranquillity and good cheer.

In fact, every detail of the Brandard picture is demonstrably false. But so, too, is the conventional account of what occurred at Kenilworth. The romantic image of the Queen's visit to the castle owes much to a hugely influential work of fiction – Sir Walter Scott's bestselling historical novel, *Kenilworth*.

The sixteenth century reality was very different. There was the rumour of a failed assassination attempt. The royal visit exploded into crisis and the entertainments programme collapsed. An anonymous hoaxer mocked the Earl's hospitality and made fun of a member of the royal household. He was tracked down and unmasked. An extraordinarily diverse collection of Tudor writing talent assembled at Kenilworth, only for it to become a snake pit of literary jealousies and animosities

1

which were still felt years afterwards.

And on the sidelines, staring at the fireworks and listening to the speeches was an eleven year old from nearby Stratford-upon-Avon… Or was he? Katherine Duncan-Jones and Stephen Greenblatt, who are both leading scholars of the period and major modern biographers of Shakespeare, each believe Shakespeare was present at Kenilworth. Other writers are either brusquely dismissive or simply ignore the possibility. One demonstrable connection between the Kenilworth entertainments and Shakespeare's *oeuvre* exists through the figure of George Gascoigne. Once the most popular writer in England, Gascoigne was centrally involved in the July entertainments and Shakespeare was unquestionably familiar with his work. Today, Gascoigne is a shadowy and largely unread Tudor writer, but as actor, poet and dramatist, he provides the foundation for the hypothesis that Shakespeare's own drama bears the imprint of the Kenilworth experience and the playwright's continuing interest in it.

Sir Walter Scott's historical romance *Kenilworth* lies at the root of modern interest in Queen Elizabeth's visit to the castle. But the truth about what really happened at Kenilworth in July 1575 is much stranger, more complicated and more interesting than any fiction. This reality has for too long been buried away in sixteenth century publications that hardly anybody reads or in scholarship known only to academic specialists. Unravelling what really did happen at the castle and afterwards involves scrutinising three anonymous sixteenth century works, two misattributed books and a stunningly successful hoax. It is a story which begins amid the windswept, melancholy ruins of a castle in Warwickshire and ends in the Rare Books room of the British Library.

In short, this book is a history, an interpretation and a speculation. It aims to provide the first comprehensive documentary account of Queen Elizabeth's nineteen day visit to Kenilworth Castle in July 1575, collating all the available sources. Two rare and little-known texts related to the Kenilworth revels are reproduced as appendices. In critically examining all these sources this book examines how the royal visit was mediated, both at the time and subsequently. Finally, it considers the impact which the revels made upon all those significant Tudor figures who were present and how, in their various ways, they responded to that unique experience.

Acknowledgements

I would like to thank the English Heritage staff at the Kenilworth Castle site for their friendly and helpful responses during my visits. I am also grateful to the staff at the Public Record Office and the British Library, in London. I owe two special debts. The first is to my brother Jim, who has been a constant source of advice and information, has supplied me with a wide range of material, and who has translated the Latin and Italian quoted in this book. I could not have written this book without his help. My second debt is to my family - Elizabeth, Daniel and Anna – who made this book possible in other but no less valuable ways. Lastly, I should mention the contribution of Dr Brian O'Kill in helping to unravel a central aspect of the Kenilworth record. I first met Brian when we were both writing our Ph.D. theses on the same twentieth century novelist, Malcolm Lowry. He was amusing company and by far the brightest scholar on the Lowry circuit. Researching this book, I was surprised to come across his name and work once again, through his involvement with Transactions of the Cambridge Bibliographical Society, of which I previously knew nothing. Less of a surprise was to encounter yet again his versatility and his genius for critical analysis. Brian O'Kill went on to become a distinguished lexicographer and editor of the New Edition of the Longman Dictionary of the English Language. He died, far too young, in 1991. I dedicate this book to his memory.

1 The castle

Kenilworth Castle is often described as the most romantic ruined castle in England. Situated alongside the old road between Warwick and Coventry, its spectacular seven acre site dominates the surrounding Warwickshire countryside. It rises up, a vast structure of walls and battlements and towers, like a castle in a fairy tale. To see Kenilworth Castle for the first time is to see the very essence of what we imagine a castle should be.

Although some sections were deliberately demolished in the seventeenth century, its main features remain substantially intact. Today, Elizabeth I would still recognise the castle she knew during her famous visit. The castle's outer curtain wall remains much as it did over four hundred years ago. The long, straight tiltyard along which Elizabeth passed on the evening of July 9 1575 is still there and, as it did for her, it functions as the main pathway into the castle. The central features of the castle complex – the Norman keep, the Great Hall and the Tudor residential block – still stand, though their roofs have gone and the interiors have been gutted.

The most obvious and biggest transformation since 1575 has been in the castle surroundings, not the castle itself. The massive artificial lake has gone, though its site remains as a natural amphitheatre of marshy, grass-covered open land. The surrounding parkland has vanished and the great swathes of forest where Elizabeth and her courtiers hunted deer have long since been felled and built on. Only a tiny fragment remains, in the form of Chase Wood, two miles west of the castle. Kenilworth itself is no longer a small, rural market town but an urban sprawl to the east of the castle, its centre by-passed by the A452 trunk road.

Long before Elizabeth's legendary visit, the historic significance and associations of the castle went back centuries. The Domesday Book of 1086 records 'Chinewrde' [Kenilworth] as a small settlement inside the Forest of Arden. An early Saxon fortress of earth and wood was constructed on a small hill surrounded by marshland. This site was massively expanded in the twelfth century, when the deep outer moat and the large Norman keep known as Caesar's Tower were constructed. Its massive, thick red sandstone walls were designed to be impregnable.

At the beginning of the thirteenth century King John enlarged the castle. The outer curtain wall was erected, enclosing the seven acre site in a vast oval of stone. Towers were added and local streams diverted and dammed to create a massive lake, sometimes called the Great Mere. This was over a mile long, to the south and west of the castle, with a broad moat on the other two sides. It was the largest artificial lake in the kingdom, covering over 100 acres. Those streams still exist today, and run across what was once the bed of the lake.

In 1253 ownership was granted to Simon de Montfort, Earl of Leicester. He died during the conflict between the barons and Henry III, and the following year, 1266, the king's forces laid siege to the castle. It was the longest siege in English history and the castle proved impregnable. The defenders only surrendered after nine months because of depleted supplies and sickness. In the peace that followed a legendary tournament known as the Round Table of Knights was held at the castle, involving 100 knights and their ladies. In a prelude to the better-known sixteenth century entertainment, it became the site of feasts, dances and jousting.

The next great period of reconstruction occurred under John of Gaunt, Duke of Lancaster, who took control of the castle in 1361 and turned it into a luxury residence. The Great Hall was built, with the largest span of any timber hammer-beamed roof in England. Today, the roof is gone, but the walls and ornamental stonework remain, together with the massive windows and the great fireplace.

It was here, to Kenilworth Castle, that Henry V retired after victory at Agincourt. Henry had a timber banqueting house constructed on the far side of the Great Mere, known as The Pleasaunce on the Marsh. It was reached by royal barge, and the outline of the harbour channel and the original earthworks can still be seen. A later royal visitor to Kenilworth was Henry VIII, who had the banqueting house dismantled and set up much closer to the castle. The king also enlarged the castle accommodation. 'Henry VIII's Lodging' was located south of the Keep and formed part of the oval-shaped wall which enclosed the inner court.

The last person significantly to develop the Kenilworth site was Robert Dudley, a man whose presence looms large in the story which is to follow.

If you enter Warwickshire on a motorway or trunk road you are greeted by blue signs welcoming you to the county of Shakespeare. Alongside the words of welcome are an uneven vertical line and the outline of a bear. When I pass these signs I sometimes wonder how many people understand what the connection is between Shakespeare, a bolt of lightning and a polar bear. Not many, I suspect. Yet if you visit Holy Trinity church in Stratford-upon-Avon, where Shakespeare lies buried beneath his famous grave slab in the chancel, you will find not far away, carved on the south side, the same enigmatic symbols.

But of course it isn't a polar bear and it isn't a bolt of lightning. It's a muzzled bear and a ragged staff (or uneven wooden stake). This was the badge of the Dudley family, whose most outstanding member in Elizabethan times was handsome, wealthy, powerful Robert Dudley, Earl of Leicester. Dudley put it everywhere – in towns he patronised, on buildings he owned, on his furniture, linen, cutlery and armour, on his portraits, and on the livery of his servants. So did his brother Ambrose, Earl of Warwick. Literally, it showed a bear and a stake, depicting the grisly Tudor sport of setting dogs on a chained bear and betting on which species would survive a fight to the death. It could also be interpreted as showing a dancing bear and the knobbly stick which the bear's keeper held. Itinerant entertainers were still travelling around with ragged staffs and dancing bears as late as the end of the nineteenth century. It was an apt symbol for Robert Dudley to use as his aristocratic logo, because he was a man very interested in entertainment. The pageantry he put on for Elizabeth I at Kenilworth Castle was, as far as England in the second half of the sixteenth century was concerned, the greatest show on earth. But he had other interests as well. He was an early friend of the English theatre, and in June 1559 he became the patron of a group of actors. They wore his livery and enjoyed his protection in an age when actors were seen in some quarters as dangerously subversive and plays a magnet for all kinds of dissolute behaviour. The Earl of Leicester was also something of an intellectual, and a sponsor of many kinds of writing. Scholars, philosophers and poets all dedicated works to him, in the hope of a tangible reward.

Despite those road signs, there was no direct connection between him and Shakespeare at all. In the second half of the sixteenth century Robert Dudley was Warwickshire's most prominent figure. He would subsequently be supplanted for all time by the glover's son from Stratford-upon-Avon. Dudley was dead before Shakespeare's career as a playwright ever began. Yet there was, oddly enough, an indirect connection between the two. What it was can be summed up in two words: Kenilworth Castle.

In July 1575 the castle was where the destinies of the most powerful aristocrat in England and an obscure schoolboy from a nearby market town briefly intersected. They never met face to face, though Shakespeare probably glimpsed Dudley from amid the crowds of spectators. And what happened there changed both their lives forever.

In 1563 the castle was returned to Dudley by Elizabeth, after its ten-year confiscation by the Crown following his father's involvement in the plot to put Lady Jane Grey on the throne. A year later the Queen made him Baron of Denbigh and Earl of Leicester.

For more than a decade Robert Dudley spent a small fortune transforming Kenilworth into a Tudor palace. Much of the stone came from nearby Kenilworth Abbey, which was almost completely demolished. Large rectangular windows were installed in the Norman keep and a columned gallery was built to link it to an ornamental garden containing walks, plants, flowers, an aviary, an obelisk and a fountain with statuary of antique marine gods. English Heritage, the modern custodian of the castle site, continues to reconstruct the Tudor garden. Though the garden is not yet as mature or as lavish as the one Elizabeth would have known, the aim is to reproduce it to a reasonable degree of historical accuracy.

Under the Earl of Leicester's ownership of the castle, the gatehouse which originally formed the rear of the castle was enlarged, modernized and turned it into the entrance. A timbered bridge 14 feet wide and 600 feet long led from it across an arm of the Great Mere to The Chase. Here there was an extensive area of parkland and forest, stocked with deer and other game. The Chase also contained many walks, arbours and bowers. A survey of the estate made during the reign of James I describes 'a Parklike ground...with 15. severall Coppisses [coppices] lyeng altogether, conteyning 789. acres within the same; which, in the Earle of Leicesters tyme, were stored with Red deere.'[1]

It also noted that 'There runneth through the said grounds by the walls of the said Castle a faire Poole, conteyning 111 acres, well stored with fish and fowle, which at pleasure is to be lett round about the Castle... The Circuits of the Castle, Manors, Parks, and Chase, lieing round, together conteyne at least 19. or 20. miles, in a pleasaunt Countrey, - the like both for strength, state, and pleasure not being within the Realme of England.'

The bridge and the Mere have gone but the great gatehouse remains completely intact today (though a gabled block was added to the east side in the seventeenth century, and the gateway arch was blocked off at both ends by bay windows and turned into rooms). The Earl's initials 'R.D.' can still be seen above the wooden doorway on the west side, with Tudor Rose roundels beside the letters.

At the head of the lake, two new towers were constructed – Mortimer's Tower and the Flood Gate or Gallery Tower, which stood at one end of the tilt yard and included a large observation room for watching displays of Tilting and Barriers. Dudley also had a large, luxury apartment block with tall mullioned windows built overlooking the lake. Its shell remains, unimaginatively known as 'Leicester's Building'. This seems to have been built partly in response to Elizabeth's dissatisfaction with her accommodation on a visit made in August 1568.[2]

The seventeenth century surveyors admired the splendour of the buildings:

> The Castle & 4 Gate-houses all covered with Lead, whereby it is subject to no other decay then the glasse, through the extremity of weather.
>
> The Roomes of great State within the same, & and such as are able to receave his Majestie, the Queen, and Prince, at one tyme, built with as much uniformity and conveniency as any houses of later tyme; and with such stately Sellars [cellars], all caried upon pillars, and Architecture of free stone carved and wrought, as the like are not within this Kingdome; and also all other houses for Offices aunswerable.

Three engravings of the castle and its environs, giving some idea of what Kenilworth looked like in the period of the Queen's visit, were printed in William Dugdale's *The Antiquities of Warwickshire* (1656).

9

These stunning panoramas make it clear what a magnificent, dreamlike place the castle was in its heyday – vastly more impressive than Windsor Castle or the Tower of London.

Robert Dudley, Earl of Leicester, was determined to exploit every aspect of this fabulous setting for the Queen's visit in the summer of 1575. The interior furnishings were evidently palatial; an inventory taken some three years afterwards lists hundreds of luxury objects. These include wall hangings embroidered with scenes from mythology and the Bible, ornate silver tableware, beds, pillows, quilts, rugs, carpets, 'Close stooles' of quilted black velvet with pewter pans, a black ebony chess board set with silver and gold chessmen, perfumed 'Swete bagges', a collection of musical instruments including a portable organ, virginals covered in black velvet, viols, flutes, 'bandoraes' (a type of early guitar) and lutes.[3] There was also an important collection of paintings, whose subjects included aristocrats and royalty, as well as such inspiring figures as Alexander the Great and an image of Julius Caesar 'enameled in brasse'. Intriguingly, the collection included the great Catholic enemy, the Duke of Alva, oppressor of the Low Countries, though this was balanced by 'the prince Orainge' (i.e. William the Silent, hero of the Protestant resistance) and 'the princes Wife'.

There was also a philosophical 'picture of occasion and time', 'a table of my lordes armes', framed pictures of five of the planets, 'a table of the risinge and fallinge of the sonne' and twenty-three 'cardes or mappes' of (unidentified) countries. Dominating this collection were four life-sized paired paintings of Elizabeth and Robert Dudley, specially commissioned for the 1575 royal visit. Two, by Federico Zuccaro, are lost (though the preliminary drawings survive) and the descriptions of the other two match paintings held by the Reading Museum and the National Portrait Gallery. These last four paintings were for more than mere show, however. Their size signified that the Leicester and Elizabeth were not simply bigger in importance than all those others but that the couple were in a sense equal. Robert Dudley had a double agenda in entertaining the Queen and his picture collection formed just one part of a wider campaign which was to become much clearer as each day of the royal visit passed.

2 The second visitor

Elizabeth I was the first of two visitors who made Kenilworth Castle a source of interest which has endured into the twenty-first century. Two contemporary accounts of what occurred there in July 1575 have survived. Both were originally published anonymously, although it is now possible to say who wrote them, and why.

The first, 87 pages long, was entitled *A Letter: whearin part of the Entertainement untoo the Queenz Maiesty, at Killingwoorth Castl in Warwik Sheer, in this Soomerz Progress, 1575, iz signified: from a freend officer attendant in the Coourt, unto his freend a Citizen and Merchaunt of London.* It gave a vivid description of what happened at Kenilworth and is the main source of modern accounts of the Queen's visit.

The second had an equally wordy title: *The princelye pleasures at the Courte at Kenelwoorth. That is to say; the Copies of all such Verses, Proses or Poeticall inventions, and other devices of pleasure as were there devised by sundry Gentlemen, before the Qvene's Majestie: in the year 1575.* It supplied many of the scripts which were enacted before Elizabeth and was the Tudor equivalent of trying to cash in on a movie by publishing the screenplay.

For the next two centuries these accounts sank into obscurity, and curiosity about Elizabeth's visit to Kenilworth faded. Then, at the end of the eighteenth century, there was a slow revival of interest. It was greatly accelerated by another visitor to the Kenilworth site, who turned it into a place of romantic pilgrimage. This person was Walter Scott, whose bestselling novel *Kenilworth* was published in 1821.

Scott's Edinburgh publisher, Constable, had urged him to write a historical novel set in the time of Elizabeth I. He suggested it should be set against the background of the failed Spanish invasion and bear the simple title *The Armada.* The idea of an Elizabethan novel appealed to Scott, but the time and subject matter proposed by his publisher did not. Instead he drew on a ballad he'd loved as a child and conflated its subject matter – the mysterious and sinister death of the Earl of Leicester's first wife, Amy Robsart – with Elizabeth's visit to Kenilworth Castle in 1575.

Scott, then 50, was at the height of his powers and commercial success. He is credited with having invented the genre of the

11

historical novel with his novel *Waverley* (1814). Scott was a prolific writer who produced 27 novels in all, as well as collections of ballads and poems, a biography of Napoleon, essays and reviews, and twelve volumes of correspondence. In his lifetime, Scott was regarded as a major figure, admired across Europe. Nowadays, like a minor rock band from the 1960s, Scott retains a small, loyal band of admirers, but his once-massive reputation has largely collapsed. No one would now seriously consider his swashbuckling romances as being artistically equal to the novels of, say, Jane Austen or Flaubert.

Interest in the Queen's visit had been reawakened at the end of the eighteenth century by the publication of John Nichols's *The Progresses and Public Processions of Queen Elizabeth* (1788). In two enormous volumes Nichols assembled all the Tudor documentary material he could lay his hands on about the official engagements of Elizabeth I, including 'other solemnities, public expenditures, and remarkable events during the reign of that illustrious princess.' This massive treasury of documentary material included both *A Letter* and *The princelye pleasures*. It renewed interest in Elizabeth I and coincided with a burgeoning interest in Shakespeare's plays as words rather than productions. 'In the eighteenth century,' Gary Taylor observes, '[Shakespeare's plays] became things; they became, primarily, books... as the eighteenth century progresses Shakespeare editions surround the text with an expanding border of annotation, an undertext of commentary that repeatedly interrupts a reading of the uppertext.'[1]

Nichols's books fed a growing appetite for knowledge about Elizabethan England, and in 1805 he brought out a third massive volume, supplementing the earlier ones, and carrying the story of royal progresses through into the time of James I. A fourth volume appeared in the same year as *Kenilworth*. After the success of Scott's *Kenilworth* an abridged second edition was published in three volumes in 1823, to cash in on the accelerating interest in Elizabeth's progresses. In fact it was probably Nichols, not Scott, who first put Kenilworth Castle on the modern tourist map. By 1813 – eight years before the first edition of *Kenilworth* – a 36-page tourist guide offering *A Concise History and Description of Kenilworth Castle, from its foundation to the present time*, with a folding plan of the site, was in its ninth edition, 'sold by the booksellers in Warwick,

Coventry and the principal inns in Kenilworth'. In 1784 an enterprising Warwick publisher, J. Sharp, had already brought out the first edition of *A Letter* to be published since the sixteenth century; another edition followed in 1794.

Scott himself was interested in the castle long before anyone suggested he write a historical novel set in Elizabethan England. He visited the site in 1815 and on at least one previous occasion. The Signet Library and the Advocates Library in Edinburgh both held copies of Dugdale's *Antiquities of Warwickshire*, which Scott almost certainly drew on for his novel. Scott's name appears in the list of subscribers to *Kenilworth Illustrated*, a lavish, illustrated volume which incorporated material from Dugdale and the Tudor sources in a new account of the castle, abbey and church. The volume was published the same year as *Kenilworth*, showing that Scott's novel tapped a growing interest in the castle, which it then hugely expanded.

The impact made by Scott's novel is indicated at one extreme by Donizetti's opera *Elisabetta al castello di Kenilworth* and at the other by the collection left by the pioneering Victorian photographer Frederick Scott Archer (1813-1857), inventor of the wet collodion process. Archer's innovation allowed exposure times of as little as a second, making it possible for the first time to photograph objects in motion, such as breaking waves and smoke rising from a steamboat. But the subject that most fascinated Archer was static. He compiled an album of atmospheric shots of Kenilworth Castle and its ivy covered walls.

For his novel, Scott diligently researched the history of the castle. His reading in a wide range of sixteenth century material underpinned his fictional Kenilworth and the characters he placed there. His description of the castle is substantially accurate, although he invented secret passages, renamed the Strong Tower Mervyn's Tower, and gave it a balcony. He also called the south wing of the Great Hall the Saintlowe Tower, by which wholly fictitious name it is still known today. The plot of *Kenilworth* intermingles historical figures and invented characters. The eighteenth century ballad 'Cumnor Hall' by William Julius Mickle supplied Scott with his heroine, Amy Robsart, and with the embryo of his plot. Leicester's wife Robsart had been found with a broken neck at the foot of a flight of stairs at their home. His enemies were quick to jump to the conclusion that he had ordered her murder to clear the way for his marriage to Eliabeth.

The ballad narrates the broken-hearted complaints of Robsart, abandoned and neglected at Cumnor Hall, while her husband is away at court flirting with the Queen. Her premonitions of death are duly borne out:

> And ere the dawn of day appear'd,
> In Cumnor Hall so lone and dreare,
> Full manye a piercing screame was hearde,
> And manye a crye of mortal feare.

After this foul play the village maids 'with fearful glance, / Avoid the antient mossgrowne walle' and passing travellers sigh and pensively weep at the thought of the countess's fate when they glimpse 'The haunted tow'rs of Cumnor Halle.'

The ballad supplies mood music more than a narrative. The Countess is murdered but though the motive is hinted at – Leicester arranged the crime in order to make him free to marry Elizabeth – the details are left mysterious. Mickle's ballad is a self-consciously 'literary' production rather than a street ballad. Its sentimentality and stock romantic properties – a lonely building on a moonlit night, a melancholy countess pining away from neglect and ill-treatment – evidently had a powerful impact on Scott's childhood imagination and temperament. It is easy enough to see how a visit to the ruins of Kenilworth allowed him emotionally to relocate the heroine of the ballad to Warwickshire.

In the early nineteenth century the Kenilworth site was massively over-run by ivy, trees, bushes and other vegetation, the ruins draped in greenery. Today, apart from a few outlying trees, this has been entirely removed, to prevent it accelerating the decay of the stonework.

In Scott's time there were grassy-coated mounds of rubble left over from the demolition of parts of the structure. These have been levelled, and nowadays the site bears a much stronger resemblance to how it looked in the sixteenth century than in the nineteenth.

Consciously or unconsciously, the wilderness of Kenilworth must have reminded Scott of the ballad's imagery of Cumnor Hall, with its moss-coated walls and haunted towers. In writing his novel *Kenilworth* Scott not only developed what the ballad left mysterious – how Amy Robsart was killed, who killed her, and why – but he also managed to link romantic Cumnor Hall with romantic Kenilworth through the starring role played by Robert Dudley, Earl of Leicester, at both historic sites.

In *Kenilworth* Amy Robsart dumps her fiancé, Edmund Tressilian, and secretly marries the Earl of Leicester, who, to avoid embarrassment at court, keeps her effectively under house arrest at Cumnor. Tressilian mistakenly believes that Amy has been kidnapped by Leicester's Master of the Horse, Richard Varney, and complains to Elizabeth. To protect Leicester, Varney asserts that Amy is his wife. The Queen demands that Amy be brought to her when she visits Kenilworth Castle. Varney plots to prevent this but is outwitted by Amy, who makes her way to Kenilworth, where she encounters Elizabeth and begs for her help.

Because Robsart won't admit to her marriage to Leicester, Elizabeth regards her as deluded, and she is returned to Varney's custody. Varney convinces Leicester that Amy has been unfaithful to him with Tressilian, and Leicester agrees to her murder.

Varney returns to Cumnor with Amy. But Leicester changes his mind and sends a messenger after Varney. Tressilian, meanwhile, duels with Leicester at the castle and is only saved from being killed when the Earl is shown a letter from Amy which clears him. Leicester confesses everything to Elizabeth, who sends Tressilian to Cumnor to rescue Amy. He is too late. Leicester's messenger has been treacherously shot and the order never countermanded. Tressilian arrives moments after Amy's murder. Varney is arrested and executed. Tressilian embarks for Virginia and dies prematurely of a broken heart. After a short banishment from the court, Leicester returns there and resumes his role as one of Elizabeth's chief advisers.

When *Kenilworth* appeared on 8 January 1821 it was another great success for Scott. Readers and most reviewers loved the novel, though some disliked the tragic ending. Only the *British Review* grumbled that the novel had been written 'in a spirit of bookmaking'. Fans made pilgrimages both to Kenilworth and the site of Cumnor

Place. At Cumnor, just outside Oxford, the landlord of the local inn hurriedly changed its name to match the one described in the novel.

Although Scott's critical reputation has declined sharply since its heyday, the book's popularity has continued. *Kenilworth* remains in print, and its modern editor has praised it as 'one of the most satisfyingly constructed of the Waverley Novels'[2] and one in which readers will find 'an unforgettable picture of a brilliant society with a "melancholy tale" at its rotten heart.'[3]

But as a fictional recreation of Tudor England in 1575, *Kenilworth* presents problems. The dialogue consists of nineteenth century English (which is not all that different from twenty-first century English), cosmetically sprinkled with words and phrases such as 'thy', 'doth', 'sirrah', 'methinks', 'I wot not', 'my pretty coz'.

Scott in fact simply copied these expressions out of Shakespeare's plays. The result is a synthetic Elizabethan dialogue which often seems unconvincing and horribly bogus, even at times unintentionally comic.

Secondly, the novel abounds in anachronisms. Its basic story is, historically, nonsense. Scott gives us an Amy Robsart who is 18 in 1575. But Robert Dudley married Amy Robsart in 1549, when they were both teenagers. It was almost certainly an arranged marriage and there was nothing remotely secret about it. Among the guests were Edward VI and the future Queen Elizabeth. Robsart was never engaged to Edmund Tressilian, who was invented by Scott.

The novelist's concern for historical accuracy in representing Kenilworth Castle is in stark contrast to his lack of attention to the biographical realities of the real Elizabethans he peopled it with. Scott puts Amy Robsart at the castle and the novel climaxes with her murder: 'The news of the Countess's dreadful fate put a sudden period to the Pleasures of Kenilworth.'[4] But Amy died in 1560 – fifteen years before Elizabeth arrived for the extravaganza at the castle.

Repeatedly in *Kenilworth*, Scott displays a cheerful indifference to the historical reality of 1575 and simply tosses in anything from the Elizabethan era that appealed to him. One minor character says that he has worked as an actor at the Globe – a theatre not built until 1599. Another quotes from Spenser's *Cantos of Mutabilitie*, first published in 1609. At court, Robert Dudley comes face to face with the bard:

Leicester's Building

- Ha, Will Shakespeare – wild Will! – thou hast given my nephew, Philip Sidney, love-powder – he cannot sleep without thy Venus and Adonis under his pillow! – we will have thee hanged for the veriest wizard in Europe.[5]

We can be confident that no such merry words as these were ever uttered, since *Venus and Adonis* was not published until 1593, by which time both Sidney and the Earl of Leicester were dead.

No modern historical novelist would dare to write with such scant regard for chronological or biographical accuracy. It would be like writing a Second World War novel featuring Prince Charles, in which the characters listen to Beatles records and play computer games.

Scott was right to put Leicester and Elizabeth at the centre of the action in *Kenilworth*. But ironically he never knew that the truth of what occurred at the castle in the year 1575 was far more curious and dramatic than the creaky melodrama he fitted around the bare facts of the royal visit. The entertainment programme *was* abruptly and dramatically terminated – but not by the murder of Amy Robsart.

3   Elizabeth and Leicester

By 1575, Elizabeth I was well used to progresses. A 'progress' was an official royal tour. Elizabeth went on them in the summer months throughout her long reign, staying at the homes of aristocrats and leading members of the gentry.

A progress served a variety of functions. It allowed the common people outside London what might literally be a once in a lifetime chance to see their sovereign. It added a useful supplement to the royal treasury: wherever Elizabeth went she was presented with lavish gifts.

A progress reinforced the legitimacy of her regime in other ways. Where the Queen went, her government went – in the shape of that trusted inner circle of advisers and administrators known as the Privy Council.   Leading members of local society who were less than sympathetic to the Protestant religion were interrogated en route and invited to mend their ways. Stubborn adherents to the old faith might find themselves obliged to go and live with a clergyman who would debate doctrine with them.   Important dissidents were sometimes imprisoned and left to confront their consciences in cold, damp unhealthy prison cells, where they were forgotten, and sometimes died.

A sinister and shadowy figure who sometimes attended progresses was Sir Richard Topcliffe, the Queen's torturer. What Scott breezily called 'the old days of merry England'[1] was a time when 800 prisoners were annually executed in public, and where branding and amputation were common punishments.

Even the most loyal subjects regarded the invitation to supply the Queen with hospitality as a mixed blessing. On the plus side there was the opportunity to impress her with a lavish gift and some suitably flattering entertainment. To have her in your own home meant you were able to press your case regarding a dispute, or perhaps plead for a favour. But on the negative side was the massive personal expenditure required to entertain her in the style to which she was accustomed.

There was also the shattering impact of the arrival of the Queen's entourage. Elizabeth took her bath, bedding, furniture and a mass of other possessions with her, which required 200-300 horse-drawn wagons. A royal visit meant spectacular upheaval for the host's household, the ruination of lawns and gardens by cart wheels and hundreds of horses, as well as a certain amount of pilfering.

Sometimes the courtiers even brought the plague with them. One third of the population of Norwich died of it after the Queen's progress there in 1578.

*

Robert Dudley, Earl of Leicester, planned his great Kenilworth entertainment long in advance of the actual visit.

He had several advantages over other prospective hosts. He'd first met Elizabeth when they were children and, as he was fond of boasting, he knew her as well as anyone in England. He had accompanied her on numerous progresses in the past. Elizabeth had also visited Kenilworth before, on four occasions. On her first visits in 1565 and 1568 the castle had not yet been transformed into a playground. In 1572 she slipped out of Warwick for a fleeting private stay, then returned soon afterwards very publicly on her royal progress. It was on this last occasion, while she was hunting in The Chase, that a messenger arrived with the news of the St Bartholomew's Day massacre in Paris. This sectarian killing of around 4,000 people was an atrocity that shocked Protestant Europe.

By 1575 the great building programme was completed and the castle was ready to receive royalty on a lavish scale. Leicester pulled out all the stops and set about organising entertainments which would amuse both the common people of the area and the royal party. Some would be private but many would be visible to onlookers. The involvement of local people was used to underline the popularity of the Queen and of her gracious host, signifying the unity of the governing elite and commoners. The entertainments were also designed to contain two coded messages from Leicester to Elizabeth, which take us to the heart of their long and vexed relationship.

The story of Elizabeth I and Robert Dudley has been told many times, but even today key aspects remain mysterious. Our image of Elizabeth is a distorted one, in so far as the official portraits endlessly reproduced in books are idealized ones, on a par with propaganda images of any leader in an authoritarian society. She is unlikely ever to have been as striking as she appears in her paintings. The most realistic image of Elizabeth is the face on her marble tomb in Westminster Abbey, which was almost certainly carved from a death mask. It shows, in Susan Bassnett's words, 'a rather coarse-featured woman with a large nose and a set mouth.'[2] This description is consistent with what is probably the only accurate image of her in her lifetime, a chalk drawing by Federigo Zuccaro, sketched for a portrait commissioned by Dudley to be used in the royal visit to Kenilworth.

Although rightly described as 'probably the most famous Englishwoman ever to have lived'[2] and the subject of innumerable biographies, novels and movies, Elizabeth's life has become encrusted with romantic myth and speculation. After reading scores of books about the Queen, Bassnett describes how she found her hard to pin down. She was left with 'an impression of a woman of energy and cunning, a woman of intelligence and feeling who was determined to survive.'[3]

Robert Dudley is elusive in other ways. He was born about 1532, the fifth son of John Dudley, Earl of Warwick, Protector of England during the reign of the young Edward VI. In 1553 the Dudley family's involvement in the plot to prevent Mary's accession by installing Lady Jane Grey on the throne led to his incarceration in the Tower of London. Robert Dudley was held in the Beauchamp Tower, close to the Bell Tower, where Elizabeth herself was placed in custody after the abortive rebellion of Thomas Wyatt. John Dudley was executed but his son Robert was among those whose lives were spared. When Elizabeth became queen in 1558 she made him Master of the Horse and a privy councillor and showered him with gifts. Robert Dudley was tall, handsome, charming, and an expert equestrian. He was also a cultured, liberal man with an interest in learning and books. It quickly became apparent that Elizabeth was infatuated with Dudley, but the sudden, shocking and suspiciously timely death of his wife was a major impediment to their marriage, reinforced by the hostility of the Privy Council.

The death of Amy Robsart remains a mystery. Sir Walter Scott's main source for his knowledge of Robsart's death, Elias Ashmole's *Antiquities of Berkshire*, derived its view of the episode from a pamphlet which has come to be popularly known as *Leicester's*

Commonwealth. Published in 1585, this was actually a scurrilous, anonymous libel - an anthology of rumours and wild, malicious speculations. Its insinuation that the Earl was fond of poisoning his enemies was absurd nonsense, but it nevertheless found its way into *Kenilworth*.

The modern consensus is that Amy Robsart, who was suffering from what at the time was called a 'malady in the breast', had a form of cancer. Her death after falling down a flight of stairs was therefore probably an accident, resulting from bones made brittle and severely weakened by her illness.

The circumstances and timing of Robsart's sudden death meant that a marriage between Robert Dudley and Elizabeth was out of the question – at least in the short term. Their close relationship dragged on, year after year, but it was now often a tense and edgy one. He was one of her key advisers and he was more special to her than any other figure at court. The Queen flirted with him and flew into rages if he ever showed himself interested in any other woman, but she continued to resist marriage to him or to anyone else. Suitors from European royal families were intermittently in the frame as potential husbands but Elizabeth became a mistress of procrastination and vacillation. It was many, many years before the recognition finally arrived that the Queen firmly intended to remain single.

Ironically, Scott's novel *Kenilworth* contained more than a grain of truth in its portrait of Leicester as a man nursing a dark secret. Eleven months before the great entertainment at the castle, Lady Sheffield secretly gave birth to Leicester's child, on 7 August 1574.

The truth about the Earl's affairs is elusive but according to one popular account Dudley started the relationship with Douglas, Lady Sheffield in 1568. She was then 25 years old, beautiful, 'feather-headed and dazzling'.[5] Her husband found out, but before he could begin divorce proceedings he fell ill and died. Leicester, it was said, had had him poisoned. Whenever the relationship really began (and it may not have been until 1573), Leicester did not deny paternity. The child, a boy, was named Robert. But both the child and the affair with Lady Sheffield were kept very secret. Elizabeth knew nothing about this matter. And for this relationship, too, Kenilworth in July 1575 was to be a turning point.

4   'a spy, an atheist and a godless person'

The Earl of Leicester planned to cram a variety of entertainments into the Queen's visit, which was probably intended to last 20 days. There would be fireworks, feasting, pageants on the lake, bear baiting, deer hunting, masques, tableaux and plays.

Where feasting was concerned, Leicester could hardly hope to surpass the food put before Elizabeth by any other grand lord in the land. Elizabeth was well used to lavish banquets. But for the other entertainments he had one great advantage: Kenilworth and its grounds. One of the Queen's favourite pursuits was stag-hunting on horseback, and The Chase supplied an extensive stretch of woodland, kept well-stocked with game.

The castle itself was more a palace than a fortress, and more a fantasy playground and holiday resort than a home. It was like a gigantic theatre, with a variety of stunning locations for staging spectacles and dramas. Its historic structure, the product of conflict and siege, had been modified for the purposes of leisure. It was a fantasy come to life: a Tudor Gormenghast, with a vast, inter-locking structure of towers and stairways and ever-shifting perspectives.

As a setting for entertainment it had unrivalled facilities for an enormous audience. The common people of the region were free to line the shores of the great lake and gaze in wonder at a sequence of colourful pageants and shows set before them, day after day. And for the privileged guests inside the castle, there were innumerable vantage points from which to gaze and observe them at close quarters. There would also be private entertainments for the elite guests, including theatre, dancing, a spectacular garden and, most probably, a gallery containing the Earl's collection of fifty curtained paintings and twenty maps.

Self-promotion was incorporated into every aspect of the castle's physical texture. The stonework, inside and out, was carved with the initials 'R' (Robert) and 'L' (Leicester) and the Dudley ragged staff. This was replicated, often using silver and gold thread, on furniture and linen in the castle's scores of rooms, together with the Earl's coat of arms and his motto 'Droit et Loyal'.

Evidently inspired by continental water fêtes, the Earl made innovative use of The Great Mere as a huge watery stage for floating pageants, as well as a vast mirror to intensify the impact of sophisticated fireworks displays. The first recorded use of the word 'firework' in English is in connection with Kenilworth Castle in 1575. An Italian specialist was hired to orchestrate this crackling celestial extravaganza. The fireworks would be enjoyed by the local population, who'd flock to the shores of the lake to watch in wonder. Underlining his self-promoted role as benevolent and generous ruler of the locality, Leicester allowed the celebration of a rustic wedding at the castle and, at very short notice, performances of the annual Hock-Tuesday Play from nearby Coventry. The most important component of the entertainments was to be the speeches, masques and pageants. These were directed at the Queen and utilised to the full the dramatic real-life theatrical props supplied by the castle and its grounds. They were planned as learned and serious entertainments, using the talents of many speakers and actors. The intention was to include elements of folklore, Arthurian legend and myths and tales familiar from the Greek and Latin classics familiar to every educated person. It is a little ironic that Scott chose to cast Leicester as a dastardly villain in *Kenilworth*, because he was in fact a friend and patron of writers – 'the greatest Maecenas of his age.'[1]

> Writers, translators, chroniclers, preachers, and poets offered him the fruits of their labours, hailing him as champion of learning and virtue and promising him eternal glory as benefactor of the commonwealth. Doctors, lawyers, actors, soldiers, printers, all who had or claimed to have special services to render, stood ready at his command. That his response was gracious and generous there can be no question.[2]

To create original and impressive dramas to set before the Queen, Robert Dudley assembled a team of writers. It consisted of William Hunnis, Henry Goldyngham, William Patten, Richard Mulcaster, John Badger, George Ferrers and George Gascoigne. This was a very diverse collection of individuals, who had never worked together before. Their job was to write speeches and to speak them, as well as producing scripts and choreographing masques and pageants and acting in them, probably with the support of professional players.

Henry Goldyngham is a shadowy figure and the member of the team about whom we know the least.[3] His starring role at Kenilworth was to act in one of its most famous water pageants, in which role, according to one anecdote, he emerged as a boisterous extrovert.

William Hunnis, on the other hand, was a professional musician who had long associations with the royal household. He was a Gentleman of the Chapel Royal in the time of Edward VI. One of his earliest publications was *Certayne Psalms chosen out of the Psalter of David, and drawen furth into English meter* (1550). In 1566, when the previous incumbent died, he was appointed Master of the Children of the Queen's Chapel – in other words, choirmaster. The royal household retained four sets of singing-boys, from St Paul's Cathedral, Westminster Abbey, St George's Chapel, Windsor, and the Queen's Chapel. If his publications are anything to go by, Hunnis was of a devout religious disposition. When Leicester hired him for the entertainments, it seems quite plausible that he hired the choir too. In short, Hunnis was there to supply highly professional musical support. The records of the Office of Revels suggest that the choirs were elaborately costumed and coiffeured for their peformances, with wigs and ornamental head-tires in use. The accounts for 1573-4 record a payment to head-tire specialists who 'attended upon Mr Hunnyes [and] his Children & dressed theire heads &c, when they played before Her Majesty.'[4]

William Patten, born around 1510, seems to have been the oldest member of the team. A quarter of a century earlier he'd published *The expedicion into Scotlāde of the most woorthely fortunate prince Edward, Duke of Soomserset*, an account of the 1547 Pinkie campaign against the insurgent Scots. His second book, *A Calender of Scripture*, was a glossary of the proper names in the Bible and was probably published in April 1575 or not long afterwards. Patten had held a number of lucrative state appointments and was for two decades lord of the Manor of Stoke Newington. Two years before the royal visit to Kenilworth he'd been effectively bankrupted. He was an old associate of Lord Burghley, and was probably there as a favour to a man down on his luck, not because he'd been actively commissioned by Leicester.

'M. Ferrers, Lord of Mis-rule in the Court' – as Gascoigne describes him – was George Ferrers, who was educated at Oxford and qualified as a barrister at Lincoln's Inn. The Lord of Misrule was basically the master of the revels in times of celebration, most often at Christmas. In his notorious *Anatomie of Abuses* (1583), the puritan Philip Stubbes raged against the figure of the Lord of Misrule, who, he complained,

> chuseth for the twentie, fourtie, three-score, or a hundred lustie guttes like to himself…Then every one of these his menne he investeth with his liveries, of greene, yellowe, or some other light wanton colour. And as though they were not (baudie) gaudy enough, I should saie, they bedecke themselves with scarffes, ribbons, and laces, hanged all over with gold rynges, precious stones, and other jewelles: this doen, they tye abouth either legge, twentie or fourtie belles, with rich hande-kercheefes in their handes… Thus   thinges sette in order, they have their hobby horses, dragons, and other antiques, together with their baudie Pipers, and   thundering Drommers, to strike up the Deville's dance withal…they have also certaine papers, wherein is paynted some bablerie or other, of Imagerie worke, and these they call my Lord of Misrule's badges; these thei give to every one that will geve money for them, to maintaine them in this their heathenry, devilrie, whoredome, drunkennesse, pride, and what not.[5]

The Kenilworth Castle guidebook identifies the poet George Gascoigne as 'pageant-master'[6] but that is to be misled by the central role which Gascoigne allotted himself in his account of the entertainments in *The princelye pleasures at the Courte at Kenelwoorth*. (Although published anonymously in 1576, the identity of the book's author was revealed when it re-appeared in an edition of Gascoigne's 'whole works' after his death.) It is far more likely that if anyone was in charge of orchestrating the shows and speeches put on before the Queen, it was Ferrers. That was his job: organising courtly entertainment. He was the man who made sure that the proceedings had more than just a splash of colour about them. It is most unlikely that events at Kenilworth were ever as anarchic as in Stubbes's hysterical vision of ordinary people having a good time.

The kind of communal revels that Ferrers organised were for courtiers, not the man or woman in the street. But no doubt they also involved music, drumming, dancing, lively processions involving physical contact and the exchange of keepsakes, 'sometimes laied acrosse over their shoulders and neckes, borrowed for the moste parte of their pretie Mopsies and loovyng Bessies, for bussyng [embracing] them in the dareke [dark].'[7]

Dr Richard Mulcaster was an eminent Greek scholar, educated at Eton, Cambridge and Oxford. In 1561 he was appointed headmaster of the newly founded Merchant Taylors' School and became known as an educational reformer. His presence at Kenilworth was presumably to lend the aura of serious scholarship to the proceedings. The Queen was multi-lingual and greatly enjoyed hearing speeches in Latin and Greek.

John Badger, 'Superior Beadle of Divinity' at Oxford University, was also roped in, presumably through Dudley's association with the university as chancellor. He, too, was there to ensure that the entertainments had a suitably learned quality.

The most important member of the team was George Gascoigne – the year's most sensational, controversial and fashionable writer. To understand what really happened at Kenilworth requires a much closer examination of this shadowy figure, who supplied important information about what happened there and who was responsible both for the incident that lay behind the rumour of a failed assassination attempt on the Queen and for the crisis that brought the entertainments to an abrupt halt.

*

Today, only two public memorials to Gascoigne exist. Both are in Walthamstow, once a tiny Essex village, now a sprawling suburb on the fringes of Greater London.

One memorial, carved into the wall of a public library on the corner of Forest Road and Wood Street, gives what was long regarded, wrongly, as his year of birth - 1525. The second, on the tower of Ross Wyld Hall, on Hoe Street, shows his coat of arms. It features an aggressive, predatory pike, with a mouthful of sharp teeth.

George Gascoigne has largely faded from modern memory, yet in 1575 he was a towering figure in English literary culture. He was born at Cardington in Bedfordshire in 1534 or very early in 1535, which made him of the same generation as Elizabeth and Leicester. He was the first born son of a leading neighbourhood family, and served alongside his father as a local MP in the last parliament of Mary.

Gascoigne followed the conventional career route of the heir to a landed estate. In his adolescence he attended Cambridge University, and was then admitted to Gray's Inn, where he trained to be a lawyer. He served as an almoner at the coronation of Elizabeth, gave up his law studies and reinvented himself as a courtier. He did so in an entirely unofficial capacity. Like many others, he was simply a hanger-on at court, dressing extravagantly, playing cards, dancing, making music, and hoping to attract Elizabeth's eye. From the Queen's favour might flow all kinds of wealth, from the granting of monopolies to gifts of land. But the problem for men like Gascoigne in the early years of Elizabeth's reign was that the young Queen really only had eyes for one person, and that was Robert Dudley. Gascoigne was wasting his time. His wealth drained away on extravagant living and he retired from the court.

In November 1561 he married a wealthy older woman, Elizabeth Breton. It subsequently transpired that the marriage was bigamous. Her existing husband turned up and the result was a savage street brawl between Gascoigne, the other man and their servants. Sir Nicholas Bacon, Lord Chancellor, intervened to sort the matter out. At this moment of crisis Gascoigne wrote 'Eyther a needelesse or a bootleesse comparison betwene two letters', which is one of his most dazzling poems It wittily contrasts 'G', which stands for everything that is good (including 'God', 'gold' and, of course, 'Gascoigne') with the despicable letter 'B', used to spell 'Black, brown and bad, yea worse than may be told', including 'Boyes', her lawful husband.

Obliged to decide between two husbands, Elizabeth chose the dashing and talented Gascoigne, who, though having squandered his fortune, came from a distinguished family. Her personal connections to Sir Nicholas ensured that the difficulties surrounding her bigamous marriage were discreetly settled. The couple moved away from London and settled in a substantial country house in Walthamstow, which in the sixteenth century was little more than an isolated group of hamlets in the Essex countryside, adjacent to what is now called Epping Forest. Although he had moved out of the city, Gascoigne maintained his association with Gray's Inn and in 1566 he was the driving force behind two plays put on there for the Christmas revels. The first, *Supposes*, was a translation from Ariosto of a lively Italian comedy centred on a master who exchanges places with his servant in order to woo an attractive young woman. The second, *Jocasta*, was a stately Greek tragedy, notable chiefly for its visually stunning dumb shows. It is likely that Robert Dudley was in the audience for both plays, which were put on for London's cultural elite. If Dudley was present, it would have supplied him with his first experience of Gascoigne's literary skills, acting abilities and dramatic flair.

In 1572 Gascoigne was about to become MP for Midhurst in Sussex when he was denounced to the Privy Council. An unsigned letter asserted that someone of Gascoigne's character was utterly unfit to serve in parliament. He was 'a spy, an atheist and a godless person' - just about the worst things you could call anyone in England at that time. In fact it was clear that Gascoigne's greatest offence was that he owed his anonymous accuser money. The denunciation began with the complaint that

> he is indebted to a greate number of personnes for the w[ch] cause he
> hath absented him selfe from the Citie and hath lurked at villages
> neere unto the same citie by a longe time, and nowe beinge returned
> for a Burgesse of Midehurste in the Countie of Sussex, doethe
> shewe his face openlie in the dispite of all his Creditors.[8]

In the sixteenth century one of the perks of being an MP was that creditors could not pursue you in the courts. Gascoigne's accuser wanted his money back and was determined to prevent him evading his debts.

Although the very serious accusations of being a spy and an atheist were empty slurs, it is clear that there was some substance to the complaint that George Gascoigne was a disreputable figure. Apart from the street brawl which resulted from his bigamous marriage, Gascoigne had been put in Bedford prison just two years earlier. He owed money to the powerful Earl of Bedford, who sat on the Privy Council and who was therefore probably sympathetic to the complaint.

The denunciation worked. Gascoigne's name was struck off the list of MPs for the new parliament. Soon afterwards Gascoigne went abroad. This may have been a new way of evading his debts or, possibly, an attempt to repair his tarnished reputation. He joined a force of 1,500 volunteers under the command of Sir Humphrey Gilbert, who went off to fight alongside Dutch Protestant rebels who had risen up against the Catholic Spanish Empire, which then ruled over the Netherlands. Elizabeth I tacitly supported the English forces, while maintaining an official position of absolute neutrality. The English campaign turned out to be an undistinguished one and by the end of the year the volunteers had returned home. But the Dutch war of independence dragged on, and the next year, 1573, Gascoigne returned, by now promoted to Captain.

One of the complaints made against Gascoigne to the Privy Council was that he was a poet and a satirist – or as his anonymous accuser furiously put it, 'a common Rymer and a deviser of slaunderous Pasquelles [lampoons] againste divers personnes of great callinge.'

The allegation must have seemed obscure, since Gascoigne, then aged about 38, had published nothing. His manuscripts had, however, clearly been in circulation, most probably among his friends and associates at the Inns of Court.

In fact before returning to the Dutch war, Gascoigne arranged to have them published. This was in itself a shocking and faintly disreputable thing to do. Gentlemen circulated their work in manuscript among their friends, but they never did anything as vulgar as sell it to a publisher. To put one's verse into print meant exposing it to the eyes of people one didn't know – something unacceptably distasteful until you were dead. But brashness and indifference to what people thought were second nature to Gascoigne – although he pretended to draw the line at some things. At a later date he indignantly denied ever accepting money for his book – a claim which, for someone as financially challenged as Gascoigne always seemed to be, needs to be taken with a large pinch of salt. The book duly appeared, probably in November 1573. By accident or design, Gascoigne was far away in the Netherlands at the time.

Though the book bore the innocent-sounding title *A Hundreth Sundry Flowers* its contents were explosive. It consisted of the two plays put on at Gray's Inn six years earlier, around one-hundred poems and a short novel, *The Adventures of Master F.J.* By sixteenth-century standards, it was a very substantial volume. *A Hundreth Sundry Flowers* was published anonymously and purported to be an anthology of writings by various gentlemen, only one of whom was named: 'Gascoigne'. In fact everything in it was by Gascoigne, and even the 'F.J' of the novel was a joke reference to 'Filius Johannus' – the son of John (the poet's father being Sir John Gascoigne).

Readers not in the know were thrown off the scent by a bogus address from 'The Printer to the Reader' – written by Gascoigne, not the printer – and, later in the volume, by an address to the reader from a pretend editor, who drew on correspondence from a wholly fictitious friend.

There had been nothing like it published before and the book created a sensation. It was a curiously double-edged volume. There was the solemn, sententious tragedy *Jocasta* side by side with the knockabout comedy *Supposes*, which was full of jokes about holes, arses and giant suppositories. There were conventional Petrarchan love lyrics, interspersed with bawdy riddles and the erotic innuendo of poems like 'Phillip Sparrow', which alludes to bisexuality, oral sex and noisy orgasms.[9] When there were attempts to revive Gascoigne's reputation in the nineteenth century, one distinguished critic bitterly protested that this Tudor writer was 'a man many of whose poems are as lewd as any others of his time, and far more filthy in expression'.[10]

Perhaps most explosive of all was *The Adventures of Master F.J.* It was a novel, but, 150 years before Daniel Defoe, it represented its fiction as fact. And what was shocking was its content. It tells the story of a young gentleman who goes to stay for the summer at a large country house in the north of England. There, Master F.J. has an affair with a promiscuous married woman named Elinor. In a raunchy, explicit scene, they first make love on the floor of the gallery. There is much bawdy innuendo about F.J. sneaking about the house at night with his 'naked sword' sticking out from under his night shirt. Elinor's great friend Frances takes a voyeuristic interest in their affair, tells F.J. about Elinor's other lovers, and makes it clear that she would also like to go to bed with him. The novel ends in jealousy, rape and bitterness.

A Hundreth Sundry Flowers created a sensation. It became the equivalent of a sixteenth century best seller. But it also attracted the attention of the body which had the power to censor books – the

Commissioners for Causes Ecclesiastical.

This was a committee of about seventy representatives of the ruling elite, including city merchants. Its membership included some of England's most senior churchmen. Traditionally, the focus for censorship had been heresy – religious ideas which offended against the theological status quo. Now, for the first time, the censors turned their attention to imaginative writing.

There was much in *A Hundreth Sundry Flowers* to offend those of a prudish, humourless or religiously strict and morally upright temperament. Most shocking of all was *The Adventures of Master F.J.*, which purported to be a true story. It showed that those at the very top of society were promiscuous, deceitful, cynical and morally dissolute. It teased readers by withholding the identities of these shocking people. But it seemed that everyone could easily identify candidates for the serial adulteress 'Elinor' and her foolish, cuckolded husband. Tongues wagged, there were winks and nudges, people sniggered. In the eyes of the censors, *The Adventures of Master F.J.* was a threatening, disturbing book which undermined decent society. As a printed text, its content was theoretically available to anyone, including those lower down the social scale. This was unacceptable.

Gascoigne returned from the Low Countries about a year after its publication to discover that he was both famous and infamous. The young bloods of the Inns of Court adored the book. So, too, did many of those at Elizabeth's court. Gascoigne was suddenly the most fashionable and popular writer in town, and he loved every moment of it. As he put it in a later poem, he relished 'To hear it said there goeth, the *Man that writes so well.*'[9] But the censors were not amused. The book was banned.[12]

Gascoigne was stunned. A book of creative writing had never been censored in this way before. He indignantly wrote that he was surprised and baffled to discover that the contents of *A Hundreth Sundry Flowers* 'have not onely bene offensive for sundrie wanton speeches and lascivious phrases, but further I heare that the same have beene doubtfully construed, and (therefore) scandalous.'[13] It was all a terrible mistake, he insisted. *The Adventures of Master F.J.* was not about any living person. But the censors were implacable.

Worse, Gascoigne returned from the Netherlands under a cloud of rumour and suspicion. Soon after the publication of *A Hundreth*

Sundry Flowers he had been detained at Delft, where the Burghers suspected him of treachery. It was a not entirely unreasonable suspicion, in so far as many of the foreign troops fighting on the Protestant side were mercenaries. These men were motivated by their pay and by what they could get from looting.

No one who knew Gascoigne at all well could have seriously believed that he was motivated by a passionate commitment either to the Protestant cause or to Dutch independence. He was a cynic, not an ideologue. And since the Dutch war did not yet have the official backing of Elizabeth I, an Englishman who worked for the Spaniards could not properly be called a traitor. Changing sides was not unknown among the English soldiers. Gascoigne's associate Rowland Yorke, mentioned in his poem 'Gascoigne's voyage into Holland', served on the Spanish side, returned to the Protestant cause, and then finally betrayed the town of Zutphen to his old masters.

As Gascoigne explained it, he fell under suspicion as a result of his involvement with a woman at The Hague, which was by then behind enemy lines. (Marital fidelity was another of his weak points.) The arrival of the woman's maid with a packet for an Englishman made the Burghers wonder if Gascoigne was involved with the Spaniards.

The packet included something far more explosive than just a love letter. It contained a passport signed by Francisco de Valdes, giving Gascoigne safe passage through the Spanish lines. Since de Valdes commanded the forces then besieging Delft, the Burghers' suspicions of Gascoigne were not unreasonable. They therefore kept the poet under surveillance and gave instructions that he was banned from all ports and not permitted to board any vessel.

Gascoigne was left angrily trapped at Delft, raging against 'the Bowgers [buggers] (Burghers should I saye)':

Well thus I dwelt in *Delfe* a winter's tide,
In *Delfe* (I say) without one penny pay[14]

He'd probably hoped to be reunited with his mistress in The Hague. Even more, he probably wanted to get back to London, where his book was the toast of the town. Instead he was stuck in the grey, dismal, low-lying coastal regions of Holland, in the middle of a war which was going nowhere. And he wasn't even getting paid! George

George Gascoigne's coat of arms, featuring a pike, on the clock tower of Ross Wyld Hall, Walthamstow

Gascoigne was not a happy man.

The rumours about him did not end there. In March more English volunteers arrived and Gascoigne and other officers were given the task of defending the new fort of Valkenburgh, some three miles north-west of Leiden in South Holland. But the fort was unfinished and had inadequate supplies of ammunition and victuals. At this point a force of at least 3,000 Spanish troops approached. As the retreat began, the enemy arrived on the scene, and soon there was total confusion and panic. When the English soldiers reached Leiden, the town hurriedly shut its gates against them. They were left stranded out in the open and spent the night there. At dawn on 27 May they were woken by the sound of approaching Spanish drums. Gascoigne and his associate Captain Sheffield went forward to negotiate with two Spanish officers. The two Englishmen requested that their force be allowed to surrender and return to England. This was agreed, and after 12 days in captivity the English volunteers were sent home. But Gascoigne and the other officers were imprisoned at Haarlem for four months. They were well treated and eventually released.

That was Gascoigne's version of what happened. In Holland, however, it was widely believed that he and the other officers had been bribed by the Spanish to surrender. The English volunteers also suspected treachery and returned to England claiming that the reason Gascoigne and the others stayed behind was to claim their reward. Gascoigne and the other officers returned late in September or early October 1574.

George Gascoigne was, therefore, a man under double suspicion of treachery, the author of a scandalous book, a bigamist, a street brawler, and someone who had been denounced to the Privy Council, accused of all kinds of wrongdoing. Yet this was the person that Robert Dudley, Earl of Leicester, chose to play a leading role in supplying and acting in many of the serious literary entertainments to be put before the Queen at Kenilworth.

It shows that Dudley had a libertarian temperament and a keen interest in contemporary writing. He was clearly not shocked by Gascoigne's risqué poetry or his scandalous reputation. Gascoigne's recent military service in the Low Countries would also have endeared him to a passionate interventionist like Dudley.

Gascoigne's biographer has suggested that his novel may even have been about Leicester's seduction of Douglas Sheffield at Belvoir Castle in 1568: 'The story…contains similarities as striking to us as they must have been to Gascoigne's contemporaries'.[15] But that parallel is far from plausible, even assuming that Dudley did begin his affair with Lady Sheffield in that place at that time. In fact *The Adventures of Master F.J.* is far more likely to be about the young Gascoigne than Robert Dudley. But the novel undoubtedly put forward a plausible account of promiscuity among the leisured upper class. If Robert Dudley liked it, it was because he appreciated both its authenticity as an account of the private lives of the landed elite and the witty originality of the way the tale was told.

5   The first day

A document has survived which gives details of the advance planning for the 1575 royal progress.[1] It deals with transport and provisions and includes a note on three possible routes from Windsor to Kenilworth, with the mileage between stopping points. One went via Oxford, another through 'Bissitor' [Bicester] and the third by way of 'Dantry' [Daventry], all three converging at Coventry, before going on to Warwick and 'Killingwoorth'.

Records of the precise itinerary which the progress followed that year are patchy. The most comprehensive account cited by Nichols simply says that 'it pleafed the Quenes Majesty to make her progress into Northamptonshire, Warwickshire, Staffordshire; Oxfordshire, Worcestershire, and so returne to Woodstock in Oxfordshire.'[2]

In fact (though no one seems to have noticed this before) the best way of tracking the Queen's movements in the summer and early autumn of 1575 is through the meetings of the Privy Council, which accompanied her on her progress. The Council met at Greenwich on 21 May, and then held ten meetings between 25 May and 13 June at Theobalds, Burghley's grand country house in Hertfordshire. On 14 June it met at Hatfield. Among those present was the Earl of Leicester. It then moved on with Elizabeth to her mansion at Grafton, sixteen miles west of Oxford, holding its first meeting there on 19 June.

When the Queen first reached Grafton, Leicester anxiously reported to Burghley her rage at discovering 'not one drop of good drink for her'. The ale was so strong 'it did put her very far out of temper'. Some weaker drink was hurriedly found 'and she is well again, but I feared greatly two or three days some sickness to have fallen, by reason of this drink.'[3] The Council held seven meetings at Grafton, the last one on 6 July.

The guidebook to Kenilworth Castle includes a painting of the Earl of Leicester standing outside, welcoming the Queen as she arrives on horseback. But this picture is sheer fantasy. The Earl had accompanied Elizabeth along the route of her progress in his traditional capacity as Master of the Horse. He welcomed the Queen to his domain long before she ever got to Kenilworth. On Saturday July 9 1575 the royal progress halted at Long Itchington, on the main highway from Coventry to Banbury.

Here, some ten miles south east of Kenilworth, a vast, palatial marquee had been erected, subdivided into rooms. A solitary statistic has survived to indicate its enormous size: putting it up required seven cartloads of tent pegs. It was now that the Earl of Leicester officially welcomed Elizabeth to the region, and gave her a suitably lavish dinner. By way of entertainment the parents of a local prodigy proudly displayed their 'great Chyld' - apparently a young man of restricted growth with learning difficulties and a 'simpl and childish' disposition.[4] In the sixteenth century, disability was a source of curiosity and amusement.

A royal progress was a leisurely affair. There was no hurry. After dinner the royal party went off hunting and did not reach Kenilworth until mid-evening. The main body of the entourage had gone on from Long Itchington, following the route of the drovers' road through Bericote. It entered the town at what is now the junction of Warwick Road, Leamington Road and Birches Lane. Here, Elizabeth, Leicester and his thirty invited guests, headed north through Kenilworth, while the bulk of the entourage turned in the opposite direction and went off to accommodation in Warwick.

It was mid-evening. Leicester's party went along Borrowell Lane and over the small bridge by the castle fishponds. Entering parkland to the south-east of the castle, Elizabeth was diverted by the sudden spectacle of ten sibyls or pagan prophetesses. The sibyls appeared out of an arbour in the park, in classical costumes.

According to the strict conventions of the age, the actors playing the part of these women, and all the others in the masques and pageants that followed, would have been men or boys. By now it was around 8 p.m. and the daylight was starting to fade.

The prophetess mouthed some conventional platitudes about the 'tenne thousand' rejoycings at Elizabeth's visit.[5] Reassuringly, 'vertue', peace and happy days were what the future had in store. Elizabeth benignly accepted this flattering doggerel, which had been penned, and the tableau choreographed, by William Hunnis.

We then reach the moment celebrated in the splendid full-colour lithograph by John Brannard. But everything in that sumptuous picture is wrong, including the geography. As she approached the castle the Queen was not greeted by fireworks. Her entourage did not stream after her from the east. She did not ride a magnificent stallion but a palfrey – a dull, safe, plodding horse for ladies. Elizabeth was late getting to the castle and there was no blue sky or sunshine.

The sibyls appeared in parkland (now vanished) close to a wide, towered gateway, leading into The Brays from the south. Today, only the foundations of this gateway remain, at the junction of Castle Grove and Castle Road. The Queen then passed on across The Brays. This was an amphitheatre-shaped area surrounded by an embankment and a moat. It was used for mélees – rough, no-holds-barred mass battles in which the participants fought for valuable prizes like horses and armour, while spectators watched from viewing areas at the edge of the arena. Nowadays this area forms the main car park for visitors to the castle.

Having crossed the Brays, Elizabeth then reached the Gallery Tower – a rectangular gateway tower designed to offer a first defence to the main entrance to Kenilworth Castle. (Today, the tower lies in ruins; only fragments of wall remain.) Here she encountered a remarkable sight. Silhouetted against the battlements were six gigantic figures holding, in the words of George Gascoigne, 'huge and monstrous Trumpettes'.[6]

As Elizabeth approached, these silk-swathed giant trumpeters seemed to blow a fanfare of welcome from their silver instruments. It was a trick, of course. The trumpeters were models, probably made out of hoops, deal boards, pasteboard, paper, cloth and buckram. The real trumpeters remained behind them, out of sight. A similar show had been put on for Queen Mary, when she passed through the London streets before her coronation on 30 September 1553. At the upper end of Grace's Street was a pageant,

> made by the Florentines, verie high, on the top whereof there
> stood four pictures, and in the middest of them and most highest,
> there stood an angell all in greene, with a trumpet in his hand: and
> when the trumpetter (who stood secretlie in the pageant) did sound
> his trumpet, the angell did put his trumpet to his mouth, as though it
> had been the same that had sounded, to the great marvelling of
> many ignorant persons.[7]

Gascoigne, remembering the spectacular Greek tragedy *Jocasta* which he'd produced nine years earlier, described the trumpeters on the Gallery Tower as a 'dum shew'.[8] Like the dumb shows of early Tudor theatre, this display conveyed a symbolic meaning. Everyone then believed that Kenilworth Castle had historical associations with King Arthur, and everyone also knew that in Arthur's day men were much, much bigger in size than they were in the sixteenth century. The message trumpeted from above was therefore simple: the castle was still safely in the hands of King Arthur's heirs and their servants. Just in case the Queen hadn't understood, the meaning was explained to her in a masque two days later:

> And what meant those great men
>   which on the walles were seene?
>   …they served
> King Arthur, man of might,
> And ever since this castle kept
>   for Arthur's heirs by right.[9]

As Elizabeth entered the gateway of the Gallery Tower she was confronted by another gigantic figure. It was Hercules – in ancient myth, the strongest man in the world. This time the giant was no dummy but someone 'tall of parson, big of lim[b] and stearn of coountinauns [countenance], wrapt also all in sylk, with club and keyz'.[10] The person playing Hercules was also the author of his speech – John Badger, M.A., Beadle of Oxford University.

Hercules pretended to be amazed and disturbed by all the fuss. 'What stirre… is here?' he cried, attempting to hold back the royal party.[11] But then he spotted 'faire Dames' and 'daintie darlings'. These were the Ladies in Waiting. But there was ('oh God') one face more beautiful and astonishing than all the others – 'a peereles Pearle'. Hercules was literally disarmed by the presence of this beautiful, gracious, heavenly, majestic figure. The lengthening inventory of banal adjectives in praise of Elizabeth climaxed with Hercules falling to his knees, laying down his weapon and handing over the castle keys. Free passage was granted to the royal party.

The Queen, accepting Hercules's apologies for his ignorance and impatience, passed under the arch. Her acceptance, however, may have been glacial rather than warm. Hercules in one sense was clearly

38

intended to represent Robert Dudley. The club could be seen as a symbol of the ragged staff. In handing it over, the master of the dancing bear was putting himself at the mercy of his dangerous creature. The initial failure to recognise the Queen, though a joke, was less than flattering. So, too, was the implicit hint that Hercules was not her inferior but her equal. Worse, in ancient myth he was a god at the mercy of a difficult, powerful woman:

> Greek myth relates how the Pythian priestess told Hercules that 'henceforth he should take the name of Heracles, meaning "Hera's Glory," undoubtedly because the Labours he was about to undertake would result in the goddess's glorification.' The hero's title, then, originates from the woman he serves. Hera instigates Hercules' labours by manipulating circumstances in order to enslave him. She both drives him to perform and impedes his performance with storms, fits of madness, and other obstacles. The strongest man in the world, Hercules must struggle in a system of power that centres on a crafty and vindictive goddess. It does not take a great leap of imagination to see a parallel between the classical hero and the English earl.[12]

Another fanfare blew from the battlements and the Queen passed on. But Elizabeth knew her mythology, and she was very shortly to show that her mood was testy.

The trumpet blasts continued to sound as Elizabeth, still on horseback, entered the Tiltyard and rode slowly across it. The tiltyard ran along the top of the dam, to Mortimer's Tower, which formed the real entrance to the castle. To her left was the Great Mere, its shore, we can safely assume, lined with spectators.

She passed through the narrow archway of Mortimer's Tower, the twin stumps of which still remain. Then she entered the base court (or outer court) of the castle. Here, a dazzling spectacle awaited the Queen. Some distance away, on the darkening waters, was a floating island, lit by blazing torches. The flickering torchlight illuminated three magical figures in silken garments.

As the Queen watched, the island began to move towards her. Neither Gascoigne nor the author of *A Letter* explain how the Queen managed to see the Great Mere from the base court. Presumably either a gateway in the curtain wall had been opened, or a temporary platform had been erected as a vantage point.

As it drew close to the castle the figures resolved themselves into 'a Ladie' and her two attendant nymphs. The island reached the shore, and the Lady called out, begging Elizabeth to wait and hear her story:

> I am the Lady of this pleasant lake
> who since the time of great King Arthur's reign
> That here with royal court abode did make
> have led a louring life in restless pain
> Till now that your third arrival here
> doth cause me come abroad, and boldly thus appear.[13]

In a rhyming verse of 42 lines, the Lady of the Lake told her sad tale. For centuries she had hidden herself away, avoiding the changing and turbulent fortunes of the castle and timidly keeping away from its fearful owners. But now the spell was broken. Elizabeth's third official visit 'doth bode thrice happy hope and voids the place from fear'.

> Wherefore I will attend while you lodge here
> (most peerless Queen) to court to make resort,
> And as my love to Arthur did appear
> so shalt to you in earnest and in sport.
> Pass on, Madame, you need no longer stand:
> The lake, the lodge, the Lord, are yours for to command.

It was at this point that something occurred to indicate that the Queen's mood that night was prickly. She thanked the Lady of the Lake, but tartly added 'we had thought indeed the Lake had been oours, and doo you call it yourz noow?'[14]

As sovereign, Elizabeth theoretically owned the entire land. She did not like someone presuming to challenge her authority in matters of land ownership, even if that person was just a fantasy figure in a masque. 'Well we wyll heerin common [commune, i.e. talk] more with yoo hereafter,' she added, ominously. It may, at best, only have been badinage, but it was not the sort to make whoever was playing the role of the Lady feel very comfortable.

After this slightly ill-tempered exchange, the mood was lightened by 'sweet Musicke'.[15] Hautboys (a wind instrument, of which there were three types: treble, tenor and bass), shalms (like hautboys, a kind of early oboe, with a double reed enclosed in a globular mouthpiece) and cornets (a horn-shaped variety of early oboe) all played as Elizabeth moved on across the great drawbridge into the inner court.

This wooden-railed drawbridge was a permanent, ornamental fixture some 20 feet wide and 70 feet long, crossing a deep ditch. It was located between the great Keep and the end of the accommodation block put up in the time of Henry VIII. The drawbridge has long since vanished, most of the ditch has been filled in – a small part remains by one corner of the Keep - and now nothing lies between the outer and inner courts but a grassy, open slope.

On that evening in July 1575 the drawbridge planks were covered in gravel for the horses. Along both sides of the bridge gifts were laid out: a pair of wire cages containing bitterns, godwits, ducks and other 'deinty Byrds'; a pair of silver bowls containing apples, pears, cherries, pomegranates and sundry other fruits and nuts; a pair of silver bowls containing wheat, barley, oats, beans and peas; a bowl of grapes; pots of white wine and claret; trays of seafood including oysters, salmon, eels and herring.[16] They were intended to represent gifts from the gods but they formed a slightly bizarre display. Elizabeth was used to being presented with valuable treasures, redeemable for cash – not perishable goods of little real value.

Beyond them lay gifts from Mars, the god of war. A pair of silver staves had been fashioned in imitation of the ragged staff shown on the Earl's coat of arms. They supported a collection of armour, including shield, head piece, gorget, corselet, spears, swords, bows and arrows. These possessed tangible value, but were not motivated by generosity. As Ilana Nash observes,

Only Mars's gift of silver – advertising Dudley with his family
badge of the ragged staffs, and indecorously reminding the queen
of his desire for a military post – has any monetary value.
Demanding and self-aggrandizing, this 'gift' is doubly ungenerous
in its positioning: what good will silver do Elizabeth when it is
stuck up on a post, out of reach, and clearly incorporated as a part

of the storytelling in a way that makes retrieving it impossible?[17]

Finally, two branches of bay were adorned with offerings from the god of music: lutes, viols, shalms, cornets, flutes, recorders and harps.

As the Queen rode between these offerings an actor dressed as a poet recited a Latin verse, telling how this homage had been commanded by Jupiter and explaining what each gift signified.

What was not spelt out but which was implicit in the display of armour was Dudley's desire for a military command. As a Protestant, he not only wanted to see Elizabeth commit herself to the war in the Netherlands, but he also wanted to command troops there himself. That was his first message to her.

But in 1575 it wasn't one she wanted to hear. The Dutch war against the Spanish had her tacit support, but nothing stronger. The exploits of the English soldiers there had so far been distinctly inglorious, as one of the onlookers, George Gascoigne, well knew. That first military expedition to the Netherlands, three years earlier, resulted in complaints of looting by undisciplined English volunteers, and ended in a disastrous rout, with the survivors fleeing home across the Channel.

A ten-foot square plaque with a stirring welcome in Latin, painted in large white capitals, had been positioned above the gateway that led into the inner court. By now it was so dark that its words, which explained the meaning of the gifts, were illegible.

Richard Mulcaster, dressed up as a poet in a long, colourful silk costume, with a garland on his head and a scroll in his hand, read aloud his own Latin poem about the gifts on the bridge.

Elizabeth passed through the gate and entered the inner court of Kenilworth Castle. Here she dismounted, while drums, fifes and trumpets sounded.

After this 'shee mounted the stayres, and went to her lodging.'[18] This was undoubtedly in Leicester's Building, a new three-storey building which supplied the most luxurious accommodation in the castle complex. Each floor consisted of a suite of rooms, including a large, light-filled room with big rectangular windows. There were bedrooms, chambers and panoramic views across the great lake. What are missing from contemporary accounts of the Queen's visit are descriptions of those rooms and their gorgeous interiors.

42

However, the inventory of the castle's contents taken some three years later lists all kinds of luxury objects including a black ebony chessboard, the tusk of a sea bear, musical instruments, curtains of crimson satin and other hangings, plates, furniture and linen. The Dudley family motto, 'Droit et Loyal', together with other reminders of Elizabeth's host, was blazoned across many of these items.[19]

The Earl owned some fifty paintings and over twenty maps, which would almost certainly have been displayed in a picture gallery, possibly located in Caesar's Tower. Here, the Queen and the most privileged guests would be treated to a very special show, the highlight of which was four new paintings of Elizabeth and her host. These had been specially commissioned earlier in the year. One can be seen today in the National Portrait Gallery and another is in the Reading Museum. Another two, by Federico Zuccaro, have been lost, though the preliminary drawings survive. But that was a treat for later in her visit. For the moment there was a more immediate entertainment on offer and Elizabeth had a grandstand view of it. The night climaxed with the Tudor equivalent of a twenty-one gun salute ('so great a peal of gunz') and a grand fireworks display. It was said that the 'noyz and flame' were seen and heard twenty miles away.[20] Everyone in the area – Stratford-upon-Avon, for instance, is twelve miles away – would have known that the Queen had now arrived.

But outside, in the darkness of the night, there was one person who was very, very unhappy about what had happened since Elizabeth had arrived at the castle. That sense of discontent was to grow and to have extraordinary consequences.

6   The savage man

The next day, Sunday, began quietly. In the morning Elizabeth travelled the short distance to the parish church, just beyond the castle walls. This involved leaving the castle through the archway of Leicester's Gateway, crossing the great bridge over the moat and heading along Bull Hill (now Castle Hill) and High Street to St Nicholas Church, in the grounds of the ruined abbey.

Back at Walthamstow, the shocking absence of George Gascoigne and his wife from St Mary's church was solemnly noted, so it seems likely he took his long-suffering wife Elizabeth with him to Kenilworth. Their absence earned them a fine but it is doubtful if it was ever paid. Gascoigne's excuse – that he'd missed church in order to entertain the Queen – could hardly have been bettered.

In the afternoon there was music and dancing for the ladies of the court and their partners. Leicester had invited some thirty guests, including his sister Lady Mary Sidney, her husband Sir Henry, and their son Philip. Also present was the Countess of Essex, whose destiny would also be transformed by the Queen's visit.

That night there were fireworks even more elaborate and spectacular than the ones seen the night before, 'with blaz of burning darts, flying too & fro, leamz [flashes] of starz coruscant [flashing], streamz and hail of firie sparkes, lightninges of wildfier a [over] water and lond [land], flight & shott of thunderboltz: all with such countinauns, terrour and vehemencie: that the heavins thundred, the waters soourged [surged], the earth shooke'.[1]

The Italian designer's blueprint for the Kenilworth displays reads as follows:

The first evening will be in the meadow. There there will be certain fireworks, where one can see certain serpents of fire move in a circle. Again, eight or ten pots, with inventions of marvellous things, which will be pleasing. Again, living birds, which will fly through the air throwing out fire throughout. Again, two dogs and two live cats which will fight artfully.

The   second evening will be in the courtyard of the palace. There you will see a fountain from which will emerge water, wine and fire for seven or eight hours continually. And this fountain will emit something worth seeing in its wonderful devices which are such as to exceed the power of description. Again, three wonderful, sweetly smelling wheels of fire, of different colours.

The third evening will be in the river. There you will be able to see a dragon as big as an ox, which will fly two or three times higher than the steeple of St Paul's, and being so high it will consume itself entirely in flames, and from its body will emerge dogs and cats and birds which will fly around and emit fire in all directions, which will be a stupendous event.

There will be many other things in this firework display, which because of their differences we will not describe in minute detail. I will make sure that all goes well, according to the payment which which has been entrusted to me for the expenses.[2]

This is much more precise than the fireworks described in *A Letter* or *The princelye pleasures at the Courte at Kenelwoorth*, but roughly consistent with them. There were indeed three great displays at the castle. The first was visible to everyone in the neighbourhood – 'the meadow' possibly refers to Castle Green or the grounds of the abbey to the east of the castle. The second display may have been restricted to Leicester's guests and held in the inner courtyard of the castle, out of sight of the common people. The third display either took place on the Great Mere or on that arm of it north of the castle. The Italian designer had evidently not seen the castle or its grounds; no doubt these proposed displays were subject to modification when they did take place.

The blueprint has sometimes been interpreted as meaning that real animals were to be used, but this is clearly wrong – what was promised were patterned representations of these creatures. Neither *A Letter* nor *The princelye pleasures* mention fireworks resembling animals, so perhaps the proposal was over-ambitious. However, it's clear that the displays were, in the event, hugely successful, impressing everyone who watched. This second display, on Sunday July 17, was out of the ordinary in another way, too. The thunderous explosions went on until well after midnight – extravagantly late by the standards of Tudor society.

*

The third day was hot and sunny and Elizabeth stayed indoors. Women of the upper class valued their pale complexions and were terrified of prolonged exposure to sunlight. A sun tan indicated a common labouring woman, who spent her days out of doors. Gascoigne poked fun at this fashion. He wrote a sonnet attacking the teasing, manipulative women of the court, describing their cosmetic-smeared faces: 'The painted pale, the (too much) red made white.'[3] They were, he wrote, 'smyling baytes to fishe for loving fooles'. He preferred an earthy, tanned country girl. Gascoigne mocked the Court and its fine ladies. His sonnet terminates with the pugnacious assertion that 'A lovely nutbrowne face is best of all'.

The Queen did not emerge from the castle until 5 p.m. She then rode out with the hounds on a deer hunt in the Chase. A deer was located, pursued and broke cover. The author of *A Letter* thought the scene was 'delectabl', with 'the earning [ceaseless calling] of the hoounds in continuans of their crie, ye swiftnes of the Deer, the running of footmen, the galloping of horsez, the blasting of horns, the halloing & hewing of the huntsmen, with the excellēt Echoz between whilez from the woods and waters in valleiz resonnding'.[4]

The animal was forced 'at last to take soil'[5] - hunting jargon for escaping into water. The deer swam across the Mere, pursued by hounds.

What happened next isn't clear, but 'the Hart waz kild'.[6] The accepted convention in such a situation was that someone rowed out in a boat and cut the creature's throat.

With the evening's hunting over, the Queen and her party returned on horseback through The Chase. But before they reached the castle Robert Dudley had arranged another tableau for her. At about 9 p.m., 'at the hither part of the Chase',[7] Elizabeth came to a glade in the woods lit by torchlight.

Here she was greeted by England's most prominent and controversial poet and novelist, George Gascoigne, dressed as a wild man of the woods. This mini-masque drew on native English folklore rather than classical mythology. The wild (or green) man signified uncorrupted pastoral innocence – the spirit of elemental nature as opposed to the fallen, artificial world of human society.

This 'Hombre Salvagio' [savage man] was 'forgrone [covered] all in moss and Ivy' and was holding 'an Oken plant pluct up by the roots in hiz hande'.[8] Presumably Gascoigne's face was suitably daubed for the part, too. Gascoigne later wrote that he'd been commanded to produce this mini-drama 'upon a very great sudden'.[9] It was plainly something the Earl of Leicester had dreamed up on a whim and at its heart was a simple message to Elizabeth: *marry me*.

This message in fact was everywhere at Kenilworth that July. The clock on Caesar's Tower had been deliberately stopped at two o'clock. (Its square site can still be seen, high up on the south-west angle turret of the Keep.) This motionless clock indicated that Elizabeth's magical presence had frozen time itself, putting the castle under an enchanted spell. But the clock hands also pointed to two to underline Leicester's unsubtle message that he and Elizabeth ought to be paired. The courtship had been going on now for some 15 years and Dudley had had enough of it. He was growing old. He wanted a decision, one way or the other. He was pulling out all the stops and giving her the greatest show on earth. If that didn't do it, nothing would. And the Earl was determined to press his suit in the most explicit ways possible.

As the Queen approached, Gascoigne began a loud half-rhyming 40-line monologue.[10] Addressing 'Thundring Jupiter' he demanded to know why 'all these worthy Lords and Peeres' were assembled in The Chase. And not just noblemen, either, but also

> glorious Dames
> As kindle might in frozen breasts
> a furnace full of flames.

But Jupiter was silent in the face of Gascoigne's questions, so instead he called on 'Echo' to help. 'Echo' – an actor concealed in the undergrowth – duly answered his plea.

What followed was an ingenious dialogue in which Gascoigne spoke 25 stanzas of verse, with Echo repeating the last word of each stanza.[11] The poem – hardly Gascoigne's most distinguished literary production – offered a racy reprise of the entertainments previously presented to the Queen. But its purpose was more than descriptive. Having reminded Elizabeth of what she'd already seen – the sibyls,

47

the giant trumpeters, Hercules the porter and the Lady of the Lake – the Savage Man interrogated Echo about the objects displayed on the drawbridge. Were they

> sent from the Gods
> As presents from above?
> Or pleasures of provision
> as tokens of true love?

Echo answered: *true love*. Robert Dudley, Earl of Leicester, was making his pitch.

But the Savage Man hadn't finished yet. 'And who gave all those gifts?' he innocently asked – although, remarkably, he seemed to know the answer:

> Was it not he? Who (but of late)
> this building here did lay?

Echo duly echoed the desperately creaky pun in those last two words: *Dudley*. The Savage Man then thundered the message which was at the heart of the Kenilworth entertainments and which would be repeated until Elizabeth grew sick of it:

> O Dudley, so me thought:
> he gave himself and all,
> A worthy gift to be received,
> and so I trust it shall.

It shall, affirmed Echo, confidently.

But in fact it never was. The moment when Elizabeth might have wed Robert Dudley had long since passed. The 'gift' of his hand in marriage would be spurned, yet again. But that defining moment had not yet been reached. For the moment, Elizabeth was merely being courted. Combining a memory of Sunday's stupendous fireworks display with the hot/cold antithesis which had become the standard template of the Petrarchan love lyric, the wild man went on to ask:

> What meant the fiery flames

which through the waves so flew?
Can no cold answers quench desire?
Is that experience true?

True, agreed Echo. But in spite of Gascoigne's sponsored optimism the 'cold answers' would continue and Leicester's 'desire' would collapse almost overnight. Besides, the Earl was driven not by desire but by ambition. It was all more to do with power and status than sexual attraction. And the final collapse of Leicester's hopes was just nine days away.

At this point the wild man pretended to discover the proximity of the Queen and fell to his knees. It seems to have been at this moment that Gascoigne did something which caused the Queen's horse to rear up, nearly unseating her. George Gascoigne came very close to going down in history as the man who broke her neck. This mishap is mentioned in most popular biographies of Elizabeth. The only source that we have for it is in *A Letter*:

> az this Savage for the more submissiō[n] brake his tree a sunder, kest [cast] the top from him, it had allmost light upon her highnes hors hed: whereat he startld and the gentlman mooch dismayd, Seé the benigniteé of the Prins, az the foot men lookt well too the hors, and he of Generositee soon callmd of him self, no hurt no hurt, quoth her highness.[12]

In other words, Gascoigne made the theatrical gesture of snapping his oak branch in two and hurling one half away. Unfortunately it flew past the head of the Queen's horse, startling it.

The 'gentlman mooch dismayd' is ambiguous. Although 'gentlman' is singular rather than plural, the passage probably refers to the assembled courtiers gasping in horror, rather than to Gascoigne's own embarrassment. Footmen rushed forward to seize the horse. But the upset was only momentary; the animal quickly settled down. Elizabeth, an expert horsewoman, was unruffled by the incident. 'No hurt, no hurt,' she called out, probably seeking to calm the fussy, exaggerated displays of concern from the assembled sycophants. The incident was quickly over. The show went on.

The self-styled 'Savage man'[13] – the description now coloured with unintended comic irony after Gascoigne's clumsiness – continued with a monologue.[14] After more platitudes about the Queen's intelligence, beauty and glory, Gascoigne informed her of a forthcoming attraction later in the week – 'sundry gladsome games'. Bidding the now silent Echo farewell, the wild man departed.

In *The princelye pleasures at the Courte at Kenelwoorth* Gascoigne made no mention of the incident with the branch, which is unsurprising since the publication consisted largely of scripts. The only noteworthy feature of the savage man masque which he thought worth mentioning, apart from his writing and acting role, was that he produced it at very short notice.

But he may well have been alluding to the near-catastrophic accident in two marginal annotations which have been overlooked in accounts of this notorious episode. The first edition of *The princelye pleasures* included eleven notes, which were not included in the text republished in Gascoigne's *Whole woorkes* (1587).

The extreme rarity of the first edition – only one copy has ever been located, and that was destroyed in a fire in 1879 – meant that virtually every reprint uses the incomplete 1587 text. Unfortunately only one later edition of *The princelye pleasures* ever seems to have drawn on the rare 1576 text rather than the 1587 edition. This was an obscure Victorian edition published in London in 1821 by F. Marshall. It has all the appearance of having been rushed out to cash in on the popularity of Scott's *Kenilworth* and is not remotely scholarly. But, remarkably, it supplies the eleven marginal notes in an appendix at the end.[15] '*In the latter ende of the Eccho her Maiesty told the wilde man that he was blynde,*' reads a note alongside the description of 'a man cladde all in Mosse...declarying that he is the wylde mans sonne'[16] in a later, unperformed play.

It repeats the information given in the first of the eleven notations: '*Here the Queene saide that the Actor was blind.*' It is not obvious what Elizabeth meant by this. At its most literal, it might mean that Gascoigne's headgear was slipping down over his eyes. Her comment apparently occurred soon after the poet had almost unseated her, so perhaps she was jokingly warning him not to repeat his earlier *faux pas*.

The first marginal note comes alongside the line 'But comely peereless Prince' and seems to bear no relation to Gascoigne's speech

50

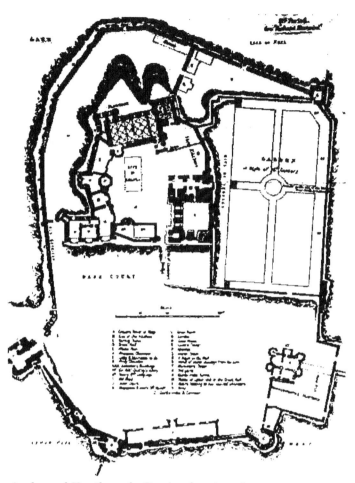

A plan of Kenilworth Castle showing the structure as it was in the sixteenth century, with the stable block at the base, the keep in the centre, the inner and outer courtyards, and the garden.

at that precise moment. It is possible that the Marshall edition is misquoting the 1576 edition, but there is now no way of telling. The note makes much more sense at the end of the dialogue with Echo some fifty lines earlier, which is where the second marginal note seems to place it. At that point, Gascoigne concluded with the words:

Well then if so myne eyes,
  be such as they have beene:
Me thinkes I see among them all,
  this same should be the Queene.

In this context, the Queen's remark makes perfect sense as a barbed comment that the wild man must be blind in taking so long to distinguish her from her ladies-in-waiting. This in fact seems to be the meaning, since 'the wylde mans sonne' was later intended to explain to Elizabeth

that his Father (uppon such wordes as hyr highnesse dyd then use unto him) lay languishing like a blind man, until it might please hyr highnesse to take the filme from his eyes.[17]

It again hints at the Queen's prickly mood, since her remark to Gascoigne supplies another example of her interrupting and openly disagreeing with someone playing a part in a masque. No doubt those who heard her comment (which the author of *A Letter* seems not to have done) all roared with sycophantic laughter.

Gascoigne himself was presumably more thrilled by being addressed in person by the Queen than by the fact that she was gently chiding him. If her comment *was* made at the end of the Echo dialogue, that might account for his over-exuberant response in breaking the branch. By mentioning it twice in marginal notes and a third time in the masque, Gascoigne showed that he was clearly very proud of Elizabeth's intervention. (We can also be reasonably sure that someone as interested in self-promotion as Gascoigne was would not have been pleased to find his marginalia missing from later editions of the text.)

News of the incident quickly filtered out to those who weren't present. Don Antonio de Guaras, the Spanish Ambassador, a man with a prodigious thirst for wild rumour, wrote a week later that 'it is said that whilst she was going hunting on one of the days, a traitor shot a cross-bow at her... The bolt passed near the Queen but did her no harm, thank God!'[18] This seems to have been nothing more than a garbled, exaggerated account of Gascoigne's clumsy accident.

7   The mermaid and the dolphin

'The next thing that was presented before her Majesty was the deliverie of the Lady of the Lake,' says Gascoigne, after his account of the wild man's speeches.[1]

What this remark reveals is the poet's indifference both to the popular entertainment that was staged and also to material not produced by himself or the other leading members of Leicester's writing team. In fact the Lady of the Lake did not re-appear for another week, during which time a variety of amusements were set out for Elizabeth.

The next day, Tuesday 12 July, there was music and dancing. At dusk the Queen walked through Leicester's Gatehouse and out on to the bridge, where she stood and listened to musicians playing 'sundry kinds of very delectabl Muzik' from a barge anchored in the moat.[2] Afterwards she went for a stroll in the parkland by the lake shore.

On Wednesday there was another deer hunt, when once again the deer fled into the water. It was captured and 'the watermé[n] held him up hard by the hed, while at her highnes commaundemé[n]t he lost his earz for a raundsum [ransom] and so had pardon of lyfe.'[3]

Even gorier entertainment was on offer the next day, when thirteen bears were assembled in the inner court and a 'great sort of bā[n]dogs' in the outer.[4] Bandogs were the Tudor equivalent of mastiffs. The bears were then 'brought foorth intoo the Coourt' - which probably means the outer court – to fight them.

Mastiffs are among the most aggressive kind of dog, with strong jaws; modern breeds include the pit bull terrier and the rottweiler. The mastiffs went for the bears' throats, while the bears slashed the dogs' scalps – 'a sport very pleazaunt'.[5] Surprisingly, *A Letter* doesn't say which animals won this bloody fight. Since Dudley's family symbol was a bear one suspects that the fight was fixed and the bears, not the dogs, survived. The bandogs were 'tyed', so perhaps they remained chained up, putting them at a disadvantage while the bears attacked.

After this an Italian acrobat put on a show in front of Elizabeth 'within'[6] (i.e. indoors – perhaps in the Great Hall). The author of *A Letter* was breathless with admiration for the man's performance, 'such feats of agilitee, in goinges, turninges, tumblinges… forward, backward, syde wize, doownward, upward, and with sundry windings gyrings and circumflexions… [I] began to doout whither a waz a man or a spirite.'[7]

That night there was a third and final fireworks display. It featured 'very straunge and sundry kindez of fier works, compeld by cunning too fly too and fro and too mount very hy intoo the ayr upward.'[8] Some fireworks burned 'unquenshabl in the water beneath: contrary yee wot [understand], too fyerz, kinde.'

This display once again utilised the Great Mere as a backdrop, and even an old theatrical impresario like Gascoigne was impressed. The fireworks were, he wrote, 'both strange and wel executed: as sometimes passing under the water a long space, when all men had thought they had bene quenched, they would rise and mount out of the water againe, and burne very furiously untill they were utterlie consumed.'[9]

The unquenchable fire may conceivably have been intended to symbolize the Earl's enduring and irrepressible passion for Elizabeth. But it raises a technical conundrum. Could rockets really have been attached to guide-wires that dipped below the lake surface? It's hard to believe that any firework could be immersed in water without it being extinguished. Since the display took place late at night, this effect may just have been a clever illusion. The displays were synchronized 'with a great peal of guns' and lasted about two hours.

*

The next day, Friday 15 July, the unbroken spell of sunshine which had accompanied the Queen's visit since her arrival came to an end. For two days the weather 'enclynde too sum moyster [moisture, i.e. rain] & wynde' and no outside entertainments were staged.

Thanks to Gascoigne, we know of one aborted entertainment which had been arranged for the Saturday. Once again, it utilised the Great Mere. The plan was for 'the heron house' at the lakeside to represent the Lady of the Lake's castle. At nightfall a captain with 20-30 men was to leave the castle and be ambushed by a similar number of troops under the command of the wicked knight Sir Bruce. There would be much skirmishing and shooting. In the end the knight's men would be driven off. The mock-battle would magically appear to take place on water, with the protagonists standing on submerged bulrushes. The captain of the victorious side would have then gone to Elizabeth and begged her to deliver the Lady of the Lake from Merlin's spell.

The verses which were to have been recited on this occasion were written by William Hunnis, George Ferrers and Harry Goldyngham, but Gascoigne was either unable to get hold of them, or chose to leave them out of *The princelye pleasures.*

The tableau appealed to the military man in Gascoigne and he regretted it was not staged: 'This had not onely bene a more apt introduction to her delivery, but also the skirmish by night woulde have bene both very strange and gallant.'

Bad weather may just possibly have been the reason for the abandonment of this mini-drama but it seems much more probable that its cancellation was deliberate and nothing at all to do with wind and rain. This 'skirmish' (with Leicester possibly in the role of the captain, dressed in a new gold suit of armour) could be interpreted as thinly-veiled advice to Elizabeth to intervene militarily in the Low Countries. Perhaps by this point the Queen was growing very tired of symbolic masques instructing her in affairs of state. Perhaps, too, she was tiring of the theme of enchanted lovers, particularly if they involved indications of the Earl of Leicester's kingly grandeur and greatness of heart. Four days later another entertainment would be cancelled. It was penned by Gascoigne and it effectively brought the Kenilworth festivities to an explosive and premature end.

*

On Sunday it went back to being warm and sunny, and, as one week earlier, there was a service, including a sermon, at the parish church. In the afternoon the entertainment consisted of what Gascoigne called 'the merry marriage'[10] and *A Letter* describes as 'a solem brydeale [wedding] of a proper coopl'.[11] But the author of *A Letter* seems to have had his tongue wedged firmly in his cheek. Judging by the description of the 'bridegroom', who 'throogh good scoolation [instruction] becam az formall in his action az had he beén a bride groom indeéd'[12] this was not, in spite of appearances, a genuine wedding party but a local folk ceremony.[13]

In permitting the participants to hold their mock wedding reception in the grounds of the castle, the Earl of Leicester was both displaying his generosity to the commoners of the neighbourhood and pointedly underlining the theme of the happiness and celebration that a wedding could bring.

The 'wedding party' lined up in the tiltyard. It was led by the 'bridegroom' and all the bachelors of the parish, on horseback. After them came six morris dancers, with Maid Marian and a Fool, followed by three bridesmaids carrying spicecakes, a tall frecklefaced red-headed man carrying the bride-cup, then 'the bride' escorted by two elderly parishioners. She was followed by a dozen bridesmaids.

They rode and marched into 'the great coourt' (meaning the base or outer court) to 'make thear [their] sheaw [show] before the Castl'. This entertainment evidently consisted of a parade, followed by the horseriders taking turns to tilt at a wooden quintain or target.

The bride was supposed to dance before the Queen, but then the entertainments programme seems to have started to go awry. So many people had poured into the outer court that it became packed with a vast, restless crowd. The description in *A Letter* is ambiguous, but either some of the 'merry marriage' party were unable to force their way through the crowd to perform, or the Queen ordered the termination of the show. Matters weren't helped by the actors for the next performance pushing forwards impatiently to get started. The wedding performers therefore lined up and marched out of the base court by Leicester's Gatehouse, across the bridge over the moat and back into Kenilworth.

By now it was four o'clock. The next entertainment was a popular play. Some men from Coventry had turned up and petitioned to be allowed to perform 'their olld storiall sheaw'.[14] This was what is usually called 'the Coventry play' – a festive history play dating from 1416, which celebrated the overthrow of the Danes. Because it showed 'how valiantly our English women for loove of their cuntreé behaved themselvez…they thought it moought [must] moove sum myrth to her Majesty the rather.'[15] The play had evidently encountered opposition from humourless Coventry ecclesiastics.

Their request was granted, and the play started. A Coventry man known as 'Captain Cox' marched across the performance space (presumably the outer court, again). He wore a velvet cap lent to him by Henry Goldyngham and flourished a large sword. Another swordsman accompanied him. Behind them came the Danish knights on horseback, followed by English knights.

Captain Cox was described by the author of *A Letter* as 'an od man I promiz yoo: by profession a Mason, and that right skilfull: very cunning in fens [fencing], and hardy az Gawin [Gawaine], for hiz tonsword hangs at his tablz eénd: great oversight hath he in matters of storie'.[16]

He was evidently the Tudor equivalent of a self-educated working class intellectual, and something of a boisterous 'character'. *A Letter* lists 33 ballads, legends, romances and collections of jests which Captain Cox knew by heart and evidently owned copies of, and a further 29 'books' (not necessarily all printed publications but probably including bound manuscripts). These included tales of King Arthur, Robin Hood and Gargantua, a life of Virgil, satires by Skelton, riddles, a medical text listing different kinds of disease, and a book about Nostradamus.[17]

Half a century later, Ben Jonson saluted this man who 'Had a goodly library' in 'The Masque of Owles at Kenelworth, Presented by the Ghost of Captaine Coxe mounted in his Hoby-horse':

Roome, roome, for my Horse will wince,
If he come within so many yards of a Prince,
And though he have not in his wings,
He will doe strange things.
He is the *Pegasus* that uses
To waite on *Warwick* muses;
And on gaudy-dayes he paces
Before the *Coventrie* Graces;
For to tell you true, and in rime,
He was foald in Q. *Elizabeths* time,
When the great Earle of *Lester*
In this Castle did feast her.[18]

It is unclear what Jonson's source was. His account of Leicester's extravaganza refers only to what happened on two days, Thursday 14 July and Sunday 17 July. Jonson displays a supercilious attitude to crude entertainment like bear-baiting, and the ghost of Captain Cox

57

explains,

> I come to play your Host;
> And feast your eyes and eares,
> Neither with Dogs, nor Beares,
> Though that have beene a fit
> Of our maine shire-wit,
> In times heretofore

Jonson says that Captain Cox fought at Boulogne with Henry VIII, a detail not found in *A Letter*. He also portrays the Captain as being mounted not on a real horse but a wooden hobby horse. But there is nothing in *A Letter* to suggest that the men of Coventry were mounted on anything other than real horses. E.K. Chambers has also suggested that only wooden horses were used, but Benjamin Griffin makes a convincing case for real horses, pointing to their use at a similar kind of show in Chester.[19]

The Coventry players performed 'under her highnes windo'[20] (meaning one of the big, modern windows in Leicester's Building). But Elizabeth was not in the mood to watch the play. She could see 'delectabl dauncing' going on 'in the chamber', and evidently wanted to participate herself.[21] The Coventry play was halted and the performers were told to come back on Tuesday.

Ben Jonson's account is a little different. According to him, Captain Cox was 'a little man', and when the battle between the Saxons and the Danes began,

> He was not so well seene,
> As he would have beene o' the Queene.
> Though his sword were twice so long
> As any mans else in the throng;
> And for his sake, the Play
> Was call'd for the second day.

It is unclear whether Ben Jonson had access to some other written source or eye-witness account, or had seen a copy of *A Letter* and was imaginatively rewriting its content. Jonson was only three at the time of Elizabeth's 1575 progress, and his explanation why the play was put on a second time seems less plausible than that contained in *A Letter*.

The 'chamber' with the 'delectable dancing' which attracted Elizabeth's attention was probably the Privy Chamber, immediately adjacent to Leicester's Building. This moment underlines the haughty indifference of the leisured upper class to the rowdy, boisterous entertainment of the common people which was going on in the outer court. Elizabeth's guests preferred to engage in some impromptu dancing inside the castle, rather than watch what was going on outside. Gascoigne may have been with them. He makes it clear in *The princelye pleasures* that he regards such crude populist material as unworthy of description, brusquely dismissing the Coventry play in three words as 'the countrie shewe'.[22] His focus, as his title states, was on material by *sundry Gentlemen*.

*

That night at the castle, after supper, a play was staged. What the play was, who performed it, and where in the castle it was put on, is not known. It seems to have been a full-length comedy and it lasted for over two hours. The play may have had nothing at all to do with the members of the writing team, since Gascoigne neither mentions it nor includes the script.

It was followed by a spectacularly lavish banquet with 300 different dishes. This must have been held in the Great Hall (which is also a likely venue for the play, though it is possible that it was staged in the 'White-hall' next door). The banquet was supposed to be accompanied, or more likely followed, by a masque, 'for riches of aray, of an incredibl cost'. But it was now so late that the performance was called off.

It is possible that this refers to Gascoigne's masque, scheduled (perhaps re-scheduled) for the following Wednesday, which involved elaborate special effects. However, that was planned for outdoors. This aborted masque may have been a completely different one, since *A Letter* refers only to the phenomenal cost of the actors' gorgeous costumes and says nothing about stage machinery.

*

On Monday 18 July the weather was hot, and, as on other sunny days, the Queen stayed inside the castle until 5 p.m. That day, according to *A Letter*, she knighted five gentlemen: Thomas Cecil (b. 1542), son of Lord Burghley; Henry Cobham (b. 1538?), a diplomat; Thomas Stanhope (d. 1596), the son of Sir Michael Stanhope; Arthur Bassett, Sheriff of Devon; and Thomas Tresham (b. 1543?), Sheriff of Northamptonshire in 1573-74.[23]

She also cured nine commoners 'of the peynfull and daungerous diseaz, called ye kings evill...without oother medsin (save only by handling & prayerz)'.[24] This refers to the popular superstition that the sovereign had divine powers of healing, and that the mere touch of the Queen's hand was enough to cure a sick person.

Elizabeth clearly believed in this nonsense, which flattered her sense of self-importance. Whether or not the 'cures' she effected were psychological or opportunistic is far from clear. The diarist Henry Machyn recorded how on one occasion a poor man with two crutches was watching Queen Mary when, transformed by her royal presence, he threw his crutches away and ran after her. Flattered by this proof of her divine powers, Mary commanded that the man be given a reward.[25] No doubt this encouraged others to discover that the sovereign's presence held astonishing healing properties.

*

What happened that evening at Kenilworth supplied the second of two moments from the July festivities which are remembered above all others. The first – Gascoigne's mishap with the oak branch – involved the Queen. The second is famous for its intriguing suggestion that William Shakespeare was present. In *A Midsummer Night's Dream*, Oberon, King of the Fairies, remarks:

My gentle puck, come hither. Thou rememb'rest
Since once I sat upon a promontory
And heard a mermaid on a dolphin's back
Uttering such dulcet and harmonious breath
That the rude sea grew civil at her song,
And certain stars shot madly from their spheres
To hear the sea-maid's music?

And Robin Goodfellow (or Puck) replies:

I remember.
(2.1.148-154)

Was Shakespeare expressing his own powerful childhood memory of
the Kenilworth entertainments? These lines in themselves prove
nothing. It's always a temptation to extract material from
Shakespeare's plays or verse and make the easy assumption that it is
directly autobiographical. Generations of scholars have squabbled
interminably over the extent to which *Shakespeare's Sonnets* are
autobiographical. His plays are full of material about war and
soldiery, but nobody seriously believes he was ever a fighting soldier.
He got what he wanted out of books. Similarly, the plays are full of
legal terminology but there is not a scrap of evidence Shakespeare
ever had any legal training. His biography has always been hard to
write because the records of his life are patchy and it seems to have
lacked the glamour of involvement in major historical events.
Shakespeare's great adventures and voyages were all in his mind.

On the surface, he was not an interesting man. In his lifetime he
was not regarded as a figure of fascination. Shakespeare had no great
compulsion to promote himself as a writer. Plays were provisional
pieces of writing, directly or indirectly collaborative, subject to cuts
and rewriting, not frozen and timeless slabs of poetry cast by a
genius. Shakespeare was an entertainer and entrepreneur interested in
making money. He may have published a number of quartos for a
literary readership but he was not a celebrity. That concept barely
existed, though it would be true to say there was just as much
contemporary fascination and rumour regarding the private lives of
Elizabeth and Leicester as there is nowadays about pop singers and
movie stars. But that public fascination involved two of the most
powerful figures in the land; it did not extend to writers. When his
poems and some of his plays were published in his lifetime,
Shakespeare felt no urge to include a portrait. Of what interest was
the personality of a playwright? None whatever. Shakespeare led a
quiet life. Much of it must have been spent reading books.

Shakespeare was a great reader. He was a sponge, a man of
insatiable curiosity and a creative plagiarist – not a man of action. It

61

could be argued that Shakespeare never went near Kenilworth Castle, and it would be impossible to prove otherwise. This is not because possible proof has vanished but because it would never have existed in the first place. In terms of documentary fact Shakespeare's childhood and adolescence is a complete blank, apart from the record of his christening on 26 April 1564 and the issuing of a marriage licence to "*willelmu*m Shaxpere" (sic) on 27 November 1582. Even the date of his birth is not known, and the patriotic orthodoxy of St George's Day, 23 April, is nothing more than colourful guesswork. We don't even know for certain that Shakespeare attended Stratford grammar school, although it is commonly and reasonably assumed that he did. Perhaps, as Katherine Duncan-Jones believes, he read *A Letter*.[26] Shakespeare almost certainly read *The princelye pleasures at the Courte at Kenelwoorth*. So perhaps he just read about the Queen's visit, and used his imagination'

Shakespeare did occasionally put obscure private material into his plays. Most scholars accept that *As You Like It* contains lines which allude to Christopher Marlowe and the ambiguous circumstances of his death. Anne Righter argues that two references to the dead dramatist 'are so diffident, so deeply buried in their own dramatic context, that one almost wonders if they were intended to evoke the image of Marlowe for the playgoers at the Globe, or whether they represented some purely personal rite of memory.'[27]

That Shakespeare sometimes included personal matter in his plays which would have been meaningless to the audience is demonstrated by *Cymbeline* (c. 1610). When Innogen, disguised as a young man, is called upon to invent a personal history, she says that her master was 'Richard du Champ' (4.2.378). This translates into English as 'Richard Field' – a London master printer who, like the playwright, came from Stratford-upon-Avon, where his father was an associate of John Shakespeare. Richard Field was the man who printed *Venus and Adonis* and *Lucrece* and he was plainly close to Shakespeare. Modern biographers believe that Field's printing house in Blackfriars supplied Shakespeare with access to the expensive books he required as source material.

The lines spoken by Oberon in *A Midsummer Night's Dream* contain two references which suggest that the Shakespearean source was in personal experience, not in a book.

The description 'certain stars shot madly from their spheres' is likely to have been drawn from the actual experience of seeing fireworks. Stephen Greenblatt, like most biographers of Shakespeare, accepts the probability that he was present at Kenilworth in July 1575 and argues that the experience evidently strongly marked his vision of the theatre. But he downplays the visceral impact of that experience, remarking that 'the fireworks were hardly stars starting from their spheres'.[28] That expresses, I think, a jaded modern sensibility. Nowadays fireworks are a familiar phenomenon, with spectacular displays on 5 November and New Year's Eve, as well as on numerous other occasions. Fireworks don't awe us any more. They are as common as aircraft flying across the sky.

What needs to be remembered is that at Kenilworth in 1575 probably none of the locals had ever seen fireworks before. Indeed, the word 'firework' enters the language at this point, in both *A Letter* (1575) and *The princelye pleasures at the Courte at Kenelwoorth* (1576). To the Elizabethans, fireworks were strange and marvellous and seen, if at all, only very, very rarely.

Shakespeare used the word 'firework' just twice in his entire career, and only once in its literal sense. In *Love's Labours Lost*, Armado says that the King has asked him to set before the Princess 'some delightful ostentation, or show, or pageant, or antic, or firework.' (5.1.103-5)

Leicester organised all of those alternatives, and the fireworks at Kenilworth were probably the finest ever seen in England in the sixteenth century. Shakespeare may have witnessed all three of the tremendous displays put on at the castle between July 9 and July 14; he certainly seems to have seen at least one of them. What is striking about *A Midsummer Night's Dream* is just how suffused with a memory of fireworks it seems to be. There is 'hail' and 'heat' and 'showers of oaths' (1.1.244-5), and Cupid's 'best arrow with the golden head' (1.1.170). And there is Lysander's sense of the powerful forces which perpetually threaten love

Making it momentany as a sound,
Swift as a shadow, short as any dream,
Brief as the lightning in the collied night
(1.1.143-5)

Even more impressively there is fate, which annihilates human achievement:

> The jaws of darkness do devour it up.
> So quick bright things come to confusion.
> (1.1.148-9)

This figurative language is surely rooted not in printed descriptions of fireworks but in the actual experience of seeing them. For reasons described later, it is highly improbable that Shakespeare ever read *A Letter*. And Gascoigne's admiring but perfunctory description of the fireworks is unlikely to have made quite the same impact that actually seeing them as a child would have done. And here I can only judge the matter by my own experience of life. When I was the same age that Shakespeare was at the time of the Kenilworth revels my parents took me on a trip to Paris. I remember little of that holiday. But what I do remember is the visit to Versailles. We stood beside the ornamental lake at night and watched a stupendous, spectacular fireworks display. Many years later, the experience is still vivid.

*

Kenilworth Castle is twelve miles north of Stratford-upon-Avon. If Shakespeare went there in July of that year, aged eleven years and two and a half months, who took him? Shakespeare's most comprehensive modern biographer, Park Honan, thinks it unlikely that in July 1575 John Shakespeare closed his glover's business and took his eldest two children to Kenilworth. It is hard to imagine the dramatist's mother Mary taking the children, since she was responsible for a baby (Richard, born in March 1574), a three-year-old (Anne, baptized in September 1571) and a six-year old (Joan, born in April 1569). But if William went to Kenilworth, it seems quite possible that his younger brother Gilbert, aged eight, went too. If so, they may have been taken by friends of his parents, or perhaps by relatives.

The Victorian scholar F.J. Furnivall was in little doubt that Shakespeare 'either went by himself or was taken over from Stratford by his father John... John Shakespeare, who had been High Bailiff of the town in September 1568-9, Chief Alderman in September 1571-2, and was still an Alderman in 1575, must have felt himself of sufficient importance to be present at a county festivity of the kind.'[29]

Another possibility (not, as far as I am aware, previously considered) is Shakespeare's uncle. Henry Shakespeare was the younger brother of the dramatist's father and lived in the small rural community of Snitterfield, where he was a farmer. He is a shadowy figure but the glimpses we get of him suggest someone with a free and easy attitude to life. In 1583 he was fined for repeatedly not wearing a cap to church. He was twice jailed for debt. He let a ditch fall into decay and failed to meet his obligations to maintain the Queen's highways, for which he was penalized by the authorities. The year before the Queen's great visit to Kenilworth, he was fined for drawing blood in a fight. He sounds like a bit of a rogue or a rascal; a scapegrace not unlike his nephew's representation of another unreformed Henry, Prince Hal.

Henry Shakespeare maintained friendly relations with his brother John; that, at any rate, is a reasonable deduction to be drawn from the fact that in 1586 the dramatist's father stood surety for a debt of Henry's. The debt was not repaid and it was John Shakespeare who found himself the subject of an action by the creditor. In short, Henry Shakespeare sounds just like the sort of person who would have abandoned his farming commitments and breezed off to Kenilworth Castle with his two young nephews. Interestingly, Snitterfield lies some four miles north-east of Stratford, on the route to Kenilworth.

There may have been a third uncle, Thomas Shakespeare, though the evidence for this is ambiguous and uncertain. For all we know he might, if he existed, have lived at Kenilworth. As it is we'll never know who took William Shakespeare to see the Queen, or where he stayed – assuming that he went at all. But there is an aspect of Oberon's speech which clinches the circumstantial evidence indicating that William Shakespeare really was present at Kenilworth in July 1575. It's not something you can pick up from sitting in a library reading books. To understand it you need to have visited and understood the Kenilworth site.

Oberon's description of 'a mermaid on a dolphin's back' quite specifically refers to the entertainments put on at Kenilworth on the evening of Monday 18 July 1575. It had been a sweltering hot summer's day. The Queen had stayed indoors all day, and no entertainments had so far been staged for her. As the sun sank over the Warwickshire countryside, the Queen emerged from Leicester's Building. Around 5 p.m. she went hunting in The Chase. Her entourage clattered through the archway of Leicester's Gatehouse, crossed the bridge, and headed west into The Chase. Once again the hunted deer fled into the water.

Returning from the hunt, Elizabeth was approaching the castle when a trumpet blast blew, attracting her attention with a 'soound very shrill & sonoroous'.[30] It was Triton, servant of the sea god Neptune, riding a boat shaped like a gigantic mermaid, eighteen feet long. The Queen had been in The Chase, to the north of the castle, and the floating mermaid was in the bay by the Swan Tower. Elizabeth reached the bridge leading to the gatehouse and the mermaid drew closer, evidently entering the moat which ran alongside the curtain wall beside the garden.

This evening's entertainment had been devised and written by William Hunnis, Master of the Queen's Chapel. Presumably he brought along with him professional musicians from the royal court; whether or not his choirboys came too is unclear, but since this was royal entertainment it seems unlikely that they were left behind.

Triton put down his trumpet, which had been made to look like a giant whelk shell, and narrated what had happened to the Lady of the Lake since her appearance on the first evening of Elizabeth's arrival at the castle. Having yielded up her lake and promised to attend Elizabeth's court, the Lady had been harassed by the wicked knight Sir Bruce, who had 'sought by force, her virgins state, / full fowlie to deface'.[31] Since the knight's men patrolled the shores of the Great Mere, the Lady had been unable to fulfill her pledge and was doomed to remain trapped there, 'Except a worthier maide then she, / her cause do take in hand.'

Triton's boat then returned from the moat and headed back towards the bay ('Mooving héerwith from the bridge & fleeting more intoo the pool'), probably to make room for the other entertainers.[32] The rowers concealed inside the mermaid then churned the water with their oars. Triton sounded his trumpet again, and commanded the winds to fall silent and the 'waters wilde' to turn calm. Shakespeare's description of how 'the rude sea grew civil' at the mermaid's song obviously echoes this moment. Stephen Greenblatt misinterprets what happened at this point, remarking 'there was no sea, only an unruly crowd by the castle lake'.[33] But to a Stratford child, the vast Mere might well have resembled a sea; in any case, *A Letter* makes it clear that its surface was disturbed for dramatic effect, and Shakespeare's 'rude sea' is a reference to this, not to the crowd lining the shore.

The Lady of the Lake, liberated by Elizabeth's presence, now appeared with her two attendant nymphs. The three figures floated across the water towards the bridge where the Queen stood. Or rather they *seemed* to. In fact they had a hidden pathway concealed just below the surface, and walked 'uppon heapes of Bulrushes'.[34] That was Gascoigne's version, anyway. The author of *A Letter* describes the Lady and her attendants 'floting upon her moovable Islands (*Triton* on hiz mermaid skimming by)'.[35]

The Lady made a short speech of thanks to Elizabeth. As a token of her thanks she presented the Queen with the gift of Arion ('that excellé[n]t & famous Muzicien') sat on a dolphin's back.[36]

The dolphin, presumably hidden out of sight in the bay beyond the Swan Tower, now sailed into view '& swymd hard by theez Ilands' (meaning the bulrushes or boats upon which the Lady and her two nymphs were standing). The giant dolphin was another disguised boat or barge, some 24 feet in length, or as Gascoigne put it, 'the *Dolphyn* was conveied upon a boate, so that the Owers [oars] seemed to bee his Fynnes'.[37] Greenblatt erroneously refers to it as a 'mechanical dolphin' which 'rose up out of the waters of the lake',[38] making it sound like an early submarine; it plainly wasn't, and was at no point submerged.

Arion greeted Elizabeth and reiterated the Lady's thanks for her release from bondage. He then began singing a song, accompanied by the music of six musicians concealed out of sight in the beast's belly. There may have been a mishap at the start of the song, if one undated, anonymous anecdote is to be believed:

There was a Spectacle presented to Queen Elizabeth upon the water, and amongst others, Harry Goldingham was to represent Arion upon the Dolphins backe, but finding his voice to be very hoarse and unpleasant when he came to perform it, he teares of[f] his Disguise, and swears he was none of Arion not he, but eene honest Harry Goldingham: which blunt discoverie pleasd the Queene better, then if it had gone thorough in the right way; yet he could order his voice to an instrument exceeding well.[39]

Walter Scott liked this story, and in *Kenilworth* (Vol. 3, Chapter 5) he gave it to his invented character, Michael Lambourne. (Scott also advanced it nine days in time and included it in his account of the Queen's initial arrival at the castle on 9 July.)

This tale of Goldyngham tearing off his mask is always enshrined as fact in accounts of Kenilworth, but it may just have been a comic story invented years later, with no basis in reality. If something like that really happened, it is odd that *A Letter* makes no mention of it. Its author usually has a sharp eye for things that go wrong.

George Gascoigne, however, half-hints that not everything went to plan, capping his regrets for the abandoned Lady of the Lake masque by the heron house with the cryptic observation, 'and thereupon her Majestie might have taken good occasion to have gone in her barge upon the water for the better executing of her deliverie'.[40]

Since 'the deliverie' of the Lady took place on the Monday, not at the heron house, it suggests that Gascoigne felt the bridge by the north gatehouse was not the best location for her to appreciate the water-based masque.

Perhaps the author of *A Letter* liked Goldyngham's singing so much he left the mishap with the mask out of the record as a kindness. He certainly seems to have been enraptured by the beauty of the song, the singing, the musical accompaniment and the setting. He called it 'delectabl', 'melodious', 'delicioously deliverd':

ye song by a skilful artist intoo his parts so sweétly sorted: each part in hiz instrument so clean & sharpely toouched, every instrument again in hiz kind so excellently tunabl: and this in the éening of the day, resoounding from the callm waters: whear prezens of her Majesty & longing too listen had utterly damped all noyz & dyn: the hole [h]armony conveyd in tyme, tune, & temper thus incomparably melodious: [41]

Arion sang of his gratitude that Elizabeth had liberated the Lady:

Ne none but you deliver us,
   from loitring life withall.
She pined long in paine,
   as overworne with woes:
And we consumde in endless care,
   to fend her from her foes.
Both which you set at large,
   most like a faithfull freend:
Your noble name by praisd therefore,
   and so my song I ende.[42]

The writer of *A Letter* describes how he was left dazed, almost literally entranced by the gorgeous song: 'As for me surely I waz lulld in such liking & so loth too leave of, ye mooch a doo a good while after, had I, to fynde me whear I waz.'[43]

Was Shakespeare present, too, and equally overwhelmed by Arion's song? In *A Midsummer Night's Dream*, Oberon describes not Arion but a *mermaid* on a dolphin's back. Had a childhood memory become blurred? A classic instance of Shakespeare's faulty memory occurs in *Titus Andronicus*, when Titus, horrified by the discovery of who his daughter's attackers were, cries out in Latin (4.1.81-2). Here, Shakespeare misquotes Seneca, blurring lines from *Phaedra* with a line from *Epistulae Morales*.[44] But perhaps in the case of *A Midsummer Night's Dream* the dramatist simply regarded a mermaid as dramatically more effective.

Elsewhere, he got it right. In *Twelfth Night* the ship's captain tells Viola that her brother may well have survived the shipwreck:

Assure yourself, after our ship did split,
When you and those poor number sav'd with you
Hung on our driving boat, I saw your brother
Most provident in peril, bind himself
(Courage and hope both teaching him the practice)
To a strong mast that liv'd upon the sea;
Where, like Arion on the dolphin's back,
I saw him hold acquaintance with the waves
So long as I could see.
(I.ii. 9-17)

The last three lines seem to describe what actually happened at Kenilworth. Shakespeare stared in wonder at the massive wooden dolphin, surmounted by its singer, until it faded in the darkness of the night. The fact that Shakespeare mentioned the dolphin, not once but twice in his plays, does strongly indicate a very personal memory.

There is also this:

You ladies, you whose gentle hearts do fear
The smallest monstrous mouse that creeps on floor
May now perchance both quake and tremble here,
    When Lion rough in wildest rage doth roar.
Then know that I one Snug the joiner am
A lion fell [fierce]
(5.1.215-20)

This has commonly been viewed by biographers as a distant echo of that comic moment when Arion is said to have torn off his mask and shouted that he was none other than 'honest Harry Goldingham'.

What no one has noticed is that these lines from *A Midsummer Night's Dream* supply another clue. Oberon says that he 'sat upon a promontory'. This is a topographical detail which exactly fits the landscape at Kenilworth on that mid-July Monday in 1575.

The great lake was not a circle or an oval but an irregular feature, formed from the damming of two local streams, Finham Brook and Inchford Brook. These streams still exist today, cutting across the marshy depression which marks the site of the Mere. Very roughly, from west to east, the lake took the shape of the number '8', pushed over sideways. The shoreline was irregular, and followed the contours of the higher ground around the course of the two streams.

The footpath which runs from The Brays still follows the zig-zagging southerly course of the old shoreline and its miniature headlands. The greatest promontory of all, however, lay just to the west, a short distance from Kenilworth Castle. It is clearly marked on pictures of the Great Mere displayed at the castle, and its outline can still easily be identified today, following the lines of the hedgerows. A narrow single-track road, Purlieu Lane, runs across it.

This promontory provided a superb vantage point for the ordinary local people who crowded the lake shore to watch the water pageant.

The view from the promontory on the west side, showing the site of the bay where the floating mermaid and the dolphin appeared.

It was also the best place to see the giant floating mermaid and the giant dolphin, since these masques were staged in the moat between the Swan Tower and the bridge which crossed from the castle green side to Leicester's Gateway. Elizabeth viewed these masques from the bridge, and they would therefore have been out of view of anyone standing on the eastern and much of the southern shore.

Oberon's words therefore provide a poetic and imaginative précis of that spectacle on the Great Mere and other Kenilworth festivities, including the fireworks. The inspiration for his speech came, I believe, from real life; from William Shakespeare actually being present on that promontory in Warwickshire when the masques took place. The impact of his presence at the Kenilworth revels was to resonate through his writing career. The word 'promontory', used only rarely by Shakespeare, on each occasion seems to carry associations with the Queen's visit to Kenilworth.

On five of those occasions (as I shall show below) those associations are to do with performance and spectacle. In short, Kenilworth haunted Shakespeare throughout his adult life as a dramatist. His engagement with his memories of the revels was complex. And, characteristically, he was able to step outside them and mock them. Nick Bottom, the weaver, is a man haunted by an enchanting experience – an experience which lies outside human understanding or knowledge:

I have had a most rare vision. I have had a dream past the wit of man to say what dream it was.Man is but an ass if he go about to expound this dream.   Methought I was – there is no man can tell what. Methought I was – there is no man can tell what. Methought I was, and methought I had – but man is but a patched fool if he will offer to say what methought I had. The eye of man hath not heard, the ear of man hath not seen, man's hand is not able to taste, his tongue to conceive, nor his heart to report what my dream was.
(4.1.201-10)

The 'dream' cannot be transmitted to others. It lies outside human communication or 'report'. Then, in comic contradiction of everything he has just said, the weaver announces that he will get Peter Quince to write a ballad about his dream: 'It shall be called "Bottom's Dream", because it hath no bottom'... I shall sing it at her death.' (4.1.211-15) A unique experience – one which is an infinite resource and 'hath no bottom' – is turned into material for a dramatic performance. This, I think, is Shakespeare wryly scrutinising his own creative endeavours. Peter Quince's ballad is a metaphor for *A Midsummer Night's Dream* itself, rooted in the Kenilworth revels.

8   The masque in The Chase

According to Alexander Schmidt's vast nineteenth century *Shakespeare Lexicon*, the word 'promontory' occurs seven times in Shakespeare's work. The usage which might seem to have least to do with Kenilworth in July 1575 occurs in the hunting scene in *Titus Andronicus:*

>   I have dogs, my lord,
> Will rouse the proudest panther in the chase
> And climb the highest promontory top.
> (2.1.20-22)

This is a Roman hunt but apart from that exotic panther the technical scenes of this scene ('uncouple', 'make a bay', *'wind horns in a peal'*) are no different to that of a Tudor hunting party. Shakespeare was plainly not intending any kind of allusion to Kenilworth, and 'promontory' is used more in the sense of 'mountain ridge' than land which sticks out into water. Nevertheless the fact that his imagination juxtaposed 'the chase' (meaning land reserved for hunting) and 'promontory' is, at the very least, an intriguing association, since it replicates the topography of Kenilworth. Close to Purlieu Lane and the land that formed a promontory into the Great Mere lie East Chase Farm and South Chase Farm, names which refer to The Chase – the deer park where the Earl of Leicester took Elizabeth hunting during those July days.

Equally intriguing are the lines in *A Midsummer Night's Dream* in which Hippolyta recalls a hunt in a Cretan wood

> With hounds of Sparta. Never did I hear
> Such gallant chiding, for besides the groves,
> The skies, the fountains, every region near
> Seemed all one mutual cry. I never heard
> So musical a discord, such sweet thunder.
> (4.1.113-17)

Did the boy Shakespeare witness the Queen hunting with dogs in the Chase? These lines are not based on anything Shakespeare found in classical mythology but were added by him.

Hunting formed a key element in the Kenilworth entertainments and in 1942, in the middle of the Second World War, Jean Robertson, a lecturer at Liverpool University, announced a discovery which significantly adds to our understanding of what occurred during the Queen's visit. She published a short article showing that the author of the anonymous 1575 hunting book *The Noble Arte of Venerie and Hunting* was not, as traditionally assumed, George Turberville, but a different George altogether – George Gascoigne.

The book, 250 pages long (with an appendix of four unpaginated pages which describe 17 varieties of hunting calls, with musical notation) is a practical hunting manual. It is mostly in prose but includes eleven poems and 53 illustrations. Much of *The Noble Arte of Venerie and Hunting* is translated from a French hunting manual, *La Vénerie de Jacques du Fouilloux*, published in Paris in 1573.

In accurately identifying the translator, Jean Robertson pointed out a fact which had been overlooked by commentators for centuries. When Gascoigne died, his friend George Whetstone published an elegy describing the lamentable circumstances of his end. The elegy is a very obscure work, of which only a single copy survives, in the Bodleian Library, Oxford. In Whetstone's elegy Gascoigne is made to say

My Doomes day Drum, from sin dooth you awake.
For honest sport, which dooth refresh the wit:
I have for you, a book of hunting writ.[1]

The first line refers to Gascoigne's theological translations, collectively published in 1576 under the title *The Drum of Doomsday*. Underlining the fact that these lines refer to two separate published books are Whetstone's printed marginal annotations. The first reads 'Drum of doomsday' and the second 'Hunting'.

Robertson concluded: 'There is little doubt that Gascoigne was responsible for both the poetical interludes and the prose translations of *The Noble Arte of Venerie and Hunting*; and an edition of his works that omits this book cannot be called complete.'[2]

This last remark was a stinging rebuke to Professor J.W. Cunliffe, editor of the Cambridge University Press edition of *The Complete*

Works of George Gascoigne, who had failed to realise Gascoigne's authorship of the hunting book. It was a careless mistake for Cunliffe to have made, for if he'd consulted the standard Victorian edition of Gascoigne's writing he would have found an association between the hunting book and the poet. Its editor, William Hazlitt, understood who was responsible for *The Noble Arte of Venerie*, accurately describing it as 'a compilation by Gascoigne'.[3]

Robertson's discovery was even more embarrassing for the twentieth century's greatest Gascoigne scholar, Professor C.T. Prouty, as the appearance of her article coincided with the publication of his major biography, *George Gascoigne: Elizabethan Courtier, Soldier and Poet*, published the same year. Prouty, like Cunliffe, had failed to perceive Gascoigne's authorship, and his biography conventionally attributed the hunting manual to Turberville

The centuries-long misattribution of Gascoigne's book stemmed from the fact that it was bound up with George Turberville's *The Book of Faulconrie, or Hawking*, which was also brought out in 1575 by the same publisher, Christopher Barker.[4] The books were obviously commissioned at the same time. But because Gascoigne's book was published anonymously, it was naturally assumed that this companion piece to Turberville's book about falconry was the work of the same author. Once paired in this way, the error became institutionalised. The second edition of Turberville's book, published by Thomas Purfoot in 1611, was also bound up with the second edition of *The Noble Arte of Venerie and Hunting*.

In fact a careful reading of the hunting book indicates that its author cannot possibly be Turberville. The preface to *The Noble Arte of Venerie and Hunting* puts forward the view that hunting is a superior sport to hawking. Beside it is the laconic marginal note, *'The Falconer sayth no.'*

Anonymity allowed Gascoigne brazenly to preface the book with a poem 'in the commendation of the noble Arte of Venerie', which he happily attributed to himself. Cheekily, he added a second pseudonymous poem, 'T.M.Q. in prayse of this booke'. 'T.M.Q' is an abbreviation of Gascoigne's motto *Tam Marti quàm Mercurio* – 'As much for Mars as for Mercury', meaning 'As much a soldier as a writer'.

Jean Robertson's attribution of this title to Gascoigne is now widely accepted as accurate in academic circles, although sometimes even leading Renaissance scholars expose their ignorance of her discovery. Gascoigne's hunting book remains little known and little read. It has not been republished for almost a century and has yet to appear in print with George Gascoigne's name on the title page. The first edition is a great rarity, and a copy of the seventeenth century second edition is, at the time of writing, on sale for £3,500.

The lack of a modern edition is easy to understand. There is little or no demand for a book on hunting conventions of the sixteenth century, particularly when it offers advice on how to kill species which are now protected, such as badgers and otters. Matters might be different if George Gascoigne was better known, but he remains a shadowy figure. Nowadays the focus falls on the writers of the second half of Elizabeth's reign – Sidney, Spenser, Shakespeare – not those of earlier generations. At the present time *The Noble Arte of Venerie and Hunting* remains Gascoigne's most obscure and least accessible work and more than half a century after Jean Robertson's discovery it continues to be misattributed. For example, H.R. Woudhuysen's magisterial Arden 3 edition of *Love's Labour's Lost* (1998) reproduces an illustration from the book, identifying George Turberville as the author. When I opened a copy of the original 1575 edition of *The Noble Arte* in the Rare Books room at the British Library it seemed as if no one had looked at it for centuries. A cloud of powdery dust erupted from its pages and I was gripped by an uncontrollable fit of sneezing.

*

This very obscure book is an important work as it supplies a missing piece of the jigsaw puzzle of Kenilworth. Gascoigne worked on the book before he went to the castle, and the note from 'The Translator to the Reader' is precisely dated 'From my chamber this xvii. of June. 1575.' *The Noble Arte of Venerie and Hunting* was therefore presumably published no earlier than that month. As some of the text appears to incorporate material from the Kenilworth entertainments the book may well not have been completed and published until a date in the last five months of 1575. This suggests that the work played no part in Leicester's commissioning of Gascoigne's talents for the Kenilworth entertainments. It was in any case published anonymously. Moreover the volume does not appear to have been a success. There were no more editions until the seventeenth century.

Gascoigne's version of *La Vénerie de Jacques du Fouilloux* was a reasonably faithful translation. However, Gascoigne partly re-arranged the order of the original, added new material and rewrote two short sections, one dealing with hunting terms. He also included six original poems: the two commendatory poems, a narrative poem about a royal picnic, and poems expressing the point of view of a hunted hare, an otter and a fox.

In 1948, without ever quite admitting that he'd made a significant blunder in his biography, C.T. Prouty made handsome amends for his error in overlooking Gascoigne's book. In collaboration with Ruth Prouty, he published a lengthy article on *The Noble Arte of Venerie*. The two Proutys ticked Gascoigne off for tricking his readers by daring to commend his own book, remarking crossly, 'What a deal of vanity and levity are here!'[5] However, they drew attention to something not previously realised. Although the hunting manual was a translation, parts of it expanded the original French text and transformed it into something new and original. Even more striking is that this part of the text, they realised, 'definitely relates the whole affair to the Kenilworth festivities'.

Two chapters of *The Noble Arte of Venerie* in fact feature material which is likely to have been written for the Queen's forthcoming visit to Kenilworth. Chapter 35 supplies the script for a masque to be staged at a royal picnic during a hunt [see Appendix Two]. Chapter 36 gives the text of a speech to be made by a huntsman in presenting the Queen with fewmishings [see Appendix Three]. This was a technical (and delicate) term for deer droppings, and formed part of the solemn ritual of the hunt. The Queen was presented with fewmishings from various deer and invited to use her great expertise in such matters to choose which individual deer was best worth hunting.

The huntsman's speech is a translation from the original French and is barely altered by Gascoigne. It would have been entirely in keeping with his character for him to have presented it as a script for use at Kenilworth, and it may well have been so used. It flattered the vanity of the recipient by conceding her great knowledge and experience in hunting matters, and we know that Elizabeth had a boundless appetite for listening to formal speeches which heaped praises upon her.

The reason why Gascoigne chose anonymity for his hunting book is probably the same reason he chose not to identify himself as the author of *The princelye pleasures at the Courte at Kenelwoorth*. He was then trying to have his banned book *A Hundreth Sundry Flowers* republished under a new title, prefaced by an address to the censors in which he claimed he was now a pious, devout and humble man. Producing entertainments for a royal progress or a hunting manual for the leisured classes didn't quite fit that image.

At the end of *The Noble Arte of Venerie*, its unidentified author looked forward to 'the nexte impression, if I lyve so long.' Those fateful words proved bitterly ironic. Two years later George Gascoigne was dead, and 34 more years passed before there was a second edition.

*

A Letter says relatively little about the Queen's hunts. It is clear that its author (who was also anonymous but who was not Gascoigne) was not a huntsman but merely a spectator at those moments when the hunt came close to the castle.

A Letter describes Elizabeth going hunting on the first, third, fifth and tenth days, but there were evidently other hunts of which the author knew nothing. Gascoigne mentions a final hunt on day nineteen. Some 37 deer were killed in all, Elizabeth accounting for six of them, including 'In ye Little Park killed by the Queen with her bows ...1 Killed by the Queen a bold buck ...1 The Queen in ye Little Park a black buck... 1'[6] 'Mr Philip Sidney' was recorded as killing one at Redfern Park, just north of Kenilworth, along with 'My Lady Sidney'.[7]

The weather was good and hunting in the Chase formed a major part of the Queen's pleasure at Kenilworth. We know that not everything in *The princelye pleasures at the Courte at Kenelwoorth* was actually presented before Elizabeth, but it is reasonable to assume that this long-forgotten masque *was* given an alfresco performance. It would certainly have met with Leicester's approval. *The Noble Arte of Venerie* fills in part of the missing picture of

Kenilworth by showing what went on during the royal hunts in The Chase. On the basis of what we know about the hunts at Kenilworth, the likeliest day on which the masque was presented and the huntsman's speech given is Wednesday 13 July, which seems to have been a day entirely devoted to hunting.

*

Chapter 35 of *The Noble Arte of Venerie* supplies an entertainment for a hunting interlude – a royal picnic in The Chase. Gascoigne sets the scene 'under shade of stately trees' and then introduces the actors. The first one to appear is the Butler, who announces the arrival of alcoholic refreshment, 'In Kilderkins and Fyrkins full, in Bottles and in Barrels.'

A kilderkin was a cask holding 18 gallons, a firkin held 9 gallons and a barrel 36 gallons. At this point servants circulated with jugs and bottles. Huge quantities of beer were consumed at Kenilworth, partly because the weather was hot, and partly because water was often not safe to drink in the sixteenth century. In just three days '72 ton of ale and beer' was consumed, and 'a relief of a forty ton' was hurriedly brought to the castle.

The Butler's appearance is followed by that of the Cook. The Cook is introduced as a captain in the great campaign against hunger. His troops then march into battle, carrying their weapons and ammunition – in other words, a vast array of food for the picnic. The Butler summons up his own forces, and a mock battle ensues. The Cook's army flees and the Butler's men 'sound their Drummes'. A third group – huntsmen – intervene and chase away the Butler's army and the remnants of the Cook's. Their leader then goes down on his knees and addresses Elizabeth:

Since golden time, (my liege) doth never stay,
But fleeth still about with restlesse wings,
Why doth your grace, let time then steale away,
Which is more worth, than all your wordly things?

Having refreshed herself with food and drink, the Queen is urged to waste no time in getting back to the hunt:

One only hour (once lost) yeldes more anoy,
Than twentie dayes can cure with myrth and joy.

And since your grace determined by decree,
To hunt this day, and recreate your mynde,
Why syt you thus and lose the game and glee
Which you might heare? Why ringeth not the winde,
With hornes and houndes, according to their kynde?
Why syt you thus (my liege) and never call,
Our houndes not us, to make you sport withall?

The huntsman's leader apologises for the 'grosse and homely'
entertainment set before Elizabeth in the form of the battle between
the armies of the Butler and the Cook, and urges her again to get back
into the saddle:

Behold us here, your true and trustie men,
Your huntes, your hyndes, your swaynes at all assayes,
Which ouerthrow them, (being three to tenne)
    And now are prest, with bloudhounds and relayes,
    With houndes of crye, and houndes well worthy prayse,
To rowze, to runne, to hunt and hale to death,
    As great a Hart as ever yet bare breath.

At this point it becomes clear that the masque involves yet another
pitch for Elizabeth's hand. The great 'Hart' – with an obvious pun on
'heart' – is none other than the Queen's host and Gascoigne's patron,
Robert Dudley, Earl of Leicester. Elizabeth is urged to hurry off and
encounter the Hart:

This may be seene, (a Princes sport in deede)
And this your grace, shall see when pleaseth you:
So that voutsafe, (O noble Queene) with speede,
To mount on horse, that others may ensue,
Untill this Hart be rowzed and brought to view.
Then if you finde, that I have spoke amysse,
Correct me Queene: (till then) forgive me this.

This masque was the second one Gascoigne produced during a writing career which probably spanned the period 1555-76. In 1572 he was commissioned to write a masque for a double wedding between a son and daughter of 'Lord Mountacute' – better known as Anthony Browne, Viscount Montague - and a daughter and son of Sir William Dormer.[8] It was an arranged marriage between two prominent Catholic families, each marrying off their male heirs.

In the preamble to that masque Gascoigne explained that remembering that there was '*a noble house of the Mountacutes in Italie*' and knowing that Viscount Montague quartered the coat of '*an ancient english gentlemen called Mountherner, and hath the inheritance of the sayde house*', he therefore devised a plot about a boy of about 12-14 years. The boy was a Montague on his mother's side and a Monthermer on his father's. His father having been killed by the Turks at the siege of Famagusta,

> *He was recovered by the Venetians in their last victorie, and with them sayling towards Venice, they were driven by tempest uppon these coasts, and so came to the marriage…*

The boy then steps forward and tells his story to the assembled wedding guests. Since he is supposed to have arrived by boat, the implication is that the wedding celebrations were put on at Montague House in Southwark, rather than the Viscount's country seat at Cowdrey Park in Sussex. This is confirmed by the boy's remark that '*London* is not far'.

But Gascoigne's masque was not one in what later became the commonly understood sense of the word. There was no dumb show, choreographed dancing, singing, stage machinery or any dramatic exchanges of dialogue. Instead, flanked by four torchbearers, the child orator simply narrated a 376-line narrative poem in rhyming couplets. It was essentially a recitation, not a visual feast of colour and movement. Its only dramatic moment came at the end when the child cries, 'lo now I hear their drum' and eight Montague men enter in extravagant Venetian costumes. There may have been scenery but none is mentioned in the text's marginalia, which describes the role of the four torchbearers and the Montague token in the child actor's cap.

The Kenilworth masque was a much bigger affair, evidently involving sixteen actors. It was both a light, comic entertainment and a way of distributing food and drink to the members of the hunt, who presumably sat around on mats on the grass, forming an open-air audience. Gascoigne reveals an aspect of courtly life on a royal progress which has long been lost sight of. In the words of Charles and Ruth Prouty,

> this charming portrayal of a *fête champêtre* with its attendant masque shows us a typical day's sport as enjoyed by the Queen and her courtiers. As well, study of it reveals once more Gascoigne's quick and dramatic imagination proceeding from translation to a pretty conceit and thence to the creation of a masque, too few of which have been preserved for us from this particular period.[9]

That this material really was written for the Kenilworth entertainments is underlined by Gascoigne's addition of a reference to Sir Tristram in the huntsman's speech. It connects it to the Lady of the Lake material, since in Arthurian legend Sir Tristram came across a knight who was being attacked by ten men under the command of the villainous Sir Bruce. Bravely, Sir Tristram fought off these cowardly attackers.

Tristram, in other words, was like Elizabeth herself – a force for liberation and justice. The sub-text of the analogy was that she should intervene in the Low Countries, against the Spanish. Ideally that intervention should be commanded by her host, Robert Dudley. In that sense, it was flatteringly hinted, they were *both* Sir Tristram. Politics and play united them as equals, since Sir Tristram was also legendary for his hunting expertise and prowess. His best known incarnation in Tudor literature is in Book VI of *The Faerie Queene*, where he describes his passion for hunting (Canto ii, stanzas 31-2).

*

Fascinatingly, *The Noble Arte of Venerie and Hunting* actually gives us scenes from Elizabeth's hunts at Kenilworth. The first edition of 1575 contains 53 illustrations, made up of 32 different woodcuts (some used up to five times). Of these, 27 were copies of the ones used in the French edition and five were original. Four of these five appear to be the work of the same artist. Three of them portray Elizabeth I at key moments of the royal hunt. The fourth (on the title page) shows huntsmen with their dogs. It is almost certain that these four woodcuts were either the work of George Gascoigne or were executed under his direction.[10] The fifth woodcut, showing an otter eating a fish, is quite different to all the others and was probably a last-minute filler derived from some other source.

The Victorian critic William Hazlitt believed that three of these original woodcuts showed Gascoigne, and Charles and Ruth Prouty likewise noted 'a certain resemblance between the huntsman and the portrait of Gascoigne on the reverse of the title-page of *The Steele Glas*.'[11] That Gascoigne intended a representation of himself is more than probable. In one woodcut a bearded huntsman presents the Queen with a knife, to make the first cut of the flesh of the dead deer. In a second woodcut a bearded huntsman kneels before the Queen as she enjoys a picnic in the woods. In the third, a bearded huntsman displays fewmishings (deer droppings) for Her Majesty's attention.

The figure presenting the Queen with a knife certainly bears a strong resemblance to the portrait used in Gascoigne's book *The Steele Glas* published the following year. The hair, beard and moustache are identical in style. The most striking similarity is that of the long slender nose. It is also significant that three of these woodcuts show a bearded figure (arguably the same man) kneeling before the Queen. That is precisely the arrangement used for the pen and ink drawing which Gascoigne did of himself and Elizabeth for the manuscript which he later presented to her on New Year's Day 1576.

Characteristically, Gascoigne represents himself as being the focus of Elizabeth's interest, at the very centre of her royal world. That such moments actually existed for him at Kenilworth that July is demonstrated by Gascoigne's wild man performance. But such episodes were at best brief. Subsequently enshrined as printed texts and in self-promoting pictorial representations, his role as a performer achieved a far greater and more enduring centrality and importance.

9   Crisis

The next day, Tuesday 19 July, was the calm before the storm. The Coventry men returned to perform their play, and this time Elizabeth watched it all. The two sides skirmished, then began to battle it out.

By the sound of it, it was the sixteenth century equivalent of the modern 'royal tournament' – a choreographed display of military action, the participants 'first marching in ranks: then warlike[e] turning, thé[n] frō[m] ranks into squadrons, then in too trianglz frō[m] that intoo ringz, & so winding oout again'.[1] These stylized mock battles between Danes and English horsemen appeared to hang in the balance. Twice the Danes seemed victorious, but in the end they were defeated, with many captive Danes led off in triumph by the women of Coventry. More than that we do not know, as no text has survived.

Elizabeth evidently enjoyed this straightforward rough-and-tumble entertainment involving real horses and the expulsion of a foreign enemy. *A Letter* describes how 'her Majestie laught well'[2] and rewarded the players with two bucks (i.e. two male fallow deer) and five marks (or three pounds, six shillings and eight pence). They, in turn, were gratified by their royal reward and cried out that she should return frequently so that they might see her again. Royal approval also ensured that moralistic attempts to suppress this traditional Coventry entertainment afterwards ceased.

On Wednesday morning another feast in a marquee or 'fayr Pavilion' had been arranged at 'Wedgnok' [Wedgnock] Park, three miles from the castle. The main amusement of the day was to be 'a devise of Goddessez & Nymphes'[3] presented to the Queen 'in the Forest'.[4] It included special effects, such as Mercury descending in a cloud and Iris coming 'downe from the Rainebowe sent by *Juno*'.[5]

Written by George Gascoigne, the 'devise' was a short, untitled play of two acts and seven scenes. The *dramatis personae* consisted of Diana, goddess of chastity and three attendant nymphs, Mercury the messenger of Jove, and Iris the messenger of Juno. The plot concerned what had happened to one of Diana's nymphs, lost to her many years before. Between the acts 'a man cladde all in Mosse'[6] was to appear, explaining that he was the savage man's son, Audax. The part may well have been chosen by Gascoigne, once again losing

84

no opportunity to put himself centre stage.

The play had been rehearsed and was ready to be performed.

But suddenly that morning there was turmoil. The feast at Wedgnock Park was abruptly cancelled. The play was called off despite (as Gascoigne plaintively put it) '*being prepared and redy*'.[7] The Queen was evidently furious about something. The author of *A Letter* hints at Elizabeth's rage: 'A this day allso waz thear such earnest tallk & appointment of remooving that I gave over my noting, and harkened after my hors[e].'[8]

What made the Queen so angry that she spurned the day's entertainments and considered cutting her visit short and storming away from the castle? Gascoigne acknowledged that his play '*never came to execution*', adding, a little evasively, '*The cause whereof I cannot attribute to any other thing, then to lack of opportunitie and seasonable weather.*'[9]

But this conjecture was threadbare and implausible. Gascoigne was justifying publishing his offensive drama by pretending that he didn't quite understand why it had never been staged. But as he surely knew, the play was the problem, not the weather.

Clearly that Wednesday morning the Queen discovered in advance the content of Gascoigne's play. Presumably someone who appreciated exactly what it signified had discovered the inflammatory theme of Gascoigne's play and reported to Elizabeth just what was to be set before her later that day.

Whoever that person was it had to be someone powerful, discreet and with access to the Queen. The likeliest candidate in such a scenario is Lord Burghley. But however Elizabeth came to find out about the play there was no ambiguity about the consequences. The result was an explosion of royal displeasure.

Her wrath was directed not at the play's author, George Gascoigne, but at the person who had plainly solicited this insulting piece of theatre. The Earl of Leicester's hand in the affair was unmistakeable. It was an almost identical repeat of what he'd done to her at court, a decade earlier. On that occasion he'd staged a play before her, involving an argument between Juno, goddess of marriage, and Diana, goddess of chastity. Diana lost.

The Queen is reported to have turned to the Spanish ambassador sat next to her and said, 'this is all against me'. But in 1565 Elizabeth's mood was more playful and light-hearted. Flirtation was acceptable. Oblique, symbolic games with figures from Greek mythology were relatively harmless fun. Marriage to Robert Dudley was a much stronger and more attractive possibility in those days.

Now the atmosphere was different. Elizabeth required deference, not symbolic instruction about her supposed inadequacy. Besides, the relationship between the two principals was much cooler, now. Ten long years had passed. The sexual electricity was largely gone. Dudley's desire for Elizabeth was probably always driven more by the power marriage to her would have given him, than by sexual attraction. As one historian of their relationship has observed, 'it is difficult to estimate the strength and sincerity of Leicester's [passion]'.[10] After the crisis of 1560 what was left was a tense, edgy relationship which mingled friendship with antipathy.

The Earl of Leicester was insufficiently deferential. He undiplomatically and egotistically regarded himself as her equal and still the only obvious candidate for her husband. But by sponsoring Gascoigne's play he had over-played his hand. The identity of the lost nymph, 'Zabeta' (a name formed from the last three syllables of the Latin version of 'Elizabeth') was all too obviously, all too publicly, the Queen herself.

That Zabeta was lost 'neere seventeene yeeres ago'[11] clinched the identification. It was 17 years since Elizabeth had become Queen and in so doing become 'lost' to her passionate friend and admirer, Robert Dudley. Just in case anyone has missed the analogy, Mercury steps forward to explain what Zabeta has been up to since the time of Elizabeth's coronation:

> For first these sixteene yeres,
> She hath beene daily seene,
> In richest Realme that Europe hath,
> A comelie crowned Queene.[12]

The most offensive part of Gascoigne's play was its final scene. Iris, messenger of the goddess of marriage, arrives with a lecture about 'How necessary [it] were / for worthy Queens to wed.'.

In an ingenious argument worthy of the trained lawyer in Gascoigne, Iris asks what the goddess of chastity ever did for

Elizabeth in the period before she became Queen:

> Were you not captive caught?
> were you not kept in walles?
> Were you not forst to leade a life
> like other wretched thralles?
> Where was *Diana* then
> why did she you not ayde?[13]

The closing lines of the play are addressed directly to Elizabeth. Iris passes on a blunt message from the goddess of marriage. Juno's advice isn't simply *get married* but *get married now to the Earl of Leicester*.

>   she bade me say,
>   That where you now in Princely port
> have past one pleasant day:
>   A world of wealth at wil,
>   you hencefoorth shall enjoy
>   In wedded state, and therewithal,
> holde up from great annoy
>   The staffe of your estate:
>   O Queen, O worthy Queen,
>   Yet never wight felt perfect blis,
>   but such as wedded beene.[14]

But joining the royal sceptre or staff to the ragged staff on the Dudley coat of arms was the last thing on Elizabeth's mind. This time the Earl had pressed his suit too hard and too often. She exploded in rage.

*

Precisely what happened next is unclear. *A Letter* says there was 'such earnest tallk & appointment of remoouing that I gave over my noting, and harkened after my hors.'[15] Its day-by-day account of the festivities comes to an abrupt halt.

The next forty pages – more or less half the book – are padding. For his part Gascoigne simply says that his play '*never came to*

87

execution' and goes on to describe 'The Queenes Majestie hasting her departure from thence…'[16]

The Queen left Kenilworth on a Wednesday, but not, apparently, for another week. Did she gallop away in a rage on 20 July before being persuaded back by Burghley and the others who had influence over her? If, as seems to be the case, Elizabeth stayed on for another seven days, then it looks very much as if she stayed in her chambers, sulking. *A Letter* is silent about what happened between 20 – 27 July, simply remarking that,

> Her highnes tarryed at Kyllingwoorth tyll the wednesday after, being the 27 of this July, and the nineténth of her Majestiez cumming thither.[17]

After twelve days of spectacle and amusement, the festivities ground to a sudden halt. It is sometimes said that bad weather both curtailed the festivities and obliged the Queen to remain at Kenilworth. The truth seems more complicated than that. A speech made to Elizabeth on the day she left refers to tears being shed

> these five dayes past and gone:
> It was no rayne of honestie,
> it was great floods of mone.[18]

That basically says that the rain wasn't just rain, it was the gods weeping for dismay at the news that Elizabeth was leaving Kenilworth. It indicates rain – perhaps heavy, if we take the speech literally - for the days Friday 22 July to Tuesday 26 July, with the weather clearing up on Wednesday 27 July, and the Queen making her final departure.

This implies that the weather was good on Wednesday 20 July, when the entertainments programme was brought to a halt. The next day, too, was fine. Elizabeth's stay at the castle in fact seems to have been planned to last 20 days, which means she left one day early. That is certainly the implication of the lines from Gascoigne's masque for a royal picnic:

> Only one houre (once lost) yeldes more annoy,

Than twentie days can cure with myrth and joy.

Twenty days. That number is not, I think, an arbitrary one. Gascoigne was a leading member of the entertainments team. He knew what was planned. But what he did not understand was Elizabeth's temperament. Leicester had pressed his suit once too often, and she was in no mood to be courted, still less to be lectured.

The author of *A Letter* clearly understood the role of Gascoigne's play in this sudden upset. He blandly refers to its 'ingenious argument'[19] but evasively declines to discuss the particulars, ostensibly for fear of misrepresenting the play's 'beauty'. Gascoigne himself grasped the potential for offence in his play's final speech. In passing on the marital advice from Juno, the actor playing the part of Iris makes a point of saying

> Forgive me (Queene) the words are hers,
> I come not to discusse.
> I am but Messenger[20]

Gascoigne could have said the same thing. It was Leicester who'd put him up to it; Leicester who'd surely sketched the plot for Gascoigne to put into verse. He was no more at fault than the player at Elsinore, mouthing Prince Hamlet's explosively provocative 'speech of some dozen or sixteen lines'. (2.2.514)

Did Gascoigne fully appreciate the offence which his play had caused? At first, perhaps not. He was present at Kenilworth as an entertainer, not a courtier. He was at best a hanger-on, not a member of that exclusive inner circle which comprised the Queen and her attendants, Leicester and his associates, and Lord Burghley and other members of the Privy Council. Gascoigne and his actors seem to have hoped that the suddenly-cancelled play might yet be performed. He describes the show as '*redy (every Actor in his garment) two or three dayes together*'[21], which suggests that the troupe waited in vain for the Queen to show herself.

Gascoigne was happy to see the unperformed play published and equally happy to take total credit for it ('*This shewe was devised and penned by M. Gascoigne*').[22] But he took the precaution of ensuring that the collection of Kenilworth scripts was published anonymously,

Leicester's Building

making it appear as if it had been edited by an unidentified third party. On other occasions, the poet always proudly referred to himself as *George Gascoigne, Esquire*, signifying that he was both the son of a knight and the proud possessor of a coat of arms. But in *The princelye pleasures at the Courte at Kenelwoorth* he was even prepared to drop that all important *Esquire* after his name to distance himself from the work.

In fact by the time *The princelye pleasures at the Courte at Kenelwoorth* appeared in print the following year, the storm had long since blown itself out. On the surface the book was nothing more than a harmless collection of masques and verses. Since they had been sponsored by one of the most powerful men in the land, who could possibly take offence? The only person likely to have been offended by its contents was the Queen, but she is unlikely ever to have seen a copy.

10   Sylvanus

There was just one final spectacle staged for Elizabeth at Kenilworth – but it was improvised at short notice on the day she left. By the sound of it, she sulked in her apartment in Leicester's Building for a week. She also seems to have vetoed any more entertainments. At any rate, there were no more spectacles on the lake, no more fireworks, no more plays – or if there were, they passed unrecorded.

The anonymous author of *A Letter* seems to have been discharged from the castle on 20 July. In place of an account of the next seven days he substitutes a comic account of an ancient minstrel, a list of the gods and the ways in which they had sponsored the entertainments, a long description of the garden, and some personal reflections. *A Letter* is silent about Elizabeth's final week at the castle and her departure, simply stating that 'Her highnes tarryed at Kyllingwoorth tyll the wednesday after' (i.e. 27 July).[1]

It appears that Elizabeth left abruptly, without much warning, on that Wednesday. Gascoigne refers tactfully to 'The Queenes Majestie hasting her departure from thence' (i.e. the castle). By the sound of it she was a day or two early in leaving, and was scheduled to go either on Thursday 28 July or on the following day.

But there is one odd anomaly which has never been noticed before, which is that the Privy Council held its tenth and final meeting at the castle on Thursday 28 July. Those present included Lord Burghley, the Earl of Leicester, the Earl of Warwick and all the other members who accompanied the royal progress. On the face of it, it seems most unlikely that they stayed behind, while the Queen travelled on alone, without any of her senior advisers. This mystery has never been noticed, let alone resolved.

Perhaps *A Letter* was wrong about the day of Elizabeth's departure (Gascoigne, unfortunately, gives no date for it). Or perhaps she did storm off that Wednesday, leaving Burghley and the others behind. If so, it supplies more evidence of her fury with Robert Dudley.

*

The Earl, anticipating her departure, had commissioned Gascoigne to stage a brief farewell entertainment. It was a last, desperate attempt to placate her.

Her original arrival at the castle had been spectacular, but there was to be no grand departure from Kenilworth. Instead it seems to have been a spur of the moment exit, without pageantry or fanfares. Elizabeth galloped off to go hunting, then continued her summer progress, without ever returning to the castle. Before she sighted any deer, however, she first had to encounter George Gascoigne and a group of actors and musicians.

Gascoigne had been loitering for days, dressed up as Sylvanus, God of the Woods. Presumably the garb, though green and leafy, was a little less primitive and a little more regal than that of his earlier incarnation as the Savage Man.

Sylvanus stepped out in front of Elizabeth, offering to conduct her 'in safetie from the perillous passages which are in these Woods and Forrests', and while doing so to recount, 'certaine adventures, neither unpleasant to heare, nor unprofitable to be marked.'[2]

The Queen had obviously taken some time to extricate herself from her black mood, judging by Gascoigne's heartfelt and slightly barbed comment that he had 'continually awayted these 3. dayes to espie when your Majestie would (in accustomed manner) come on hunting this way.'[3] He also seems to have been again referring to the original scheduled length of her stay when he remarked that it was 'not yet twenty daies past'[4] since he was summoned to appear before the Gods.

Sylvanus explained to Elizabeth that when he met the gods the scene he encountered there was the divine equivalent of what was going on at Kenilworth Castle:

There was nothing in any corner to be seene but rejoysing and mirth, singing, daunsing, melody and harmony, amiable regardes, plentiful rewards, tokens of love, and great good wil, Tropheys and triumphes gifts and presents (alas my breath and memorie faile me), leaping, frisking, and clapping of hands.[5]

The gods were thrilled to hear that the Queen was visiting Kenilworth. They were so happy they staged their own celestial celebrations. But when Sylvanus was summoned a second time to heaven, he was shocked to discover that everything was changed:

for when I came there, heaven was not heaven, it was rather a verye Hell. There was nothing but weeping and wayling, crying and howling, dole, desperation, mourning and moane. All which I pereceived also here on earth before I went up, for of a trueth (most noble Princesse) not onely the skies scowled, the windes raged, the waves rored and tossed, but also the Fishes in the waters turned up their bellies, the Deere in the woods went drowping, the grasse was wery [weary] of growing, the Trees shooke off their leaves, and all the Beastes of the Forrest stoode amazed.[6]

Gascoigne was flattering the Queen in the accustomed manner: her departure from Kenilworth made the gods weep and caused a convulsion in nature. That there had been a spell of unseasonal weather, with wind and rain seems plain. But the hyperbole and the pointed reference to Kenilworth having become 'a verye Hell' hints strongly at Elizabeth's recent outburst of rage.

The Queen's fury literally brought everything to a halt. Gascoigne himself was suddenly a redundant figure, hanging around with nothing to do. The actors were *'prepared and redy (every Actor in his garment)'* but they waited in vain. Even the grass stopped growing, in Gascoigne's phrase. Elizabeth had plainly had quite enough of Kenilworth Castle and its didactic entertainments, even though Sylvanus explained that he had been sent by the gods – i.e. Robert Dudley – 'to beseech your Majestie that you would here remaine.'[7]

Evidently by this time Gascoigne was beginning to sweat and pant. He was, after all, in his early forties, and by Tudor standards was a man well into middle age. 'Here her majestie stayed her horse to favour *Sylvanus*, fearing least he should be drivẽ[n] out of breath by following her horse so fast.'[8]

But Gascoigne was tall and probably fit. Evidently he was proud of his stamina – or was yielding to the *gascon* ('boaster') in the family name: '*Sylvanus* humbly besought her Highnesse to goe on, declaring that if hys rude speech did not offend her, he coulde continue this tale to be twenty miles long.'

So the Queen rode on, and Gascoigne ran on beside her. It was like a symbolic expression of the poet's lifelong quest for patronage, as he panted after wealth and power, pouring out words. But Gascoigne could be cheerfully brash, as well as sycophantic (and it is part of his charm that deep down he really didn't care what people thought of him, no matter who they were).

Provocatively, he returned to the story of Zabeta, pointing out that among her other names was '*Ahtebasile*' ('Elisabetha' spelt backwards). In this account, Diana's nymph was someone who had 'rigorously repulsed, or rather (to speake playne English) so obstinately and cruelly rejected' certain 'noble and worthy personages' that it made Sylvanus 'sigh to thinke of some their mishaps...the teares stande in mine eyes (yea and my tongue trembleth and faltereth in my mouth) when I begin declare distresses wherein some of them doe presently remayne.'

This was dangerously close to being a description of Elizabeth's recent anger with Leicester. Zabeta had, Sylvanus emphasized, turned 'sundry famous and worthy persons...into most monstrous shapes and proportions'.[9]

Gascoigne pointed to a massive oak. That, he explained, was Constance - a faithful follower and trusted servant of hers, turned into a tree by 'a strange and cruell metamorphosis'.

This parable about Elizabeth's treatment of Leicester was becoming more and more explicit. But Gascoigne moved on – literally – and defused the tale, making it blandly unspecific. Near the mighty oak was Inconstancy, turned into a poplar tree, 'whose leaves move and shake with the least breath or blast'. A nearby ash tree represented Vainglory – the first plant to bud 'and the first likewise that casteth leafe.' As for 'that busie elfe *Contention*'[10] – Zabeta had turned him into a bramble bush.

And so it went on, with Gascoigne pointing to tree after tree, explaining what each one represented. Ambition was a branch of ivy; 'Due Desert' a laurel. But there was a twist in the tale. This botanical disquisition was a prelude to the Earl of Leicester's final and rather more muted attempt to entice Elizabeth to stay on at Kenilworth.

Gascoigne led the Queen to 'a close Arbor, made all of Hollie, and whiles Silvanus pointed to the same, the principall bush shaked.'[11] This trembling bush represented Zabeta's transformation of Deep Desire - a 'wretch of worthies and yet the worthiest that ever was condemned to wretched estate'. Deep Desire was obviously intended to signify Robert Dudley, Earl of Leicester, here making his last pitch

94

as a devoted lover, in the style of Petrarch. He was such a man, explained Gascoigne, 'as neither any delay could daunt him: no disgrace could abate his passions, no tyme could tyre him, no water quench his flames.'[12]

Gascoigne claimed that his speech to the Queen was extempore and there is no reason to disbelieve him. The published text, then, is a reconstruction after the event, and not an accurate transcript. Gascoigne presumably polished and revised his prose before seeing it into print. On the face of it, it seems unlikely that he really told Elizabeth that there were male and female varieties of holly and that 'the she *Holly* hath no prickes'.[13] Bawdy innuendo like that would surely not have amused the Virgin Queen, who had a haughty sense of her own dignity and importance.

Sylvanus suddenly realised that the holly's animation indicated 'that Deepe desire hath gotten leave of the Gods to speake unto your excellent Majestie…me thinkes I heare his voice.'

Gascoigne then stood aside and let Deep Desire do the talking. Although the voice booming out of the holly represented Robert Dudley, it clearly wasn't the Earl crouching in an undignified posture behind the prickly bush. Desire spoke of Leicester in the third person as 'the Knight'. There was a cryptic reference to grieving and tears 'these five dayes past and gone' – ostensibly at the news of the Queen's impending departure but perhaps another tacit acknowledgement of her recent sulks and anger.

Though the message hadn't really changed, the invitation to marry Dudley was implicit rather than explicit ('Live here good Queene, live here, / you are amongst your friends'). There was no attempt to lecture her; no mention of Juno. On the contrary, 'Diana would be glad / to meet you in the Chase'.[14]

Musicians hidden behind the bush began to play and Deep Desire sang a melancholy song of farewell:

> Come, Muses, come, and help me to lament,
> come woods, come waves, come hills, come doleful dales…[15]

The song ended; the music ceased. Gascoigne stepped forward to wrap the proceedings up.

The metamorphosis of Deep Desire into a holly bush was, he

emphasized, 'very lamentable'.[16] He humbly craved that the Queen intervene on his behalf with the gods or at the very least consent to transform him back into human form,

> Whereat your highnesse may be assured that heaven will smile, the earth will shake, men will clap their hands, and I will always continue an humble beseecher for the flourishing estate of your royall person.[17]

The Queen presumably nodded and gave a glacial smile at this last, muted attempt to promote Leicester's cause. Then she rode on her way. The great Kenilworth extravaganza was finally over.

11   The great hoax

Shakespeare seems to have understood very clearly that Kenilworth signalled the annihilation of Leicester's dream of marrying Elizabeth. Oberon, King of the Fairies, recalls the time he saw

> Flying between the cold moon and the earth
> Cupid all armed. A certain aim he took
> At a fair vestal thronèd by the west,
> And loosed his loveshaft smartly from his bow
> As it should pierce a hundred thousand hearts;
> But I might see young Cupid's fiery shaft
> Quenched in the chaste beams of the watery moon,
> And the imperial votaress passed on
> In maiden meditation, fancy-free.
> (*A Midsummer Night's Dream*, 2.1.156-164)

In other words, Cupid (alias Robert Dudley) shot his arrow at Elizabeth and missed. The passage also seems suffused with memories of the fireworks – an arrow/rocket soaring across the sky, 'a hundred thousand hearts', a 'fiery shaft / Quenched'. The metaphors express a historical truth: the brilliant display was in vain. Elizabeth was untouched by it. She shunned the Earl's advances and moved on. It marked the end of Leicester's royal marriage fantasy.

Katherine Duncan-Jones has suggested that the contemporary context of the first staging of Shakespeare's play should not be forgotten in understanding its meaning. *A Midsummer Night's Dream* was 'performed for the Queen's cousin and half-brother Henry Carey, Lord Hunsdon, as part of the celebrations of his grand-daughter's wedding. Older members of the aristocratic audience in 1596 would certainly have picked up Shakespeare's allusion to the Earl of Leicester's most conspicuous display of desire for Elizabeth.'[1]

That desire, however, was not sexual. What Leicester was primarily interested in was power. Essentially, he wanted to be king. But unlike his father he was not prepared to stage a coup. His only aspiration was to achieve power through marriage to Elizabeth. His sexual needs were met elsewhere.

Shakespeare was not the only one to perceive the Queen's visit to Kenilworth as a failure. The first account of the visit, *A Letter*, seems to have been published not long after her departure from Kenilworth. In its own, idiosyncratic way it is a minor masterpiece of sixteenth century prose and it underpins every modern description of events at the castle that July. But *A Letter* is a curiously double-edged production. It is both a vivid, chatty account of the Earl's entertainments and a veiled satire on them.

An unmistakeable seam of sarcasm and comic irony runs through the narrative. The author seems to take a malicious delight in describing everything that went wrong, including Elizabeth's ill-tempered rejoinder to the Lady of the Lake and Gascoigne's bungled throwing of the oak branch. The cupbearer at the country wedding had his freckled head 'sumwhat unhappily infested' with flies that swarmed around the cup. The bride is 'il[l] smelling' and 'ugly foou ill favord'.[2] The 'princely pleasures' seem far from princely. The bridegroom blows his nose and wipes his face on his father's jacket.

A Letter describes three deer hunts. On each occasion the hunted animal flees into the Great Mere and swims away. The third time this happens, the author says it 'reyzed [raised] the accustomed delight'.[3] But it is extremely unlikely that the hunters were delighted that the deer kept escaping in this way. On the contrary, it was a frustrating end to a hunt. The thrill of the chase was supposed to climax with the deer brought down by the hounds or shot with an arrow, not in sending a boat out after it. It was another example of how things repeatedly went wrong at Kenilworth that July.

A Letter describes 'a most deliciouz' banquet of 300 dishes, and then goes on to radically undercut that admiring description. The author says that, 'for my part I coold little tel thé[m], and noow less, I assure yoo' - in other words that he found the dishes wholly unmemorable. He continues:

Her majesty eat smally or nothing: which understood, the coorsez wear not so orderly served & sizely [neatly] set dooun, but wear by and by az disorderly wasted & coorsly consumed, more courtly [curtly] me thought then curteously. But that was no part of ye matter, moought [might] it pleaz and be liked & do that it cam for, then waz all well inough.[4]

98

This insinuates that the Queen was less than impressed by what was set before her (although in fact we know that Elizabeth always ate very sparingly). It tells us that the courses were served in an erratic and clumsy fashion and that the food was eaten by the diners in a coarse, discourteous, gluttonous manner. The final sentence pretends to shrug off this blistering description with the breezy remark that since everybody was having a good time what did it matter? This is (to mix languages) *schadenfreude* masquerading as *bonhomie*.

As a satire *A Letter* targets three people in particular. The book is prefaced by an epigraph consisting of three lines of Latin, no doubt coined by its author.

DE REGINA NOSTRA ILLUSTRISSIMA

Dum laniata ruant vicina ab Regna tumultu:
Laeta suos inter genialibus ILLA diebus,
(Gratia Diis) fruitur: Rumpantur et ilia Codro.

This translates as:

ON OUR MOST ILLUSTRIOUS QUEEN

While neighbouring kingdoms collapse in butchery from tumult,
SHE, thanks to the gods, amidst her people happily enjoys
genial days. May Codrus's innards burst.

Conventional pieties end with an obscure outburst of spleen. In fact, this ostensibly harmless salutation is razor-edged: 'genialibus' is ambiguous. It can simply mean 'genial days', but it can also be translated, much more explosively, as 'days pertaining to marriage'. *That*, of course, was what all the trouble was about.

Arbitrarily tacked on at the end of these lines to her illustrious majesty is a sudden spurt of venom: *Rumpantur et ilia Codro* – 'May Codrus's innards burst'. In Latin literature Codrus was the archetype of a talentless poet. Who did the author have in mind in those final, not quite grammatical, and slightly hysterical Latin words?

The answer is George Gascoigne, then the most fashionable and successful poet in England. Gascoigne had authored the most offensive of the masques intended to be put before the Queen – the one that lectured her on her inadequacy as a single woman. Not that the author of *A Letter* really cared about whether Elizabeth married or stayed single. The animus towards Gascoigne was personal, not political.

Some of the details of the description of the grotesque bridegroom at the country wedding sound very much like a dig at Gascoigne. The man is clumsy and ridiculous and 'brake hiz spear' at quintain, though he 'had no hurt as it hapt, but only that hiz gyrt burst, and lost his pen & inkhorn that he waz redy to weep for.'[5] The scene reads like a calculated mockery of Gascoigne's mishap with the oak branch, complete with the phrase *no hurt*.

The emphasis on how the bridegroom had 'a pen & ink[h]orn at his bak, for he woold be knowen to be bookish'[6] makes one wonder if Gascoigne was already proudly showing his associates the engraved portrait used to preface *The Steele Glas*, published the following year. It shows Gascoigne with a pen and a pot of ink dangling from a bookshelf behind his left shoulder.

The digression about the 'auncient minstrell'[7] whose 'ridiculoous devise' was never performed also sounds suspiciously like a skit at Gascoigne's expense, particularly as it immediately follows the account of how his play about Zabeta was aborted. The preposterous minstrel has a 'smugly shaven' beard, a stiff, starched ruff and a 'side gooun of kendall green…gathered at the neck with a narrow[w] gorget, fastned afore with a white clasp and a keepar close up too the chin'.[8] All this sounds suspiciously like a parody of Gascoigne's portrait, and the emphasis on the minstrel's fondess for green may allude to Gascoigne's self-representation as 'the green knight'.[9]

The minstrel also sports 'a greén lace' and wears 'a Schoochion, with mettall & cooler [collar] resplendant upon his breast of the auncient armez of Islington'.[10] This, too, was perhaps intended to mock the intolerable pretensions of George Gascoigne Esquire, pictured in his armour. Islington of course had no 'ancient arms'. Nor does it seem to have had a very good reputation. One day in 1581 the Queen rode out to take the air and, near Islington, 'she was invironed with a number of begging rogues (as beggars usually haunt such places), which gave the Queen much disturbance.'[11] The authorities moved swiftly and next day 'took seventy-four rogues, whereof some were blind, and yet great usurers, and very rich. They were sent to Bridewell and punished.'

George Gascoigne gets off lightly compared with the book's two other targets. The biggest was the Earl of Leicester himself, and here the author had to be very careful in conveying his disdain for Dudley and all his works. Pretending to be deliberately obtuse, the *Letter*'s author describes the clock with its hands stopped at two and purports to be baffled by what this freezing of time can mean. He concludes that it's Leicester's way of signifying that visitors are welcome at any time, early or late, 'whither cum they to stay & take cheer, or straight to returne: too see or too be seéne: cum they for duty too her Majesty or loove too hiz Lordship, or for both.'[12]

This description is far from innocent. It hints at the Earl's delusions of grandeur in regarding himself as the Queen's equal. The fact that some visitors may be there simply 'to be seen' points to their shallow vanity. And why would anyone arriving at this magnificent castle wish 'straight to return' (i.e. back to wherever they came from)? Underneath the Earl's magnificent enterprise something is horribly wrong.

The afternoon of Sunday 17 July, we're told, was spent 'in woorship of this kenelwoorth Castl, and of God & saint kenelm'.[13] That is a very strange order of priorities. It puts the worship of a castle before that of God. Indeed, the act of worshipping a castle is both absurd and blasphemous, indicating that Kenilworth is a place where material show is far more important than spiritual values.

A Letter repeatedly puts forward a discreet, comic alternative meaning to the magnificence it describes. What other than a lampoon of Robert Dudeley, Earl of Leicester, is the 'great Chyld of Leyceter shire…of a foour foot & four inches hy…simpl & childish'?[14]

The extensive description of the grotesque country wedding ridicules the solemn marriage theme which the Earl was keen to promote, and the remark that 'it woold have mooved sum man too a right meéry [merry] mood, thoogh had it be toold him hiz wife lay a dying'[15] is clearly a barbed allusion to the scandal surrounding the mysterious death of the Earl's wife, Amy Robsart.

To Leicester's enemies the 'thing that could not bee hidden from ony [anyone]'[16] was not, as *A Letter* mock-naively goes on to explain 'hoow carefull and studious hiz honor waz' in amusing Elizabeth, but the cold fact of his ruthless murder of Robsart in order to make himself available as the Queen's prospective husband. Leicester's 'carefulness' is that of a clever killer.

Later, *A Letter* tells us that 'though the day took an eénd, yet slipt not the night all sleéping awey: for az neyther offis nor obsequy ceassed at any tyme too the full, to perform the plot hiz honor had appoynted'.[17] It poses as the innocent preamble to a description of the play put on after supper on Sunday 17 July but it's a razor-edged remark. The 'plot' might mean the play or the entertainments, but it could just as easily be read in its most literal and basic sense. In other words, the 'plot' is Leicester's plan to marry Elizabeth – something he works for day and night, using any means necessary, including murder, which requires a continual 'obsequy' or funeral rite. The ghost of Amy Robsart hovers over this sentences, as it does over others. Passages like these are the verbal equivalent of giving someone a friendly handshake – and squeezing so hard it hurts them.

A Letter notes the 'immens & profuse a charge of expens'[18] involved in the festivities, and with wide-eyed mock-innocence asks 'what may this express, what may this set oout untoo us?' The obvious answer would be that it expressed the Earl's extravagance, vanity and overweening ambition - the exact opposite, in fact, of 'a magnifyk minde, a singuler wizdoom, a prinsly purs, and an heroicall hart'.[19] The author tacitly concedes as much, adding (with a verbal wink) after the conventional, safe response, 'yet coold I say a great deel more.'

A Letter applauds Leicester's 'wizdom and cunning in acquiring things so rare, so rich'.[20] Although it could be glossed as 'skill', it is difficult to read that slippery word 'cunning' in any other sense than a negative one: 'craft', 'dissimulation' or 'falseness'.

*

Two other features of *A Letter* point to Leicester being one of its satirical targets. Firstly, its author twice describes himself as the Black Prince. This apparently baffling historical identification only makes sense in relation to the Earl of Leicester and the history of Kenilworth. Leicester was heir to John of Gaunt, who was the last person before him to renovate the castle. But John of Gaunt's bitter enemy was the Black Prince. In adopting this persona, the author of *A Letter* signals his antipathy to Gaunt's successor.

Secondly, *A Letter* competes with Gascoigne by punning on the Earl of Leicester's name. But whereas the Savage Man's *did lay/Dudley* dialogue with Echo was flattering, *A Letter* is sarcastic, describing the Fates accompanying the Queen on her grand entry to Kenilworth as being 'duddld with such varietee of delyghts'.[21] 'Duddld' – an obvious play on 'Dudley-ed' – was, even in the sixteenth century, an extraordinarily obscure word, meaning 'confused' or 'muddled'. What they see at the castle leaves the Fates 'gigling' – hardly a very deferential response to the Earl's munificence and effort.

*

The third target of *A Letter*'s satire is its ostensible author.

No name appeared on the book's title page, which merely states that it is 'from a freend officer attendant in the Coourt, untoo hiz freénd a Citizen, and Merchaunt of London.' This friend is identified on the opening page: 'Master Humfrey Martin Mercer'.

There really was a mercer, or dealer in textile fabrics, of that name. He was the son of a former Master of the Mercers' Company, and by 1575 was an affluent London merchant, probably aged in his mid-twenties. But Humphrey Martyn plays no part in the text and there are no jokes at his expense (except possibly once). He is simply the addressee, there to give the book plausibility as a straightforward, chatty letter from one man to another.

Who, then, was the book's author? Within the text he identifies himself on four occasions. On page 44 of what is probably the first edition he writes 'my name is Laneham' (changed to 'Langham' in what is almost certainly the second edition). On page 84 he calls himself 'Langham'. On page 87, the final page, he is mentioned as 'Ro. La.' In the book's final paragraph he signs himself off to Humphrey Martyn as

Yoor countreéman, companion, & freend assuredly: Mercer, Merchauntaventurer, and Clark of the Councel chamber door, and also keéper of the same: *El Prencipe negro. Par me.* R.L. Gent.

Mercer.

These clues are enough to identify the man as Robert Langham (c. 1535-80). He was admitted to the Mercers' Company in 1557. In 1573 a warrant was issued for £10 to be paid to Langham for his position as Keeper of the Council Chamber – a sum paid annually for the rest of the decade. However, by 13 April 1580 Langham was dead, and that year's payment went to his widow.

Robert Langham was never, as *A Letter* claims, clerk of the Council chamber door, which implies that he controlled access to the room where the Privy Council – the sixteenth century equivalent of the Cabinet - held its regular meetings. Instead his role as keeper was merely to furnish the Privy Council's committee room with flowers, fire-tongs and other minor comforts. Entries in the *Acts of the Privy Council* list eight payments to Langham. The one for 15 April 1576, covering the previous twelve months, reads:

A warraunt to the Threasurer of the Chamber to pay to Robert Langham, Keeper of the Councell Chamber, the somme of x^{li}, in consideracion of his paines taken and provisions made of bowghes [boughs, presumably either for decoration or firewood], flowers, and others, &c., for that Office, and also $xiij^s$ $iiij^d$ for a fier shovel, peyer of tonges, bellowse and forke for that Chamber.[22]

Authorship of *A Letter* is still sometimes attributed to 'Robert Laneham' but it's clear that 'Laneham' was an isolated misprint and that the correct form of this surname should be 'Langham'.

The English Heritage guidebook to Kenilworth Castle, like many other publications, describes Langham as 'Gentleman-Usher to Robert Dudley'. He is also commonly referred to as a 'protégée' of the Earl of Leicester. Such identifications are very questionable. There is not a scrap of evidence that Langham was ever a member of Leicester's household. The 'Gentleman-Usher' myth is derived solely from *A Letter*. Langham's role at Kenilworth has also become blurred as a result of that scene in Scott's *Kenilworth* (Vol. 2, Chapter 17), in which 'Master Robert Laneham' confronts Leicester in the royal palace at Greenwich and begs the Earl to grant him 'Licence to attend the Summer Progress unto your lordship's most beautiful, and all-to-be unmatched Castle of Kenilworth' – which Leicester testily grants.[23] But the real Robert Langham was part of the official entourage and did not need to ask Dudley's permission to be present.

If the book was really written by Robert Langham, what are we to make of him? For a long time readers have sensed that there is more to *A Letter* than meets the eye. Muriel Bradbrook concluded that 'There is something about this whole piece which makes it sound like the *jeu d'esprit* of a more practised hand than that of a mercer.'[24] But even if the author really *was* a mercer, what kind of man was he? The Victorian editor F.J. Furnivall thought that *A Letter* revealed him to be 'a most amusing, self-satisfied, rollicking chap.'[25]

Sir Walter Scott's verdict was harsher. He wrote that 'There has seldom been a better portrait of the pragmatic conceit and self-importance of a small man in office'.[26] In *Kenilworth* Scott portrayed Langham as a buffoon:

Then the Earl was approached, with several fantastic congees [bows], by a person dressed in a doublet of black velvet, curiously slashed and pinked with crimson satin. A long cock's feather in the velvet bonnet, which he held in his hand, and an enormous ruff, stiffened to the extremity of the absurd taste of the times, joined with a sharp, lively, conceited expression of countenance, seemed to body forth a vain, hare-brained coxcomb, and small wit; while the rod he held, and an assumption of formal authority, appeared to express some sense of official consequence, which qualified the natural pertness of his manner. A perpetual blush, which occupied rather the sharp nose than the thin cheeks of this personage, seemed to speak more of 'good life,' as it was called, than of modesty; and the manner in which he addressed himself to the Earl, confirmed that suspicion.

'Good even to you, Master Robert Laneham,' said Leicester, and seemed desirous to pass forward, without further speech.

'I have a suit to your noble lordship,' said the figure, boldly following him.

'And what is it, good master keeper of the council-chamber door?'

'*Clerk* of the council-chamber door,' said Master Robert Laneham, with emphasis, by way of reply, and of correction.[27]

This is a convincing dramatisation of the person who ostensibly wrote *A Letter*. It is precisely how Langham comes across – vain, pompous, boastful and self-regarding.

The very first sentence of the book, addressed to Humphrey Martin, reads: 'After my harty commendacionz, I commend me hartely too you.' It is a comically preposterous sentence, the second half of which pointlessly repeats the first half. It signifies that the speaker is a loud, *hearty* backslapper. And it gets worse. The next sentence begins:

Understand ye, that syns throogh God and good friends, I am placed at Coourt heer (as ye wot) in a woorshipfull room: Whearby, I am not only acquainted with the most, and well knoen to the best, and every officer glad of my company...

This manages to combine vanity, snobbery and self-satisfaction. No less a power than God has taken the trouble to get involved in finding Langham his position at court. There, Langham knows just about everyone and is himself very familiar to 'the best' (which implies the Queen, Lord Burghley, the Earl of Leicester, Sir Nicholas Bacon, the Earl of Bedford and other leading figures). What's more, every other court official is 'glad' of his company. It's a highly unlikely scenario, given that the court was a place of sycophancy, intrigue, back-biting, power struggles and naked ambition.

But in fact the book was a hoax. The real Langham had nothing at all to do with it. *A Letter* is a satire. It mocks Leicester and Gascoigne but it also makes fun of Robert Langham and sets him up as the fall guy.

A Letter was, revealingly, a furtive, anonymous publication. It lacked a printer's name, or a date of printing, or the traditional 'colophon' or ornamental tailpiece identifying its source. Two early editions survive – almost certainly the first and second.[28] One is an octavo in fours with half-sheet imposition – technical details which suggest that the book was produced by a printer with a small shop who did it as an unexpected rush job. The second, a normal octavo in eights, has sometimes been regarded as a pirated version of the first. No one knows which edition came first, though since the octavo in eights incorporates corrections, it is almost certainly a second edition.

It is unlikely that either edition was registered with the Stationers' Company, as every publication was supposed to be by law.

A Letter drops a number of hints to the reader that all is not quite as it appears. A description of the Italian acrobat's agility – 'sundry windings gyrings and circumflexions' – leads on to a reference to 'men that can reazon & talk with too [two] tongs [tongues], and with too parsons [persons] at onez [once]'.[29]

This is essentially what happens in *A Letter*, which is a double-edged, many-tongued, slippery verbal performance. The person who wrote it is a ventriloquist. He is pretending to be Robert Langham talking to Humfrey Martyn. But he is also talking to a different kind of reader, giving nods, and winks, and dry smiles. Two-tongued men, *A Letter* informs us (with another sly wink), 'dwel in a happy Iland (as the booke tearmz it) four moonths sayling Southward beyond Ethiop'. This island is obviously a satirical version of England – a land of two-tongued men where men say one thing and mean another. This condition in the narrator is exemplary – in others, less so.

Twice the narrator casually asks, with a wink, 'perceyve ye me?' In other words: *do you get the joke?* There is a good deal of sexual innuendo. When 'Langham' boasts that '(as partly ye kno) have I traded the feat of marchaundize in sundry Cuntreyz' there is clearly an obscene hint that he, and perhaps also Humfrey Martyn, is a user of whores.[30]

Gascoigne and Shakespeare also thought it side-splittingly funny to pun on 'country', 'compt' [count], 'content' and 'account'. Nor should one overlook the Elizabethan male's fondness for sniggering over 'quaint' as slang for the vagina. The joke was still going strong in the seventeenth century and crops up in Andrew Marvell's 'To His Coy Mistress': '... then worms shall try / That long-preserv'd virginity, / And your quaint honour turn to dust'.

Nor is this the first use of *double entendre* in *A Letter*. On the second page, Langham's boast that he 'occupied Merchaundize, both in Frauns [France] and Flaunders (long and many a day)' hints that he is an incorrigible and regular user of whores when away from home. This innuendo reaches, so to speak, a climax with the section on Langham's skills as a musician and his popularity with the fair sex. Langham's boast to his fellow 'cuntreman' that he is a great success with the ladies, who adore his singing and playing, hints that musical ability is being slyly used as a metaphor for lovemaking skills.[31] Langham complacently congratulates himself: 'it dooth me good to heer hoow well I can do'. We can find a similar sort of bawdy wit in Gascoigne's novel, published two years earlier. Elinor gives up Master F.J. and goes back to her old lover, who

> did now pricke such faire large notes, that his Mistres liked better to sing faburden [the undersong] under him, than to descant any longer uppon F.J. playne song: and thus they continued in good accorde, until it fortuned that Dame *Fraunces* came into hir chamber uppon such sodeyn [with such suddenness] as shee had like to have marred all the musick.[32]

After proclaiming his great popularity with women, Langham goes on stoutly to deny a fondness for over-indulgence in liquor. But these final three pages of *A Letter* are comically garrulous, as if mimicking the rambling, unstoppable flow of words from someone who is cheerfully tight. He claims to drink no more sugar and sack (a dry Spanish wine) than malmsey (a strong sweet wine), and then only in company. It sounds very much like the bluster of a heavy drinker, an interpretation reinforced by his breezy acknowledgment that one friend calls him 'Ro[bert]. La[ngham]. of the Coounty Nosingham Gentlman' (meaning that he has a heavy drinker's bright red nose).

In short, the 'Robert Langham' that emerges from *A Letter* is full of himself - vain, pompous, boastful, insufferably smug, half-drunk, utterly unaware of what a clown he is.

What happened next was perhaps inevitable. The real Robert Langham read *A Letter*. He was not pleased. He complained bitterly about it. Lord Burghley became involved. And the hunt for the hoaxer began.

*

What happened *after* Kenilworth is in some ways just as important to our understanding of the real significance of Elizabeth's nineteen days there as the bare record of the entertainments put on for her.

From Kenilworth the royal progress headed north to Lichfield, where the Privy Council held three meetings between 30 July and 3

The coat of arms of William Patten, a member of the group of writers assembled by the Earl of Leicester for the Kenilworth revels. St Mary's Old Church, Stoke Newington.

August. After Lichfield, Elizabeth visited Chartley Park, in the valley of the Trent. Chartley was the home of the Earl of Essex (who was then away in Ireland) and the Countess of Essex. The Countess, born Laetitia Knollys, was Elizabeth's second cousin; her grandmother, Mary Boleyn, had been Ann Boleyn's sister. Lettice was eight years younger than Elizabeth, and her portraits have been described as showing 'an extraordinary degree of sexual magnetism'.[1] In 1565, when Lettice was twenty-four, the mother of two small children and the wife of Viscount Hereford, she seems to have had some kind of relationship with Robert Dudley, which aroused Elizabeth's jealousy. The Queen demanded that the affair be terminated: 'A blazing quarrel took place, in which both parties cried with anger and wounded feeling; the result of it was that Lord Robert returned to his former favour.'[2]

After Douglas Sheffield gave birth to his child, she seems to have lost her attraction for Leicester, and he returned to his old love, Lettice. Her husband had been created Earl of Essex in 1572 and the following year he was despatched to Ireland, to try and colonise Ulster. When he returned to England in 1573 it was rumoured that Leicester had put pressure on to have him sent back to Ireland as quickly as possible. One painting in the Earl's collection which was perhaps *not* put on display for the Queen was 'the picture of the countesse of Essex'.

Whatever the truth of the matter, Kenilworth was a turning point for Robert Dudley in his relationships with the three women in his life. The July entertainments at the castle amounted to his very last and most extravagant marriage proposal to Elizabeth. When she repeatedly rebuffed his offers and finally cut short the programme in a display of ill-temper, he at long last gave up. After Kenilworth his interest unambiguously focused on Lettice. The truth, grossly magnified by rumour and tittle-tattle, seems to have become known to everyone at Court except Elizabeth. In December 1575, Antonio de Guaras passed on the gossip:

As the thing is publicly talked of in the streets, there can be no harm in my writing openly about the great enmity between the Earl of Leicester and the Earl of Essex, in consequence, it is said, of the fact that while Essex was in Ireland his wife had two children by Leicester. She is the daughter of Sir Francis Knollys, a near relative of the Queen and a member of the Council, and a great discord is expected in consequence.[3]

That 'great discord' did indeed occur – but not just yet.

12   Woodstock

From Chartley the progress went on to Stafford Castle, where the Privy Council held a meeting on 8 August. Four days later it met at Sudeley Castle, and two days after that at Worcester. There were five meetings of the Council at Worcester, between 14 and 20 August. On 29 August Elizabeth arrived at her estate at Woodstock in Oxfordshire. Here the entertainments were managed by Sir Henry Lee, who was both the royal champion and Lieutenant of the Royal Manor of Woodstock.

The royal progress of 1575 is nowadays always remembered for Kenilworth. But from Elizabeth's point of view, what was on offer at Woodstock was far, far more interesting and satisfactory. Indeed, the Woodstock entertainments were both informed by a wry knowledge of the offence caused to the Queen at Kenilworth, and a calculated attempt to win her favour by offering her an agreeable alternative.

The strategy succeeded. On her very first day at Woodstock the Queen was presented with an entertainment which was seen visibly to excite and move her. Although the festivities put on by Sir Henry Lee could hardly hope to compete with the grandeur and extravagance of Leicester's, it's plain that Elizabeth was altogether happier at Woodstock than at Kenilworth. Perhaps it had always been planned that way, or perhaps she extended her stay deliberately – whichever is the case, she remained at Woodstock twice as long as at Kenilworth, arriving in late August and not departing until October 3.

The show that thrilled her was a romantic tale of thwarted love and self-denial, told by an actor dressed up as a hermit. The Queen was led into woodland on the estate, as usual still on her horse. There she was confronted by the spectacle of two knights in armour having a sword fight.[4] As she approached, a hermit stepped forward and called out, 'No more, most valiant knights!' The fight was halted.

By 1575 hermits had virtually ceased to be a part of contemporary life. They belonged to the middle ages and existed in late Tudor times largely as folklore. The hermit announced that his name was Hemetes – itself a play on the word 'heremyte' and equivalent to calling himself 'Hermit the hermit'. The actor playing Hemetes was dressed in a lavish costume, loaded down 'with beads and other such ornaments of his profession.'

111

'Violence must give way to virtue, and the doubtful hazard you be in, by a most noble help, must be ended,' cried the hermit. The knights dutifully lowered their swords and kneeled. Hemetes turned to Elizabeth, hailing her as 'bound to the immortal gods'. He then announced that he would tell her an instructive tale. It went like this:

Not long ago, in the country of Cambia, situated near the mouth of the River Indus, lived Duke Occanon, who was its ruler. His only heir was his fair daughter, Gaudina. She fell in love with a poor but noble and honourable knight named Contarenus, and he with her. When the Duke discovered his daughter's secret love he said nothing but was nevertheless determined to separate the lovers. At his bidding, and for a fabulous sum of money, an enchantress caused Contarenus to be swept into the air and carried to the furthest boundaries of the ocean. Depositing the knight on the ground again the enchantress advised patience, promising him that before seven years had passed his dearest wish would come true. But before that happened he would first see 'the worthiest lady in the whole world' and have to do combat with its 'hardiest knight'. At the same time Contarenus would also have to help a blind hermit who would recover his sight at the very moment that his wish came true.

Gaudina, meanwhile, grew restless. Eventually she discovered what the Duke had done. 'Farewell, unhappy country and most cruel father!' she cried, and set off to find her lover, accompanied only by a single maid. Dressed in simple clothes they fled over the border and eventually arrived at Sibyl's grotto, where they encountered the noble knight Loricus. Loricus explained that the lady he loved regarded him as unworthy of her and that he was travelling the world to win a great reputation and impress her.

The Sybil told Gaudina and Loricus that their destinies were linked and that they would not be parted until they came to a place where the men were strong, the women very fair, the land fertile, the people wealthy, the government just and the sovereign most worthy. There Gaudina would find that which would content her and Loricus that which would comfort him.

The hermit then interrupted his tale to explain his own role in the story. Though old and wrinkled in appearance and 'cast into a corner'

Hemetes revealed he was himelf once a knight. Not only a knight but one known and accepted with the best in the world, who resided at a famous court among many knights and ladies of great worth and virtue. There, Hemetes had fallen in love with a lady who, alas, kept changing shape when touched. When Hemetes embraced her she finally metamorphosed into a terrible tigress and he had to let go.

In the face of such a doomed love Hemetes went on a pilgrimage to the temple of Venus on Cyprus. Entering the temple, Hemetes was suddenly struck blind. He was ejected from the temple for his folly and presumption, and told that Venus was not honoured by 'parted affection'. Weeping and sighing, Hemetes begged Apollo for help. Apollo's priest took Hemetes by the hand and told him that the god was sympathetic to his plight and had granted him the gift of foreseeing the destiny of every lover. What's more Hemetes would recover his sight but only in a wonderfully tranquil land, in the presence of the most virtuous lady in the world, when two very valiant knights fought and two constant lovers came face to face. Until that happy moment Hemetes must live as a solitary hermit in the wilds.

As the priest's words ended, Hemetes found himself suddenly transported to a nearby hill, where he'd subsequently spent many winters in seclusion from the world.

While the hermit was talking, Gaudina presumably silently entered and joined the other three actors in the masque. Hemetes now dramatically announced that the prophecies had come true. The two knights had fought and the lovers been reunited. And he, Hemetes, had recovered his sight. And all thanks to the presence of her gracious and most virtuous majesty!

More flattery. But there is no evidence that the ageing Elizabeth, who was just days away from her forty-second birthday, ever grew tired of being praised for her great beauty, virtue, wisdom, learning or benignly transformative presence.

The main characters in the tale had been brought face to face, and their destinies transformed. But the climax was inconclusive. What happened next? Elizabeth was not to be disappointed by the twist in the tale – but she'd have to wait. The intense excitement produced by this fable was glaringly obvious to everyone who saw her.

Apologising for tiring the Queen's 'noble ears' with the length of his tale, the hermit beseeched her to honour his home with her presence. He then offered to lead the way and began to stagger off, evidently weighed down by his beads 'and other such ornaments'. Perhaps the actor playing the part of this old and wrinkled hermit was himself elderly. Whatever the reason, Elizabeth then did something extraordinary. *She got off her horse and walked.*

She was evidently in a bubbly, animated mood. As the hermit escorted her through the trees to his home she 'fell into some discourse and praise of his good tale.' The romantic tale of Gaudina and Contarenus had struck a powerful chord. Elizabeth was keen to know more. The story was thrilling but, frustratingly, had been left open. What happened when Gaudina was at last reunited with Contarenus?

*

As the Queen chatted to the actor, the crowd of privileged onlookers, including the French ambassador and George Gascoigne, trooped after them.

At Woodstock, Gascoigne was reduced to the role of passive spectator. It was others who organised and starred in the entertainments. From Sir Henry Lee's perspective, Gascoigne was heavily implicated in the débâcle at Kenilworth. Sir Henry's agenda was simple, which was to flatter, not lecture, the Queen. But even in this unfavourable situation Gascoigne managed to press matters to his own advantage.

Almost at once they reached the poor hermit's home amid the trees. Here the hermit explained to Elizabeth that the hour approached when he had to say his prayers, according to a vow he had sworn never to break. He bade her farewell, and left her to enjoy the comforts of his 'simple hermitage'. The actor slipped away, and presumably Sir Henry took over as Elizabeth's guide.

The hermitage was scarcely in keeping with the bleak, ascetic tradition of the hermit in his stony, inhospitable cave. A 200-yard perimeter of ornamental latticework surrounded a spectacular ivy-draped entrance. The entranceway was decorated with loose gold plate on strings, creating a fabulous shimmering effect. Once through the entrance, the Queen walked along a pathway made from fresh turf. Railings draped with flowers and ivy offered protection as the grassy path ascended some forty feet off the ground. At the top Elizabeth came to the hermit's home: a cavern of greenery fashioned from an oak tree. The tree's topmost branches had been bent over and tied down with ropes, forming a curving roof of natural foliage.

At one end of this fantastic green chamber was a table in the shape of a half moon. The tablecloth was made of freshly cut turf and on it was enough food for a royal banquet - scores of fish and meat dishes, pastries and delicacies. At the other end was a round table with a chair covered in crimson velvet and embroidered with a leaf design enclosing scenes of wild beasts and trees. On the 'walls' hung allegorical paintings of noblemen and other 'men of great credit'. The French ambassador was particularly impressed by the pictures and 'made great suit to have some of them'.

The Queen then sat down to eat – presumably in the velvet chair, at her own table. Sir Henry and the other chief guests sat down at the other table.

During the banquet there came 'a divine sound' from musicians concealed 'in the hollow roome under the house'. Then 'the fayery Queene' herself arrived on the scene, in a wagon with six children, 'the Boies bravely attired, & her selfe very costly apparrelled'. The fairy Queen made a rhyming speech of welcome, acknowledging that 'no man throughout the worlde hath seene / a prince that may compare with th' English Queene'. She presented Elizabeth with a gift: 'a goune [gown]... of greate price'. The ladies in waiting were presented with scented nosegays 'made of all cullers to every one whereof was annexed a posy of two verses, given by a handmayde of the fayry Queene, and one above the rest of greatest price for the Queenes Majestie with her posie in Italian'.

With the day's entertainment at an end, Elizabeth got into her coach. It was observed that she took 'joy in remembring what had passed, recounting with her selfe and others how well she had spente the after noone'.

*

Before she finally left, there was one other diversion. Leicester's nephew Philip Sidney had a new friend with him, Edward Dyer –

later to make a name for himself as a poet. Dyer hid in an oak tree and as the Queen's coached passed by he sang a song of melancholy 'Despair' at his sad neglect.

The Queen was evidently in an ebullient mood. Dyer's request for preferment was granted. A little over three months later he was granted a 'licence to pardon and dispense with tanning of leather' – a lucrative monopoly.

Sidney, too, got something out of his attendance at the progress. He was made a royal cupbearer – a worthwhile post but disappointingly badly paid by the standards of a member of the ruling class.

On her way back to Woodstock that evening the Queen made 'earnest command that the whole in order as it fell, should be brought to her in writing'. George Gascoigne took note of Elizabeth's enthusiasm for the hermit's fable and decided to exploit it for his own purposes. He received nothing as tangible as the gifts given to Dyer and Sidney, but he'd made his mark. After the scandals associated with his private life and his writing, his social rehabilitation was almost complete. The following year was to show that he was regarded as someone whose talents were worth deploying on behalf of the Tudor state. Like the characters in the masques which were set before Elizabeth that summer, his proximity to the Queen had wrought a transformation. He ended up working for Lord Burghley and Francis Walsingham. He became *respectable*.

13   A satirist unmasked

Meanwhile, back in London, the publication of *A Letter* had had predictable repercussions. If its author had used an invented and wholly fictitious pseudonym he would probably have got away with it. But by adopting the persona of a real person for his satire he invited a response which swiftly came. The real Robert Langham was evidently not amused to discover he was the supposed author of a book which portrayed him as a hard-drinking, philandering, self-satisfied fool.

The culprit was quickly unmasked. The real author's fingerprints were all over *A Letter*, to anyone who knew his other writings and his obsessions and interests. But it was probably through the printer that the man behind *A Letter* was swiftly tracked down and identified.

Although *A Letter* had appeared anonymously it contained a clue which allowed the identification of the printer. The book's use of a particular design of decorated initial 'A' showed that it was the work of a minor printer named John Awdely. However, Awdely died during the summer of 1575 and much of his small printing business was then acquired by John Charlewood. The book was essentially vanity publishing with a small print run and tracing its author through the Awdely household or John Charlewood would have presented the authorities with few difficulties.

The author was identified, copies of the book were immediately suppressed, and the matter was successfully hushed up. A second, revised edition was slipped out at a later date. This, too, was an anonymous publication.

Many mysteries surround these two editions. One theory, which I don't share, proposes a vanished first edition, with the surviving copies later editions.[1] The publication dates for these editions are also hotly contested. My own view is that the first edition came out in late August 1575 and that the second edition did not appear until the following decade, probably some time between 1584 and 1589. A total of seventeen copies survive but it is impossible to draw any firm conclusions about the book's circulation or popularity from this, since there are so many variables involved in the survival of books from this period. However, the absence of further editions during Elizabeth's reign suggests it was not a popular text or if it was, only briefly.

The Queenes Majesties Entertainment at Woodstocke, about her 1575 visit, appeared in 1585 and has been interpreted as an attempt to cash in on a successful second edition of *A Letter*. A.W. Pollard argued that since *The Queenes Majesties Entertainment* took the form of a letter to a friend, it was 'obviously modelled on the account given by Robert Laneham of the much more famous revels at Kenilworth'.[2] This is debatable; the two texts are very different in form, language and tone. It could equally be argued that the appearance of *The Queenes Majesties Entertainment* encouraged the republication of *A Letter*. Another spur to republication might have been the reappearance of *The princelye pleasures at the Courte at Kenelwoorth* in *The Whole woorkes of George Gascoigne Esquyre* two years later, in 1587.

By the end of the following year, 1588, all three of the main satirical targets of *A Letter* were dead, which meant that was no one left to complain about a new edition. However, its author was still taking a risk, in view of what happened in 1575, which would explain why the second edition was also a furtive, hole-in-the-corner publication, not officially licensed and not listed in the Stationers' Register. This sort of publication risked a fine, but by 1588 *A Letter* may well have seemed an innocuous book, its explosive content defused by time. What obsessed the censors were libels against the Queen, heretical theology, and licentious and immoral literature. An obscure unlicensed account of a long-ago royal progress can hardly have seemed like something worth suppressing; even assuming that anyone in authority noticed its existence.

The second edition of *A Letter* evidently made as little impact as the republication of Gascoigne's *The princelye pleasures at the Courte at Kenelwoorth*. The Elizabethans were far less interested in the subject than later generations. (There is not a scrap of evidence to support Stephen Greenblatt's assertion that *A Letter* was 'widely circulated'.[3]) The next edition of *A Letter* did not appear until the end of the eighteenth century. By this time the knowledge that *A Letter* was a satirical hoax and that Robert Langham was not in fact the real author, had long since been buried in a dusty archive of Tudor correspondence.

For almost four centuries the truth behind *A Letter* was lost. Then, in 1962, the eminent Shakespeare scholar M.C. Bradbrook suggested in her book *The Rise of the Common Player* that it was unlikely that Robert Langham had really written the book.

She rightly sensed that the narrator is not quite as stupid as he seems, and that the book's 'merriment is by no means naïve, but conceals a sting.'[4] Proof of the book's satirical bent, she argued, was indicated by the way 'Langham' called the mercer he had served as a young apprentice 'my Master Bumstead' when his name was actually Christopher Bompstead. It hinted (hinted Bradbrook, unable to bring herself to use such an indelicate word) at a pun on 'bum'. 'If there is one thing which even the most careless writer would not mistake, it is the name of the master to whom he served his seven years of apprenticeship...To choose a name that was nearly, but not quite, that of a well-known citizen was a familiar clown's jest.'[5]

She concluded that the clue lay in the book's single use of the name 'Laneham'. Its true author was not Robert Langham but one of Leicester's players, John Laneham (or Lanham). *A Letter* represented 'the common player's point of view...it is a social document of importance for the historian of the theatre.'[6]

Unfortunately for Bradbrook her central piece of evidence was erroneous. In her enthusiasm for her theory she had misread the text. The spelling 'Bumstead' is simply not used in any edition of *A Letter*. The book only ever talks of 'my Master Bomsted', which is a perfectly acceptable sixteenth century spelling of Christofer Bompsted, as he was generally called. There was no hidden pun.

Bradbrook also failed to appreciate that 'Laneham' was not a deliberate signalling of the real author's name but a misprint. And if the book was, as she claimed, written by one of Leicester's players, why did it have nothing at all to say about their contribution to the entertainments at Kenilworth, and make only the most perfunctory reference to the full-length professional play performed on Sunday 17 July?

Bradbrook was correct in her belief that the book was not what it purported to be, but the conclusions she reached about the true author were thin and implausible, and her faulty scholarship ensured that her theory collapsed like a house of cards. Once this was noted, it seemed to be the end of the matter.

The first significant step in unravelling the truth behind *A Letter* came six years later, when a scholar named Betty Hill published an article in the specialist journal *Transactions of the Cambridge Bibliographical Society*. It was entitled 'Trinity College Cambridge MS.B. 14.52, and William Patten' and discussed additions and glosses made to a small manuscript volume which included a collection of 33 Middle English homilies and the *Poema Morale*. Among the later insertions were a six line Latin poem attributed to 'W.P.' and a note addressed to 'yoʳ grace' which read:

> Manye will Bragge of there knowledge and haweinge of Antiquities
> but the writer of the verses above is the onlye man that ever I cold
> be aquainted with for the readonge of this boke and other
> Antiquities his Calender of the Byble maye apere to yoʳ grace but I
> most humblye besiche yᵉ that yᵉ paynfull work   by him gathered
> after yoʳ grace hath perused might not be wraped upp in oblivion
> how he hath travelled in the Armenian tounge may apere

Betty Hill concluded that the note was addressed to Archbishop Whitgift around 1583 and that the 'W.P.' who wrote the poem and who was being recommended as an expert antiquarian and scholar was William Patten.

Patten was the author of *The Calender of Scripture* (1575) and the first English student of Armenian, producing an Armenian alphabet and vocabulary in 1570. Both achievements are clearly what the unknown author of the recommendation to Whitgift was alluding to.

Betty Hill praised Patten as 'one of those sixteenth-century humanist-scholars to whom antiquarian studies owe so much' and sought to rescue him from obscurity. She corrected many inaccuracies in descriptions of him in standard reference works, listed three manuscripts by Patten and supplied a new and authoritative account of his long career.

Without Betty Hill, the truth about *A Letter* would probably still be unknown. Unfortunately she overlooked Patten's connection with the Kenilworth entertainments, identified by Gascoigne in *The princelye pleasures at the Courte at Kenelwoorth*. In a passing reference to a manuscript, Hill simply noted that 'In 1575 he wrote to William Cecil, his fellow on the expedition to Scotland, about the suppression of a book.'

This referred to a letter from Patten to Lord Burghley, dated 10 September 1575, which had lain ignored among the Cecil papers at Hatfield House for centuries.[7] Its contents were in their own way as revelatory as those of the long lost inquest report into the death of Christopher Marlowe, only rediscovered in 1925. The letter, addressed to Lord Burghley, who at that time was with the court at Woodstock, read as follows:

May it lyke yoor honorabl Lordship. This day receyved I aunswer fro my good freend the m^r of Requests hoow the book waz too be supprest for that Langham had complaynd vpon it, and ootherwize for that the honorabl entertainment be not turned into a iest. May it pleaz yoor honor, excepting the vj vntoo m^r Wylson, too yoor Lordship and vntoo my Lord Kepar, I haue not let three more pass me, but haue & suppress them all. I indeed prayd m^r Wylson too gyve Langham one, for that of woont he woold haue taken more vpon him. sory I am that he takez it so noow. And for the rest, I humbly submit myself too yoor honor, mooch less to stand at ony point of defens, but rather beseeching the continuans of yoor favour, whearof my poor estate hath so mooch need of, God healp me. Thus ending vntoo yoor good Lordship, encreas of mooch honor and continuauns of good health must humbly & hartely wish I. From London this xth of Septembr 1575.

> yoour honorabl Lordships allweyz
> humbly at comaundment
> W Patten

This item of correspondence is an extraordinary document to have resurfaced after four centuries. It is the Rosetta Stone of the Kenilworth revels, because it finally allows us to decipher their central text. This letter firmly establishes a number of things.

Firstly, Robert Langham had seen a copy of *A Letter* shortly after publication and had understood all too well that it was a satire, and that one of its targets was himself, the ostensible author.

Secondly, Langham had complained about the book, evidently to the Court of Requests. Members of the Privy Council had become involved in the matter. These included two of the most powerful

121

figures in the land – Lord Burghley and the Lord Keeper (or chief law official) Sir Nicholas Bacon – as well as Thomas Wilson, one of the four Masters of the Court of Requests.

Thirdly, William Patten, a member of the entertainments writing team, had been identified as the book's true author.

Fourthly, Patten acknowledged that one argument for withdrawing *A Letter* from circulation was that 'the honourable entertainment [i.e. the royal visit to Kenilworth] be not turned into a jest'.

Fifthly, the book had been suppressed and Patten ordered to return all his copies.

*

This single tantalising letter is all that has survived (or has so far been discovered) from what must have been a chain of correspondence about *A Letter* involving Lord Burghley and other court officials.

Evidently attempting to pass the matter off as a harmless jest, Patten says that he asked the Master of Requests 'too gyve Langham one, for that of woont he woold haue taken more vpon him.' The meaning of this sentence is fuzzy but it probably indicates that Langham, having discovered the hoax, not only complained about it to someone in authority, but tried to lay his hands on every copy he could get hold of in order to prevent others reading it. Patten meanwhile, exposed as the hoaxer, passed a copy on to Wilson, asking him to give it to Langham to add to his collection.

The next sentence in the letter reads simply: 'sory I am that he takez it so noow'. This could be interpreted in two ways. It might mean 'I'm sorry Langham is offended by the book, I've apologised and anyway it was only a lighthearted joke', or equally it could be read as signifying 'I'm sorry Langham feels he had to take that extra copy from Wilson, he needn't have worried because the book has now been suppressed.'

The letter ends on a slightly blustering, unapologetic note: 'And for the rest, I humbly submit myself too yoor honor, mooch less to stond at ony point of defens, but rather beseching the continuauns of yoor favour, whereof my poor estate hath so mooch need of, God healp me.'

The letter has an evasive, conspiratorial tone. It talks of 'the book' but scrupulously avoids giving its title. Perhaps unsurprisingly, since her scholarly expertise and interests lay in different areas, Betty Hill made no connection between 'Langham' and Kenilworth. Her article appeared in a small circulation specialist academic journal and attracted no wider attention.

*

Another nine years passed before the importance of the letter was properly appreciated. By one of those strange quirks of literary history, two renaissance scholars independently published articles in 1977 identifying William Patten as the real author of *A Letter*.

Writing in the same journal as Betty Hill, Brian O'Kill announced that *A Letter* was the 'most startling and intriguing addition to the Patten canon. Although it has been reprinted many times in the last two centuries, and is well known to historians and philologists, its authorship and purport have never previously been realized.'[8] Simultaneously, the Canadian academic David Scott published an article in the North American journal *English Literary Renaissance*, also identifying Patten as the true author of *A Letter*.

The arguments of both men overlapped at certain points. Both pointed out the significance of the September 1575 letter to Burghley and the fact that Patten was present at Kenilworth castle that July. They also noted strong similarities between the unusual semi-phonetic spelling system used in *A Letter* and other works by Patten, and the strong similarity between Patten's handwriting and the handwritten corrections in an early edition of *A Letter*. Scott noticed striking parallels with Patten's *Expedicion into Scotlāde* (1548) and O'Kill spotted similarities with *The Calender of Scripture* (1575).

The matter seemed to be decisively resolved. Then, in 1983, *A Letter* was republished, with a scholarly introduction and notes. The book's editor, R.J.P. Kuin, acknowledged the essays by Scott and O'Kill, but asserted that they were wrong. As far as he was concerned, the writer of *A Letter* really was Robert Langham.

Two years later, Kuin published an article which set out further to demolish their case for Patten's authorship of *A Letter*. He rebutted the handwriting argument, saying that the evidence was inconclusive. He argued that Patten's letter to Burghley could not possibly refer to

A Letter, since the text was completed no earlier than 20 August and there would not have been time for it to have been printed and suppressed by 10 September. Patten must therefore have been referring to some other book about the 1575 Progress – perhaps *The Pastime of the Progresse* mentioned in the printer's note to the reader in *The Princely Pleasures at Kenelworth Castle*. No copy of *The Pastime of the Progresse* is known to exist and this apparent one-off edition is presumed lost.

Kuin admitted that *A Letter* was remarkably similar to the orthography used by Patten and shared a number of his idiosyncratic interests, but explained that since it was clear Langham knew Patten, then he might well have derived these aspects of the book from this acquaintanship. Kuin also asserted that the book could not be a satire, because if it was it would have publicly insulted by association many prominent people, not to mention risked incurring the wrath of the powerful Mercers' Company. In conclusion, Kuin argued that most of *A Letter* is 'perfectly straightforward, with no great attempt at humour' and that it was not a parody.[9]

And there, for over twenty years, the matter has uneasily rested. There have been no further substantive contributions to the debate, and scholars have adopted various positions as to who they side with. Recently, the distinguished renaissance scholar G.W. Pigman acknowledged in passing the 'strong case' for Patten put forward by David Scott but concluded that Kuin 'makes a more convincing case for Langham'.[10] However, Benjamin Griffin is in no doubt that *A Letter* 'is the production of William Patten' and a 'satire'.[11] Alan Stewart notes the scholarly disagreement but avoids taking sides, remarking that 'although [*A Letter*] records the events faithfully enough, the tone has been read as dripping with satire.'[12]

14   The mysterious *Pastime of the Progress*

I believe that David Scott and Brian O'Kill were right all along in attributing *A Letter* to William Patten and that R.J.P. Kuin was wrong in thinking that Robert Langham was its author. I will explain why, and then go on to answer two very pertinent questions. Who was William Patten? And what motivated him to write *A Letter*?

It is an odd and perhaps revealing coincidence that the publication which did most harm to Leicester's reputation was entitled *The Copy of a Letter written by a Master of Art of Cambridge to his friend in London*. This was published anonymously in 1585 and is now better known as *Leicester's Commonwealth*. It supplied an inventory of all the rumours and innuendo which had accumulated around the life of Robert Dudley, with the intention of discrediting him as treacherous and wicked. Although there is no connection between *A Letter* and *The Copy of a Letter*, in the sixteenth century the genre clearly held some attraction for those motivated by malice. It was also a useful medium for disguising a political critique. As James Shapiro has noted, when the Earl of Essex was accused of war-mongering he wrote an *Apology* in his own defence, 'ostensibly...written as a letter to a friend'. It was widely circulated, originally in manuscript form and then in print. Similarly, Francis Bacon set out the official version of Catholic assassination attempts on Elizabeth in the form of the anonymous publication *A Letter Written out of England...Containing a True Report of a Strange Conspiracy.*[1]

This narrative form – almost a minor genre - is, as Terence Hawkes has commented in words which seem very relevant to the meaning of the Kenilworth *Letter*, a 'paradoxical mode':

> As a document whose standing is both private and public at the same time, it 'means' both by what it is seen to offer, in confidence, and by what it is seen to withhold, in public. It operates, that is to say, both directly, by intimate revelation, and indirectly by evident obfuscation and suppression. The two methods of signifying are equated and intimately involved. What such a letter says and what it does not, its utterances and its silences, are both meaningful: each becomes an aspect of the other.[2]

The utterance becomes yet more complex if the narrating voice purports to represent an individual who, all the time, is being slyly mocked. The way in which published 'Letters' were used as propaganda in the sixteenth century reinforces the case for the Kenilworth one being a satire. But how can we be sure that the author really was William Patten and not Robert Langham?

In establishing the authorship of *A Letter* there is little point in getting bogged down in arguments over handwriting. To my eyes there is indeed a striking similarity between the handwriting of William Patten and the handwritten corrections, very probably by the book's author, in the Huntingdon library copy of the book. But every individual's handwriting can vary according to time and circumstance, and deciphering Tudor handwriting requires an expertise which very few people have. Let us grant that this argument either way is inconclusive.

This leaves five main planks to Kuin's case for Robert Langham. His first argument seems persuasive. The time scale appears too short for the manuscript to have been taken from Worcester on 20 August, printed in London, read by Langham, and suppressed within the space of just three weeks. However, Kuin makes some very questionable assumptions, such as that Thomas Wilson consulted the Privy Council, which then 'discussed and decided upon it'.[3] But this is wholly conjectural. There is no real reason to believe that the Privy Council was involved and no evidence at all that the matter was brought before it. Burghley dealt with the matter personally and, as we shall see, he had good reasons for doing so.

A printer could easily have produced the book in days. If it was a vanity publication, it almost certainly had a very small print run. Assuming that the dating of William Patten's letter to Burghley is accurate, then the time scale is tight but it is not absolutely out of the question for it to be referring to *A Letter*. Besides, if the book *was* a hoax, there is no reason to believe that its sign-off date 'At the Citeé of Worcester, the xx of August. 1575.' is any less bogus than the name of the supposed author. Kuin's argument assumes a *terminus a quo* which is actually very questionable.

If Patten was the author of *A Letter*, he probably left Kenilworth as early as 20 July, when the entertainments programme was abruptly curtailed and his services were no longer required. Even if he did stay on until the day Elizabeth left the castle he was then free to return to London with his narrative largely completed. The letter to Burghley indicates that the book was in circulation while the royal progress was still making its slow, cumbersome way around the Midlands.

A lot depends on how fixed the royal itinerary was, which is far from clear. If Elizabeth was scheduled to be at certain locations on certain fixed days (and on the face of it, this seems a reasonable supposition), then Patten could easily have found out the future route and timing of the royal progress. His lifelong friendship with Lord Burghley gave him access to the very best information, even assuming that the schedule of the progress wasn't already known to everyone at Kenilworth that July. Although clearly the book would not have been released until after its sign-off date, Patten could therefore have quite easily dated his manuscript 'Worcester, the xx of August' while organising the printing of the book in London early August. It seems Elizabeth *was* in Worcester on that date, so in theory Patten was taking a risk of the book being exposed as defective if the Queen arrived at the town after that date or left before it. On the other hand, it is not unusual to find quite glaring errors and misprints in Tudor books. Besides, readers back in London would probably not have known where Elizabeth was on her progress on a particular day.

One good reason for Patten to have inserted 'Worcester, the xx of August' at the end would be to throw Robert Langham (and, perhaps, the authorities) off the scent, when they tried to find out who had *really* written the book. If he'd put 'Kenilworth, the xx of July' that would have narrowed the list of suspects down considerably, with the risk of speedy exposure. Langham evidently saw a copy of the book soon after it was printed, and the likeliest scenario is that Patten made sure he received one. There would have been no point in writing a blistering satire on Langham if the man himself never saw a copy. *A Letter* was designed to mock him – and to enrage him. It plainly succeeded in achieving this. However, Patten could not have anticipated that he would be swiftly identified through the printer rather than the book's contents.

Besides, if whoever wrote the book remained with the royal tour until 20 August, why does his account of it terminate a month earlier, on Wednesday 20 July? The author of *A Letter* clearly knew nothing of Elizabeth's departure from the castle, when Gascoigne ran along beside her and led her to 'Deep Desire' and the concealed band of musicians. If the book is simply an innocent account of a royal progress, why doesn't it say anything about what happened in those four weeks between 20 July and 20 August? The answer, I think, is obvious. The author of *A Letter* was no longer with the royal tour.

*

Kuin argues that Patten's letter to Burghley must refer to a hypothetical third book, which Patten was involved in and in which he pilloried Langham: 'This third book on some aspect of the 1575 Progress might well have been the subject of a formal complaint, suppressed, and withdrawn: so effectively, in fact, that no further mention of it appears.'[4] Kuin adds, 'One possible clue to its identity may be found in the Preface to Gascoigne's *Princely Pleasures* of 1577…where the printer Richard Johnes, refers to and discredits a now-lost account which he calls the *Pastime of the Progresse*… there is a remote possibility that the two lost accounts are one and the same.'[5]

On the face of it, this is an attractive hypothesis. The conventional story of the progress is that no less than three accounts appeared of what happened at the castle during the Queen's nineteen-day visit in July 1575. It is often asserted that they testify to a strong contemporary interest in a celebrity visit to a spectacular pleasure palace and the revels which took place there. *A Letter* and Gascoigne's *The princelye pleasures at the Courte at Kenelwoorth* have survived, but not the *Pastime of the Progresse*. Its disappearance is commonly regarded as a sign its popularity, with copies being read, passed on, and re-read, until they fell apart. Alternatively, as Kuin suggests, it may have been that this was the book which was suppressed. If it wasn't, it would indicate that *four* published accounts of the Kenilworth entertainments originally existed, of which only two have survived.

There are two other possibilities, which neither Kuin nor anyone else involved in this debate has considered. The first is that the *Pastime of the Progress* never existed in the first place. What Kuin fails to appreciate is that the introduction 'The Printer to the Reader' in *The princelye pleasures at the Courte at Kenelwoorth* was not written by Richard Johnes but by George Gascoigne. (Kuin also, incidentally, gets the year of publication wrong.)

Gascoigne was an old hand at tricking his audience with bogus addresses to the reader. The first one he ever set before the public was 'The Printer to the Reader' at the start of his first book, *A Hundreth Sundry Flowers* (1573). This is now commonly acknowledged to be by Gascoigne, as is all the other extra-authorial commentary in that book, including 'H.W. to the Reader', the letters of 'G.T.' and the linking editorial passages which speak of Gascoigne in the third person.

Gascoigne was a slippery and elusive figure, who was keen to market his work in any way possible. The reason he chose anonymity for *The Noble Arte of Venerie* was because a book about a pleasurable leisure activity did not fit in with the pious, devout image of himself put forward in his letter 'To the reverende Divines' which prefaced *The Posies of George Gascoigne Esquire* (1575) and which was shamelessly and cynically designed to make the ecclesiastical censors think that he was a reformed character. (He wasn't.)

In 'The Printer to the Reader' Gascoigne revealed the marketing strategy behind his equally anonymous book *The Princely Pleasures at Kenelworth Castle*:

Being advertised (gentle Reader) that in this last progresse, hir Majestie was (by the Ryght Noble Earle of Leycester) honorably and triumphantly receyved and enterained, at his Castle of Kenelwoorth: and that sundry pleasaunt and Poeticall inventions were there expressed, aswell in verse as in prose. All which have been sundry tymes demaunded for, aswell at my handes, as also of other Printers, for that in deede, all studious and well disposed yong Gentlemen and others, were desirous to be partakers of those pleasures by a profitable publication: I thought meete to trye by all meanes possible if I might recover the true Copies of the same, to gratifye all suche as had required them at my handes, or might hereafter bee styrred with the lyke desire. And in fine I have with much travayle and paine obtained the very true and perfect Copies, of all that were there presented & executed: Over and besides, one Moral and gallant Devyce, which never came to execution, although it were oftĕ in a readinesse. And these (being thus collected,) I have (for thy cõmoditie gentle Reader) now published: the rather because of a Report thereof lately imprinted by the name of the Pastime of the Progresse: which (in deede) doth nothing touche the particularitie of everye commendable action, but generally reherseth hir Majesties cheereful entertainment in all places where shee passed: togither with the exceeding joye that her subjects had to see hir: which Report made verye many the more desirous to have this perfect Copy: for that it plainlye doth set downe every thing as it was in deede presented, at large: And further doth declare, who was Aucthour and deviser of everye Poeme and invencion.

This is vintage Gascoigne. He conjures up the image of readers thirsting to read the text of the material set before the Queen at Kenilworth – the sixteenth century equivalent of a blurb screaming 'the number one international bestseller!' He presents himself not as George Gascoigne the scandalous poet but as an impartial third party who has gone to considerable trouble to gather together a comprehensive collection of the material set before the Queen – material which is in fact far from comprehensive, and which just happens to put Gascoigne centre stage.

He reveals himself to be still grumpy about the aborted performance of his play about Zabeta. In addition, recently scorched by the experience of having both *A Hundreth Sundry Flowers* and *The Posies of George Gascoigne Esquire* banned by the censors, Gascoigne piously emphasizes the moral worth of a publication which is strictly for 'studious and well disposed yong Gentlemen'.

Lastly, he refers to a 'Report…lately imprinted' which speaks only in general terms of what was set before Her Majesty and which has whetted the appetite of readers for a more detailed account of what occurred at Kenilworth. It is possible that such a publication existed. However, it may well be that it didn't. This hitherto unconsidered possibility would certainly explain why no library anywhere in the world holds a copy. Gascoigne may simply have been trying to create the image of a keen readership for material on Kenilworth when no such readership existed. He may also have been trying to corner the market against any future publications by other writers by emphasizing that he had the monopoly on the scripts enacted before the Queen – and who could better that?

If 'the Pastime of the Progresse' was a fictitious title with no tangible existence as a publication it would certainly not be the first time Gascoigne had used this ploy. In the preamble to *The Adventures of Master F.J.* the editor 'G.T.' describes 'two notable workes' written by F.J.: *Sundry lots of love* and *The clyming of an Eagles neast.*[6] These texts existed nowhere outside Gascoigne's own imagination.

The possibility that 'the Pastime of the Progresse' is a fiction is strengthened by two other occasions on which Gascoigne supplied bogus reasons for producing a particular work. His pioneering essay on prosody is entitled '*Certayne notes of Instruction concerning the making of verse or ryme in English, written at the request of Master Edouardo Donati.*' It begins with a flowery paragraph addressed to 'Signor Edouardo', describing how Donati has held him to a promise to supply him with advice on how best to write poetry in English. But no one has ever been able to identify Donati, for the simply reason that he was fictitious. Gascoigne gives himself away by explaining that the word 'ballad' was '(I thinke) derived of this worde in Italian *Ballare*, which signifieth to daunce'.[7] But as Donati was an Italian, why did he need to have his own language translated for him? Answer: *because Donati never existed.*

Gascoigne's essay is a passionate defence of English verse, urging would-be poets to avoid obscure words, to understand the requirements of different sorts of metre, and remarking that 'the more monasyllables that you use, the truer Englishman you shall seeme'.[8] But why should an Italian want to seem like a true Englishman? Donati was an exotic phantom, conjured up by Gascoigne to create a reason for writing what was by the standards of the time a revolutionary and experimental piece of writing.

Gascoigne used the same device in the final part of his little-read theological book *The Drum of Doomsday* (1576). The last part consists of 'A letter written by I.B. unto his familiar frende G.P. teaching remedies against the bytternesse of Death.' It is a kind of sequel to *Certayne notes of Instruction concerning the making of verse or ryme in English.* Like the essay on prosody, this short prose essay purports to have been written at the request of a friend. 'G.P.' 'I.B.' – who is almost certainly Gascoigne – explains that his friend

131

asked him to write 'a meditacion of contented death, or at the least to diminish the desyre of long lyfe.'[9] It was a request that with a suspicious neatness coincided with Gascoigne's translation work for *The Drum of Doomsday* and the poet's own bout of sickness. 'G.P.' is almost certainly just as imaginary as Edouardo Donati.

*

There is a second possibility, also never previously considered in connection with the Patten v. Langham debate. This is that Gascoigne had heard something about *A Letter* and its suppression, without ever seeing a copy. He knew that a book about Kenilworth had appeared, and was determined to cash in on this subject himself. If he knew that the book had been suppressed, that would explain why he avoided referring to it by its real title, and instead substituted the much blander *Pastime of the Progresse*. The word 'pastime' is used in the sense of 'amusement' and irrespective of whether or not Gascoigne knew the identity of the author of *A Letter*, he would have known that no one else but himself was in a position to marshall the scripts which he regarded as central to the revels – including his own.

Gascoigne's description of the book is oddly vague and general, almost as if he'd never read it. The 'Pastime of the Progresse' was, then, perhaps simply *A Letter*, referred to in a deliberately muffled form. This conclusion was reached by a Victorian editor of *Gascoigne's Princely Pleasures* as long ago as 1821. He took it for granted that the two titles were one and the same, and assumed that the printer was helpfully pointing out that Gascoigne's book complemented *A Letter*: 'In the printer's preface…is another allusion to the incompleteness of Laneham.'[10]

The 'Pastime of the Progresse' never existed. Gascoigne either mischievously fabricated it for marketing reasons, or it was his way of referring to *A Letter*, a book which he had heard of but never seen. Either of these two possibilities seems to me just as credible as the hypothesis that there were as many as four accounts published of what happened at Kenilworth in July 1575, of which only two survive.

15   Subterranean textual blues

Hardly anybody nowadays reads *A Letter*, either in its original published form - 88 pages, in a punishing deep black gothic typeface - or in the modern scholarly edition of 1983, which has for many years been out of print. This has little to do with the rarity of the book or the difficulties that sixteenth century prose presents to the modern eye and everything to do with the extraordinarily bizarre language in which it is written.

Even by the standards of Tudor English, which, notoriously, uses a flexible phonetically-based spelling system, *A Letter* is an eccentric production. Most Tudor prose is about 95 per cent intelligible to modern readers, and no particular specialised knowledge is required to tease out the meaning. Gascoigne's prose supplies a prime example of how little the English language has altered over 450 years. The main problems for modern readers are likely to be in the areas of vocabulary (specialist terminology to do with hawking and deer hunting, for example) or cultural and social allusion.

What has changed much more than the language are the *conventions* of the printed book. Books nowadays have traditional sizes and formats, including paperback and hardback, and much smaller fonts. Nowadays we abide by rules of grammar, punctuation, paragraphing and correct spelling. In the sixteenth century writers spelled words according to how they sounded and largely left punctuation to the printer. But even this ostensibly anarchic system conformed to certain standards and accepted conventions.

What is distinctive about *A Letter* is that its phonetic spelling is idiosyncratic and bizarre, even by the standards of the author's contemporaries. Some nineteenth century critics originally believed its odd appearance was because the book was written in a distinctive local dialect, restricted either to Warwickshire or Nottinghamshire. This turned out to be a completely baseless speculation. Its author had in reality spent most of the previous quarter of a century living in a village in Middlesex, three miles from the city of London. *A Letter*'s distinctive style is in fact totally synthetic and every bit as invented as the somewhat similar semi-phonetic language used in Iain M. Banks's inventive science fiction novel *Feersum Endjinn* (1994).

Some features of the language of *A Letter* occur again and again, resulting in what Brian O'Kill rightly calls 'a bristling barbarous surface effectively obscuring anything that may be underneath it.'[1] Even sixteenth century readers must have struggled to plough their way through *A Letter*. Its orthography (or spelling system) is characterised by the use of 'z' instead of 's' for plurals and a disinclination to use one 'o' when two could be slotted in, as in 'oour, 'doo', 'untoo'.

Common words are spelled according to the author's own distinctive formula: 'elz' (else), 'proez' (prose), 'olld' (old), 'nien' (nine), 'sum' (some), sheauwze' (shows), 'fier' (fire), 'callmd' (calmed), 'toong' (tongue), 'boll' (bowl), 'rein' (reign), 'doon' (done), 'knu' (knew) and 'poour' (power).

As O'Kill dryly notes, 'the cumulative effect is very distinctive.'[2] Matters are further complicated by the author's fondness for archaic and obscure words: 'steed' (room or place), 'leemz' (rays of light), 'steeven' (voice).

One man alone was responsible for inventing this orthography. His name was William Patten, and he was, of course, a member of the entertainments team at Kenilworth Castle in July 1575. Even R.J.P. Kuin is forced to concede that where *A Letter* is concerned, 'the orthography was indeed Patten's'.[3]

Kuin's way round this difficulty is to argue that Patten's system was briefly fashionable in the mid to late 1570s and that Robert Langham must have written *A Letter* under its influence. It is at this point that Kuin's case for Langham seems to me to be at its weakest. Where *A Letter* is concerned, the medium really is the message, in the sense that the quirky, obsessive nature of its spelling and narrative interests are perfectly in keeping with what we know of the character of William Patten and his writings.

At this point it is appropriate to step aside from *A Letter* and ask: *who was William Patten?*

*

There is a small corner of England where the name William Patten is still honoured and remembered. To find it you have to go to the oldest street in Stoke Newington, in what is now part of the dense urban sprawl of the London Borough of Hackney. If you turn into Stoke

Newington Church Street from the High Street you will soon come to a blue sign with six cartoon ducks pictured above the words WILLIAM PATTEN DAYCARE. It's a children's nursery, in the same building as the adjacent William Patten School. Continue on, past Defoe Road and a blue plaque commemorating the site of a house once lived in by the novelist, and you will eventually arrive at a building with a more immediate conection to the great Kenilworth hoaxer.

In 1550 Patten became the first secular lord of the Manor of Stoke Newington, which in the sixteenth century was a tiny rural village in the county of Middlesex. It lay in wooded countryside well beyond London's city walls, some three miles north east of St. Paul's Cathedral, and east of Ermine Street, the Roman road from London to Lincoln. The residents of Stoke Newington, who numbered around 100 adults in the mid-century, were probably a mixture of affluent city merchants and commoners engaged in traditional rural occupations.

Patten was then aged about 40 and about to enjoy two decades of affluence and social success. He seems to have been born around 1510, the son of a London cloth worker. He was the great-nephew of William Patten or Waynflete, Lord Bishop of Winchester, twice Lord Chancellor of England and founder of Magdalen College, Oxford. This ecclesiastical connection may have helped Patten in his early career in the church. Between 1528 and 1540 he was associated with the church of St Mary at Hill, Billingsgate, where he held a succession of positions, including Parish Clerk.

In 1544 he was secretary to the Earl of Arundel in France, and in August and September 1547 he took part in the English army's punitive march into Scotland – the so-called Pinkie campaign - under Protector Somerset. Someone else who participated in this military venture was William Cecil, who would later become famous as Lord Burghley, Elizabeth's most important adviser.

Cecil lent Patten his diary when in the following year he published his first book, a narrative of the campaign based on his notes. It was from the parsonage of St Mary at Hill that on 28 January 1548 William Patten dedicated the book, to John Russell, first Earl of Bedford. It was entitled *The expedicion into Scotlāde of the most woorthely fortunate prince Edward, Duke of Soomserset…made in the first yere of his Majesties most prosperous reign, and set out by way of diarie, by W. Patten, Londoner.*

By 1548 Patten was thriving. Through the patronage of the Earl of Warwick he was appointed to be one of the two 'Judges of the Marshalsey'; the other judge was William Cecil, strengthening the association between the two men. In 1549 he was appointed as 'collector of petty custom and subsidy in the port of London'.

He suffered bereavement in 1549-50, when his first wife died. She was buried at St Mary at Hill. Her death may have had something to do with his decision to leave the city and move to the countryside. In 1550 he became lord of the Manor of Stoke Newington. There he lived in the manor house beside the parish church of St Mary.

His social position and wealth continued to expand. In 1558 he was appointed 'receiver of the revenues of the late Court of Augmentations in the County of York, the City of York and the archdeaconry or Richemonde'. He remarried and a son, Thomas, was baptized at Stoke Newington on 11 January 1561. In the years 1559 to 1562 William Patten served on commissions surveying property of the Bishopric of London. In 1562 he received a 'grant for life...of the office of a teller of the receipt of the exchequer'. He was also given positions with the Mines Royal and the Mineral and Battery Works. In the 1560s William Patten was also a local Justice of the Peace. It was during his affluent Stoke Newington years that Patten sent his eldest son to Trinity College, Cambridge. With a wackiness that was characteristic of some of his writings, Patten had named the boy 'Mercury'.

Some of the fruits of the wealth which Patten accumulated were showered on Stoke Newington. He paid to have the decayed parish church torn down and rebuilt, in the process eliminating almost all trace of the original medieval stone building.

The work was completed in 1563 and the church remains standing today, in the south east corner of Clissold Park. It is now known as St Mary's Old Church, to distinguish it from the much bigger Victorian gothic church of St Mary's, erected directly opposite in 1858. Over the door in the south wall leading to the chapel, a small plaque still exists, bearing Patten's coat of arms, sandwiched by the initials 'W' and 'P'. At the base is the motto'Prospice' (literally 'look out' - in the sense of 'have foresight' or 'be aware') – strangely apt in relation to

A Letter. St Mary's Old Church is the only church of the Elizabethan period left in London and one of only a handful in England (however, the square tower put up by Patten has now been capped with a Victorian spire designed by Sir Charles Barry). Patten also added a schoolhouse on to the western aisle in 1563, for which act of philanthropy he is still remembered locally in the form of the William Patten School.

Patten also had the manor house rebuilt in brick. It was evidently a very substantial dwelling, with a gallery, a great dining room and a 'little' dining room, some twenty other rooms, as well as a kitchen, a buttery, a milk house, a storehouse, stables, a wood yard, a barn and a wash-house. The brick gateway of the old manor house, with its pointed arch, was still there in the nineteenth century but along with the rest of the building has now vanished. Its site alongside the church is now occupied by council offices.

*

There are aspects of Patten's career which tie in perfectly with certain aspects of *A Letter*. Unlike Robert Langham, who was a former mercer and a minor royal official, Patten was a man who had had first-hand contact with the law, both as a judge and as a Justice of the Peace. As O'Kill suggests, Patten may well also have received some legal training in his younger days, perhaps at one of the Inns of Chancery.

Patten's legal background fits in perfectly with the description of the dog and bear fight in *A Letter*, which is presented with heavy-handed humour as resembling a court case, with a 'pannell' (or jury list), 'a Queast' (or inquest), a 'challenge' (or charge), a 'forman' and 'Jury', 'sharp and byting arguments a both sydes' and 'if the dog in pleadying woold pluk the bear by the throte, the bear with travers would claw him again by the skalp' ('with travers' being legal jargon for a formal denial of a fact alleged by the other party).[4]

Patten was also a man of the church, who knew his Bible as well as anyone. Between the ages of 18 to 30 he was employed by St Mary at Hill, he took a keen personal interest in renovating his local church at Stoke Newington, and in April 1575 he published *The Calender of Scripture. Whearin the Hebru, Challdian, Arabian, Phenician,*

Syrian, Persian, Greek and Latin names, of nations, cuntreys, men, weemen, idols, cities, hils, rivers, & of oother places in the holly Byble mentioned, by order of letters ar set, and turned into oour English toong.

This was a glossary of proper names in the Bible, listed alphabetically in their original language, and annotated. It is the work of a man with a keen interest in Holy Scripture. Patten's theological zeal helps to make sense of a moment in *A Letter* which, when it has been noticed at all, has been dismissed as a printing error.

The description of how, on Monday 18 July, the hunted deer yet again fled into the Mere, is accompanied by a marginal gloss 'Psal. 24.' (Psalm 24). On the face of it this makes no sense and does indeed appear to be a misprint for Psalm 42, which begins 'As the hart panteth after the water brooks, so panteth my soul after thee, O God.' The Biblical allusion seems gratuitous, even faintly mocking. It may hint at the writer's anger and satirical spleen, since it goes on to ask, 'Why art thou cast down, O my soul? And *why* are thou disquieted within me?'

What is strange is that the apparent misprint was not corrected in the second edition of *A Letter*, even though The Psalms were known to everyone in the sixteenth century and even though someone, probably the author, went through the text making numerous changes.

It was, I think, a deliberate, super-subtle 'mistake'. The joke ramifies if we look at what Psalm 24 is about. It consists of a hymn of praise to the Lord, 'the King of glory'. God, we are told, has founded his world 'upon the floods. Who shall ascend into the hill of the LORD? And who shall stand in his holy place?' In directing us to this Psalm the author of *A Letter* mockingly hints that it applies to Kenilworth castle itself – built on a hill, surrounded by floodwater – and that the ruler of this world, Robery Dudley, thinks of himself as God's equal.

This was satire at its most blasphemous and dangerous. It could only be written obliquely. It is almost a private joke. To unlock it is to unlock the real meaning of *A Letter*, which is that it is as much a satire as a straightforward account of Elizabeth's visit to Kenilworth.

It is also the case that *The Calender of Scripture*, which was probably published about four months before *A Letter*, contains strong similarities to the later work. The phrasing of the sign-off date at the end of *A Letter* – 'fare ye hartely well...the xx. of August. 1575' – echoes almost exactly the words, 'Fare ye hartely well in Christ, this. ix. of Aprill. 1575.' which conclude the preface to the earlier work.

Both books also contain two of Patten's particular theories and obsessions – that the English language was largely derived from the Germans and that in Hebrew the Queen's name, Elizabeth, signifies seven, and that this number has a mystical significance which can be found everywhere in her honour. That Robert Langham exactly imitated William Patten's writing style is a remote possibility; that he also identified with Patten's idiosyncratic beliefs and theories seems to me so unlikely that it conclusively rules him out as the author of *A Letter*.

The parallels between *A Letter* and Patten's first book *The expedicion into Scotlāde* are even more striking. *The expedicion* has a diary format, based on notes. It is also characterised by rambling digressions. Both books were rushed out soon after the events they describe.

David Scott argues that the two works have in common 'the adoption of the viewpoint, for literary effect, of a somewhat naïve participant-observer; an erudite preface...a conscious reliance on superb descriptive passages to form high points in the literary structure; a continual attention to the minutiae of personal appearance and behaviour; and a degree of overt personalization highly unusual at this date in English histories of warfare or entertainment.'

There are also striking similarities in vocabulary. *The expedicion* has 'importable [intolerable] pride and execrable arrogancie', *A Letter* has 'outrage & importabl insolency'.

Furthermore, it is a stunning concidence that the archaic and extraordinarily rare verb 'to duddle' (meaning to confuse or muddle) occurs in both books, and these are the *only* examples cited by the Oxford English Dictionary.

*

Internal evidence indicates that the author of *A Letter* was far more likely to have been a member of the Earl's team of Kenilworth writers than a minor government official like Langham.

Whoever wrote *A Letter* had knowledge of the content of Gascoigne's unperformed play. Patten would have known that, but not Langham. The author of *A Letter* also knew that a masque had been planned to entertain the banqueters on the evening of Sunday 17 July, which was then called off.

In fact the identification of Patten as the author of *A Letter* throws one other aspect of what happened at Kenilworth into sharp focus. It is now obvious that it must have been William Patten who tipped off Burghley about the 'Zabeta' masque. Burghley – who certainly had no desire to see his monarch marry Robert Dudley – in turn told Elizabeth. If Dudley and Gascoigne were instrumental in creating a text which was dangerously explosive, it was Patten who wilfully detonated it. His evident antagonism towards Gascoigne provided him with quite sufficient motive.

The author of *A Letter* also had knowledge of incidental details such as the trumpets having a diameter of over 16 inches, indicating someone involved with the organisation of the entertainments rather than someone involved in seeing that a room was tidy and properly furnished.

All this raises the central question: if William Patten was the real author of *A Letter*, what was his purpose in writing it?

*

In 1568 Patten's world began to fall apart.

This was the year in which Patten lost his position as teller of the receipt of the exchequer, 'indebted to the Queen in £7928 7s. 11½d' – a truly phenomenal sum. In 1570 he was sacked from his post as receiver general of the revenues of York. On the face of it, he was either a grossly incompetent financial manager or an accounts-fiddling fraudster, siphoning off cash which he couldn't repay. In 1571 he was forced to give up his lease of Stoke Newington, presumably in an attempt to clear his massive debts (which would today be equivalent to around half a million pounds or more).

The following year he produced a Latin poem addressed to Elizabeth, entitled *Supplicatio Patteni*. It was never published but Patten later recycled some of it in his rambling section on 'Elizabeth' in his *Calender of Scripture*. He apparently presented the poem to

140

her in person at Hampton Court on 16 November, 1572. Patten offered extravagant praise of Her Majesty and her advisers but lamented 'the cruel fate of unfortunate Patten...the sorrowing father of seven children', who had been stricken down by disaster.

He seems to have received some kind of royal pardon, though it did not benefit him financially. By 1573 all Patten's remaining estates and offices were sold or confiscated.

At the age of about 63 his fortunes had hit rock bottom. His affluence and social position had melted away. From being lord of the Manor of Stoke Newington and the holder of a clutch of lucrative government offices, he was suddenly an impoverished nobody. Brian O'Kill has conjectured what may have happened next:

> A possible situation takes shape: Patten, still brooding over his disgrace and the apparent injustice of the world, returns to Court and finds an idiotic upstart mercer flaunting his little brief authority as Keeper of the Council Chamber. Robert Langham now takes precedence over William Patten, grand-nephew of a Lord Chancellor and Archbishop, true gentleman and devoted friend of great men! So the faithful servant of the old order rails against the newcomer who denies him his place, as Kent against Oswald in *King Lear.* [5]

This is plausible, though it is a speculation for which any tangible evidence is lacking. But plainly, for whatever reasons, Patten had a very strong animus against Robert Langham. As O'Kill remarks, 'Is there not, underneath the high spirits, another voice throughout the book suggesting to us that the man really is an ignoramus, a drunkard, a philanderer, a toady, and a base mercer?'[6]

One passage in *A Letter* underlines just such an interpretation:

> It pleazed his honor to beare me good wil at fyrst, & so too continu. To have givē me apparail eéven from hiz bak, to get me allowauns in ye stabl, too advauns me unto this worshipfull office so neér the most honorabl Councell, to help me in my licens of Beanz (though indeéd I do not so much uze it, for I thank God I need not) to permit my good Father to serve the stabl. Whearby I go noow in my sylks, y^t else might ruffl in my cut canves: I ryde now a hors bak, that els

many timez mighte mannage it a foot: am knoen to their honors &
taken foorth with the best, that els might be bidden to stand bak my
self: My good Father a good releéf, that hee farez mooch the better
by, and none of theez for my desert, eyther at first or syns [since]:
God hee knoez [knows].[7]

That the Earl of Leicester really gave away his cast off clothes to
Robert Langham must be doubted. What the image really symbolizes
is that Langham is just a shabby, second-hand clone of the
contemptible Earl.

For 'Langham' to boast that he has 'allowauns' (allowance,
meaning 'authorisation' or 'acknowledgement') in the stable is self-
evidently absurd. The Tudor stables still survive at Kenilworth Castle.
They are where a mass of common servants were lodged, in the roof,
well outside the large, exclusive residential complex which
surrounded the inner court.

As O'Kill rightly observes, 'This is surely a satirical portrait of a
social upstart aping his betters and displacing worthier men; a person
who has indeed no desert, who really ought to be on foot rather than
on horseback, and so on. I am tempted to think that the "licens of
Beanz" (never satisfactorily explained, to my knowledge) is a joke
about Langham's flatulence; and the equally obscure but disturbing
picture of his father serving the stable could be a pointed allusion to
his ignoble ancestry.'[8]

But if Patten chose to satirise Langham because of his insufferable
pomposity, what were his motives in also slyly mocking his writing
associate George Gascoigne, and his ostensible patron, Robert
Dudley? After all, Leicester had hired him to help write the
entertainments for Her Majesty. Moreover, Patten had once enjoyed
the patronage of Dudley's father, the Earl of Warwick. Why the sour
grapes?

In fact Patten probably got his employment at Kenilworth through
Burghley's influence. He had been a lifelong protégée of Burghley,
not Leicester. Burghley was simply doing his old acquaintance a good
turn by getting him paid employment at a time of severe financial
distress. And Burghley had long been a rival of Leicester's at Court.
In satirising Leicester and his desire to be king through marriage to
Elizabeth, Patten was aligning himself firmly with the Burghley

camp.

However, there is no reason to believe that Burghley was in any way complicit in the production of *A Letter*. It was strictly a one-man job by a maverick loner. There is also a very relevant fact which has not been considered before. When Patten had to leave Stoke Newington the person who took his place and moved into the grand manor house which he'd built was none other than Lord John Dudley, another member of the Dudley clan. To Patten it must have seemed, sickeningly, as if the Dudleys had all the luck.

*

But why would William Patten want to satirise George Gascoigne?

Pride and hurt feelings, one suspects. Of the seven members of the writing team, Patten, though at sixty-five the oldest, was probably also its most junior. Compared to the others, he was a bankrupt nobody. In a society as hierarchical and status-driven as Tudor England the others in the team may not have bothered to conceal their disdain for Patten's lowly status. He was Burghley's man, not Leicester's. He was there as a favour to Burghley, not because Leicester particularly needed him.

The man Leicester wanted was that season's literary celebrity – George Gascoigne, tall, handsome, witty, talented and the author of some scandalously risqué material. Gascoigne was sexy – something that could not be said of the sixty-five years old, impoverished William Patten, whose interests included Biblical commentary.

Gascoigne made sure that the lion's share of the writing set before the Queen was his own. He also made sure that he had a starring role in the proceedings. By contrast, Patten was marginalized. His only contribution to the entertainments that we know of is the Latin verse on the board above the gate, which the Queen was unable to read because by then it was too dark.

In *The princely pleasures* Gascoigne gives writing credits to Hunnis, Ferrers and Henry Goldyngham, but is strikingly offhand and casual about Patten's contributions to the entertainments. Describing the moment that the Queen passed along the drawbridge he quotes a Latin verse by Mulcaster, adding: 'other verses to the very selfe same effect were devised by M. *Paten*, and fixed over the gate in a frame. I am not verye sure whether these or master *Patens* were pronounced by the Actor, but they were all to one effect.'[9] The tone here is one of casual disdain and barely-concealed indifference.

A Letter says that because the verse on the plaque above the gate couldn't be read in the darkness, not even by torchlight, 'the same wear [were] pronoounced' by Richard Mulcaster, who was ostentatiously dressed-up in a costume designed to indicate a poet. But it is highly unlikely that Mulcaster read another man's poem when he'd penned a near identical one himself. Even Kuin is forced to concede this point, remarking that 'In fact, the "Poet" may have read a different set of verses.'[10]

In his anthology of the entertainment's scripts, Gascoigne didn't even bother including Patten's contribution. If it hadn't been quoted in *A Letter* it would have been lost to posterity. In reality it very strongly reinforces the case for Patten's authorship that the *only* text from the Kenilworth entertainments quoted in *A Letter* just happens to be one written by William Patten.

Patten not only quoted it in full but evidently instructed the printer to give it typographical prominence. This is an aspect of the work which is lost unless the book is read in its original published form. Unlike anything else in the text, Patten's verse is italicised and eye-catchingly set with narrow margins at the top of page 14. In his own way he was as proud of his own work as Gascoigne was of his, and just as keen to promote its importance. And, like Gascoigne, he was happy to heap praises on his own writing, under the guise of a pseudonym. The author of *A Letter* admires the plaque for being 'beautifully garnisht' with the royal arms 'and featly [neatly] with Ivy wreathz boordred aboout'.

But Patten had to come up with an explanation for quoting his own writing while pretending to be speaking in the voice of Robert Langham. He therefore claimed that 'becauz it remaynd unremooved, at leyzure and pleasure I took it oout'. It is an unlikely scenario. The plaque specifically referred to the presents laid out for the Queen on the bridge that night. It was not a decoration relevant to the rest of her stay and it was surely removed when the presents were, later that night or early the next day. That the plaque stayed up for nineteen days is as improbable as Richard Mulcaster reading Patten's verse before Elizabeth rather than his own.

Patten's ingenious excuse for quoting his own verse is matched by the opening words of the book's penultimate paragraph, ostensibly from Robert Langham to Humfrey Martyn:

Heérwith ment I fully to bid ye farewell, had not this doubt cum to my minde, that heer remains a doout in yoo, which I ought (me thought) in any wyze to cleer. Which, iz, ye marvel perchauns to seé me so bookish.

This is both a joke at the expense of Langham's shallow intellect and a laconic recognition on Patten's part that he has to find some way of explaining why the cluttered product of his own congested sensibility and orthography should apparently be the work of someone who had supplied no previous evidence of such interests.

*

Where William Patten and Robert Langham are concerned, R.J.P. Kuin concedes 'an acquaintance between the two men and a certain influence'.[11] He is forced into this by the curious parallels between *A Letter* and Patten's other work. But the argument cuts both ways. If the two men *were* friends and *were* both at Kenilworth, why doesn't Langham boast of being a personal friend of the man responsible for that magnificent welcoming plaque? That is what you would expect from the persona of 'Langham' which *A Letter* constructs.

'Langham' is a namedropper, so why doesn't he acknowledge his close friendship with William Patten, the great-nephew of a former Lord Bishop of Winchester, a good friend of Lord Burghley and the author of a distinguished work of military history?

In fact there is something even odder about the case for Robert Langham's authorship. It amounts to a glaring inconsistency and it is has never been noticed before. The 'Langham' of *A Letter* boasts that 'if the Councell sit, I am at hand'.[12] In other words, where the Privy Council goes, so goes Robert Langham, Keeper of the Council Chamber. There is no reason to doubt this, and it means that Langham went on the royal progress of 1575

What is never mentioned in any popular or scholarly accounts of what happened at Kenilworth that July are the actual sittings of the

145

Privy Council held there. In fact this body met at Kenilworth castle on 12 July, 14 July, 15 July, 16 July, 18 July, 19 July, 20 July, 22 July, 25 July and 28 July – a grand total of ten meetings.[13] Each of these meetings of the Privy Concil was attended by between six and eight people: The Lord Treasurer, Burghley; the Lord Chamberlain; the Earl of Warwick; the Earl of Leicester; 'Mr Treasurer' (i.e. Sir Francis Knollys, Treasurer of the Household; 'Mr Comptroller' (i.e. Sir James Croftes, Comptroller of the Household) and two principal secretaries – Francis Walsingham and Thomas Smith.

Extraordinarily, 'Langham' mentions none of these meetings and none of these people. You would expect him to boast of how busy he was at the castle, and how his services were constantly required. But he says nothing. It is a remarkable omission. The narrator possesses privileged knowledge of the entertainments but knows nothing at all about the meetings of the Privy Council. This makes no sense at all if 'Robert Langham' wrote *A Letter* but it makes perfect sense if William Patten was the real author.

The picture of Langham as a self-important busybody, who hangs around outside the Council chamber ticking people off if they 'make babling' and sternly telling them 'woot ye whear ye ar?'[14] supplies the clue to Patten's motivation in writing *A Letter*. Clearly he knew Langham at court before he ever went to Kenilworth Castle. He knew the world that Langham inhabited and knew that he was a friend of Humfrey Martyn (if he didn't, he learned it at Kenilworth from Langham's boasting). What motivated Patten to write *A Letter* in the form it eventually took was plainly some kind of slight suffered at the hands of the intolerably pompous, self-important Robert Langham. It may well have been just such the kind of ticking off complacently described in *A Letter*. It is easy enough to imagine Patten going to seek out his old friend Lord Burghley, only to be chastised by Langham. Hence Patten's sarcastic promotion of Langham to the non-existent office of 'Clark of the Council chamber door'.

Probably at first Patten intended to write nothing more than a sequel to *The expedicion into Scotlāde*. But at some point – either at the castle, or later, back in London – he decided to write up his notes in the form of a satire, using the adopted persona of 'Robert Langham'.

Up to this point in his life Patten had been something of an oddball. His writings were not particularly distinguished and had earned him neither fame nor fortune. But in choosing to write under the pseudonym of a real person his creativity was let loose in a brilliantly original and unique way. *A Letter* became less of a straightforward account of the entertainments set before the Queen and much more of a retaliation against Langham, against Leicester and against George Gascoigne. It was the sly, bitter, jeering revenge of an angry, clever and envious man.

What we have no way of knowing is just how accurate Patten's portrait of Langham is. Quite probably it is substantially a caricature. Patten can have known nothing about Langham's activities abroad, and the innuendo that he was a regular client of prostitutes may just have been an empty slur. But in its essentials 'Langham' is a brilliantly convincing comic creation, as vivid as a comic character in a Dickens novel. 'Langham' is a type, the kind of loud, pompous, self-important person most of us will have encountered at some point in our lives.

What, then, of the important people that Patten dragged into his satire? Arguing against his authorship, Kuin asserts that 'it is scarcely probable that he would have permitted himself, in the process, gratuitously and publicly to insult by association a number of prominent people'.[15] But of course Patten sought to avoid detection by hiding behind a pseudonym, and could therefore do and say what he wanted in his book. He may even have hoped that Langham would get blamed for it and lose his position.

Secondly, none of these prominent people mentioned in *A Letter* is a target for satire. When 'Langham' talks of being indebted to Lady Sidney and of spending time in the company of Sir George Howard, these people are not themselves mocked. Patten was almost certainly simply recycling genuine boasts of Langham's. His satirical gibes against Leicester are extremely oblique, as they are against Gascoigne. The major target throughout is Robert Langham.

A Letter was plainly a book written at speed. Its chronology of the entertainments at Kenilworth is at times erratic and about half of the book isn't about events at the castle at all but consists of rambling digressions. In writing it, Patten hoped to avoid detection, but clearly part of him didn't give a damn. He had lost everything. Moreover, he had even survived losing half a million pounds worth of other people's money. And he had a powerful protector in Lord Burghley.

When his identity as the hoaxer was exposed, it was Burghley who moved to bring the matter to a swift conclusion and ensure that his old associate escaped punishment.

William Patten was surely the classic outsider, silently consumed by private discontents. He was the oldest member of the writing team, but regarded as its least important contributor, and his only known individual contribution was restricted to a hand-painted plaque. He was marginalized and never given the opportunity to perform solo before the Queen. Even a virtual nobody like Robert Langham treated him with haughty disdain.

Worse, Patten had to tolerate the presence of the most successful writer of the day, and there is nothing quite like someone else's success to bring home to a failed writer the acuteness of his disappointed hopes. Patten's literary career had, in truth, been undistinguished and unprofitable. His antipathy to Gascoigne probably wasn't personal so much as professional – sheer jealousy and envy. This kind of situation is not exactly unknown among writers. And in reality, Patten's equation of Gascoigne and Codrus was not unjustified. There was nothing particularly memorable about the lines which Gascoigne penned at Leicester's command. It was hack work. Patten might have been able to produce speeches that were just as good – but he wasn't asked. Instead he produced *A Letter*.

The abrupt way in which *A Letter's* description of proceedings at Kenilworth terminates on Wednesday 20 July 1575, a week before the Queen departed, strongly suggests that his services were dispensed with. All the more reason, then, for Patten to return to London, smouldering with sundry discontents, bent on his revenge. Oblivious to all this, the 'real' Langham travelled on with Elizabeth.

Ironically, *A Letter* is William Patten's one and only masterpiece. The combination of a sharp eye for detail, a lifetime of literary aspiration, his presence at a major royal event, and a raging sense of humiliation and injustice, all combined to set his creative juices flowing. To be patronised by a loudmouthed pipsqueak like Robert Langham was plainly the last straw. The consequence was a stunningly vivid, clever, funny, complex piece of prose, denied a wider readership in later centuries only by its bizarre and idiosyncratic spelling style.

16 Gaudina and Contarenus

Back at Woodstock, Elizabeth had to wait just over three weeks for the climax to the thrilling story of Gaudina and Contarenus.

This was set before her on 20 September in the form of a play. The long wait suggests that the play may have been hurriedly composed and rehearsed in order to answer those questions left unresolved at the end of the tale. Though it is sometimes attributed to him, Gascoigne plainly wasn't involved in the writing of this play. Its style is wooden and banal, and had he been in any way involved as a co-author he would almost certainly have trumpeted the fact and arranged for the work's publication.

In reality the striking thing about the Woodstock play is that it is very obviously a retort to Gascoigne's aborted drama about Zabeta. It climaxes with Gaudina suppressing her passion for Contarenus and giving him up out of duty to the state. Sir Henry Lee substituted a tale of romantic self-denial for Leicester's waspish critique of Elizabeth's status as a spinster, and the Queen was delighted.

Lee's flattery hit the spot. There was a reflection of her contorted, difficult relationship with Dudley in the play, but it was a safe, soothing one. It told her she was right to remain single. Not just right but thrillingly and nobly self-sacrificing. It reinforced her deepest beliefs and imbued them with a sort of poetry. It was an entertainment which meant much more to her than high-tech stuff like fireworks or floating dolphins.

*

Meanwhile, as the great royal progress of 1575 began to wind down at Woodstock, *A Letter* was being effectively suppressed. It was a private publication; only a handful of copies were in circulation.

Langham's anger over *A Letter* was, essentially, a storm in a tea cup. Burghley moved quickly to defuse the situation. If Leicester had become involved then Patten might have been in much more serious trouble, but Dudley, away from London, is unlikely to have known about *A Letter*. Similarly Gascoigne probably never saw a copy of the book. If he did, he was surely unaware that he was one of its satirical targets. The book's clotted surface texture deterred casual readers

149

from venturing very far into the text or its oblique ironies. On the face of it the joke was strictly at the expense of Robert Langham and it requires a much sharper eye to see the broader satire at work or the sustained, double-edged quality of the narrator's posture of garrulous, wide-eyed innocence.

Quite probably there was some truth in Patten's portrait of Langham as a puffed-up, self-important nobody. When Langham discovered the satire he protested bitterly, and Burghley intervened to calm him down and have the book withdrawn. It was all done very quietly, and the main organ of state censorship – the High Commission – never became involved.

Burghley, though he might well have privately smiled at a satire on Leicester's overweening egocentricity and pretensions, would hardly have involved himself in such surreptitious manoeuvering. His role in the affair was to soothe Langham's ruffled feelings, suppress the book and protect his elderly and somewhat eccentric friend.

That *A Letter* was successfully suppressed in 1575 is plain. Only three copies of what is probably the first edition survive, and they were doubtless among the ones left in Patten's own possession. Patten himself may well have promised to get rid of them but no author is very willingly going to destroy a book he wrote, valued and had paid to have published. Fourteen copies of a possible second edition survive. This was just possibly a pirated edition, though given the murky circumstances surrounding the publication of *A Letter* Patten may well have been perfectly happy to see his book re-appear at a later date when the fuss had died down. Robert Langham died around 1579-80, after which republication would have been a much safer bet.

*

The last meeting of the Privy Council at Woodstock was held on 2 October. It met again at Ricot on 7 and 8 October, and on 14 October at Windsor. And so the great summer progress of 1575 came to an end.

Ironically, at the time, it was not regarded as a progress that was in any way out of the ordinary. William Patten's motives in rushing out a book were a swirling mix of personal obsessions and emotions, and

150

his book no sooner emerged into the light of day than it was stamped on and vanished. Gascoigne brought out his own Kenilworth book the following spring but this again was perhaps as much a moneymaking exercise and an attempt to promote himself as a leading royal entertainer, rather than the action of a man who had been impressed and awed by what he'd witnessed. *The princelye pleasures at the Courte at Kenelwoorth* does not seem to have been a commercial success, and it was only republished after his death, in a volume which advertised itself as containing the poet's 'whole works'.

Gascoigne returned to Walthamstow that autumn aware of a new opportunity to promote himself at court. He had seen with his own eyes that Elizabeth had much preferred her stay at Woodstock to her nineteen days at Kenilworth. The Queen had publicly requested a written account of the first day's entertainment at Woodstock. Gascoigne decided to do better than that. He would supply her with a beautifully produced manuscript presentation copy of the hermit's tale, in four languages – English, Latin, French and Italian. A gift of this sort was a conventional way of ingratiating oneself with the monarch. Decades earlier Thomas More had presented Henry VIII with a lavishly decorated copy of a Latin poem he'd written celebrating the king's coronation.

'The Tale of Hemetes the Heremyte' is not, as is often assumed, an original piece of writing by Gascoigne. He nevertheless decided to stamp it as a distinctively Gascoignean production in other ways. Since the Queen admired and respected learning, he produced a multi-lingual manuscript in 38 folios. It is quarto size, 8¾ inches x 6½ inches – about the size of a modern notebook. It even resembles a notebook, in so far as Gascoigne only filled half of it. The remaining 38 folios are blank. It has commonly been assumed to have been produced by a scribe on the poet's behalf but there seems no real authority behind this belief. It is just as likely to be entirely Gascoigne's own painstaking work.

The narrative is accompanied by his own translations of the tale into Latin, Italian and French. In addition, the versions of the tale are divided by three emblematic pen-and-ink drawings accompanied by verses in Latin, Italian and French. On the first page another quasi-emblematic drawing portrays the poet presenting 'The Tale' to the Queen. It is followed by a sonnet and a prose address 'To the Queen's

151

Most Excellent Majesty', ending with an 18-line rhyming epilogue. The prose preface amounts to a request for employment. Gascoigne concedes his 'youth myspent', his 'follys laughed att' and other errors, but the key item in his list of personal failings isn't really a failing at all: 'my trewth unemployed'. What he wants is patronage and sponsorship, and he isn't too choosy whether it's for his writing or his soldiering:

> Behold here (learned pryncesse) nott *Gascoigne* the ydle poet, writing trifles of the green knighte, but *Gascoigne* the *Satyricall* wryter, meditating eche *Muse* that may expresse his reformation/ fforgett (most excellent lady) the poesies which I have scattered in the world, and I vowe to wryte volumes of profitable poems, wherewith your majesty may be pleased/ Only employ me (good Quene) and I trust to be proved as dillygent as *Clearchus*, as resolute as *Mutius*, and as faythfull as *Curtius*/ Your majesty shall ever fynde me with a penne in my righte hand, and a sharpe sword girt to my lefte side, *in utramaque paratus* / as glad to goe forwards when any occasion of your service may dryve me, as willing to attend your person in any calling that you shall pleas to appoint me/ my vaunting vayne being nowe pretyly well breathed, and myne arrogant speeches almost spent, lett me most humbly beseche your highness, that you may vouchsafe to pardon my boldness, and deigne to accepte this my simple new yeres gifte/

The Queen did deign to accept it and today this unique and priceless manuscript is held by the British Library. The preface is dated 'this first of January 1576' and it is conventionally assumed that the manuscript was presented to Elizabeth on this date, although there is no concrete evidence of this.

It turned out that Patten's *Letter* was not the only questionable text to emerge from the royal progress of 1575. Someone managed to get hold of either the original or a copy of Gascoigne's gift to the Queen, and reproduced the English and Latin versions of the hermit's tale. Falsely attributed to 'Abraham Fleming' they appeared, with surrealistic incongruity, bound up with a tract by Synesius of Cyrene entitled *A Paradox, Proving by reason and example that Baldnesse is much better than bushie haire*. Gascoigne would no doubt have protested bitterly about this pirate edition but it did not appear until 1579, by which time he was dead.

The handsome manuscript was also signed by Gascoigne. His signature is big and bold, as if indicating a solid confidence that the Queen knew exactly who he was. He wasn't, like Robert Dudley, addressing her as an equal, but neither was he beseeching her favours as an unknown outsider. Indeed, in the prefatory sonnet he even seems to have been reminding her of the mishap in The Chase at Kenilworth:

Behold (good Queen) a poet…

In doubtful doompes, which way were best to take
with humble heart, and knees that kiss the ground
presents himself to you for duty's sake.
And thus he saith, no danger (I protest)
shall ever let this loyal heart I bear
to serve you as may become me best
in field, in town, in court, or anywhere.

Gascoigne is referring to the pen and ink drawing of himself kneeling and presenting the manuscript. But indirectly he seems to be echoing that moment when, as the savage man, he startled Elizabeth's horse. He is, as he says, down in the dumps or depressed and uncertain about 'which way were best to take'. The Queen's cry 'no hurt' seems to reverberate in the poet's insistence that 'no danger' will attend his future service on her. As an actor he rather botched the job. What, then, of the future? Gascoigne puts forward the 'strange sight' of 'a poet with a spear' who is simultaneously

A soldier armed, with pencil in his ear,
with pen to fight, and sword to write a letter,
his gown half off, his blade not fully bound

The Gascoigne portrayed in the drawing is an armed warrior. But he is also a poet and he presents, as Hamlet was to do, an artfully dishevelled appearance. This is a man of possibilities, multi-talented, equally at home on the battlefield or in the study. By 'pencil'

Gascoigne means an artist's brush – something used in drawing (the modern meaning doesn't begin until the eighteenth century). He is, and is not, a soldier, a writer, an artist.

This drawing is much reproduced in books about the Tudor age, as if it was the sixteenth century equivalent of a photograph. Modern monochrome reproduction has the effect of making the picture seem sharper and fresher than in the original, which has a faded brown-grey appearance, the colour of a soup stain. The caption usually reads something along the lines of: 'George Gascoigne presenting Elizabeth I with the gift of a book.' But this is not really true. What the drawing expresses is George Gascoigne's *fantasy* of himself presenting the Queen with the manuscript of 'The Tale of Hemetes the Heremyte'.

The scene shown is an extremely stylized one. Prouty rightly comments that 'the drawing is practically an emblem'.[1] The Queen, wearing her crown, sits on her throne beneath a fringed canopy. A winged griffin with naked female breasts squats beside her like a guard dog. Elizabeth ceremonially clutches her orb and sceptre, almost as if she was undergoing her coronation all over again. Gascoigne kneels before her. In his left hand he holds what he called 'a spear' (but is really a small lance) and in his right hand his manuscript.

Although obviously intended to feature the interior of one of the royal palaces, the whole scene is intensely theatrical. It's almost like a two-person dumb show from a static, gloomy play like *Jocasta*. Elizabeth and Gascoigne are pictured entirely alone (a wildly improbable scenario), as if on a small stage. They appear to be facing each other but on closer examination the perspective is wrong. The enthroned Queen is tilted to her right and Gascoigne, his right shoe resting (oddly) on the right corner of her outermost robe on the floor, is actually positioned looking to the left of the griffin.

Two steps lead up to this stage-like room, which is viewed from about the height of Gascoigne's head. It's like looking at a scene onstage at London's rebuilt Globe theatre, from a very good seat in the middle stalls.

Flagstones or tiles stretch to the rear of the room, where an open doorway set in a curtained partition reveals a cloister-like scene of pillars receding into the distance along a walkway or corridor. To the right another open doorway shows a tiny part of an apparently deserted antechamber. The ceiling of the room consists of exposed crossbeams. From a large black hole cut in the beams an outsize hand dangles the snake-like arm of an ornamental hook. From it dangles an elaborate frame bearing the words of Gascoigne's motto *Tam Marti quàm Mercurio*, with a tassel drooping beneath it. Above Gascoigne's head, like a saint's halo, floats a crown of laurel leaves.

The artificiality of this frozen, strangely exaggerated, theatrical scene is accentuated by an outer frame of elaborate scrolled patterning. It looks like a three dimensional scene on a page from a book – which is, of course, exactly what it is. The circumstances were probably quite different to those portrayed in Gascoigne's fantasy drawing. The room – whether at Whitehall or Greenwich or one of the other royal palaces – was probably bigger, less intimate, crowded with Ladies in Waiting and courtiers and other servants of the royal household. Gascoigne is hardly likely to have been admitted to Elizabeth's presence armed to the teeth, gripping a lance. It must nevertheless have been an odd moment when the Queen took delivery – almost like one of those strange tales of receding realities by Jorge Luis Borges. She accepted a manuscript showing her accepting the manuscript in a drawing which even portrayed the brush used to draw the drawing of her accepting the book which she held in her hand.

Perhaps the most interesting feature of the scene is Gascoigne's representation of himself. We only have two conclusive images of the poet – this one and the portrait printed in *The Steele Glas*, which was apparently the work of another hand. That portrait shows a lean, trim man in armour. Age is creeping up on him. There are lines under his eyes. He looks wary. This is a man who has experienced much and who wears it in his face. It is a portrait which lives up to the book's title: the steel mirror – the mirror that reflects the hard, realistic, unembellished truth.

Since *The Steele Glas* portrait was probably done at about the same time as the drawing in 'The Tale of Hemetes the Heremyte' it is instructive to compare them. The image of Gascoigne in his self-penned drawing is similar but with revealing differences. In both he has a full head of hair, a moustache and beard. There is the same fine, sharp nose. But the Gascoigne who kneels before her looks healthier and more robust. His hair is fuller, even curly. It comes down in an exaggerated fashion to just above his eyebrows, whereas in the portrait the forehead is much more expansive and the hairline higher, almost on the brink of receding around the crown of the head. The kneeling poet looks strong and vigorous, apt for a man seeking military service. The calf of his exposed right leg and the thigh of his left leg look muscular and strong. These are the legs of a regular horse rider.

George Gascoigne: the 'Steele Glas' portrait (1576)

The image is likely to have been a flattering, slightly exaggerated one. This is Gascoigne as he liked to imagine himself. Compared with the man in the portrait he looks unwrinkled and younger – a fine strapping man in his prime and surely no older than his thirties. But of the two images, the portrait is likely to have been much closer to the reality. Looking at the portrait it is not hard to believe that it shows a man in his early forties. Nor is it hard to believe that it shows a man who, whether he knew it or not, was not far from death.

17   Philip Sidney's revenge

William Patten was evidently not the only person present at Kenilworth that July who felt a pang of jealousy regarding George Gascoigne's success and reputation as a writer.

The Earl's twenty-year-old nephew Philip Sidney was present at the entertainments and can hardly have been unaware of Gascoigne's dominant presence. Nine years earlier, the young Sidney may well have been in the audience at Gray's Inn when Gascoigne's productions of *Jocasta* and *Supposes* were staged.

After his early death in 1586, Sidney's poetry, criticism and fiction was published and he was elevated to the status of a classic English writer. But though Sidney wrote an essay about the state of contemporary English poetry you would never know from that or any of his other writings that George Gascoigne had ever existed. After Sidney's exposure to Gascoigne in the summer of 1575 his subsequent absolute silence about his literary achievements is strangely eloquent.

That Sidney and Gascoigne would not have enjoyed each other's company is hardly surprising. Gascoigne was handsome, easygoing, extrovert, fond of a bawdy quip, whereas Sidney, by all accounts, was priggish, uptight and solemnly 'serious'. Someone who knew him recorded that Sidney's face was 'laid waste, as with little mines' by the ravages of smallpox, which you would never know from portraits of him.[1] He became an icon of beautiful youth, but according to William Drummond (cited by Ben Jonson) 'S[ir] P[hilip] Sidney was no pleasant man in countenance, his face being spoiled with pimples and of high blood and long'.[2] One of Sidney's biographers calls him 'a hot-tempered, arrogant, and in many ways "difficult" young man, who was not liked by all his contemporaries.'[3]

Sidney was a haughty aristocrat who disdained the common vulgarity of publication. When he died in 1586 none of his manuscripts had been published. But if, as seems certain, Sidney and Gascoigne fell out with each other at Kenilworth, they each took an oblique revenge on the other.

One of the illustrations to *The Noble Arte of Venerie* shows the Queen picnicking during a hunt at Kenilworth, surrounded by courtiers. Katherine Duncan-Jones has suggested that the two bearded courtiers with garters on their left legs may be Sidney's father and Leicester. She adds,

> A group of courtiers sitting and picnicking to the right ought, if precise identifications are intended, to include Sidney. The most noticeable of the group, and the youngest-looking, bears some slight resemblance to the 1577 portraits of Sidney. He is shown, unglamorously, about to stuff a large piece of meat into his mouth.[4]

Duncan-Jones's hunch is certainly a possibility. In fact the Sidney figure is duplicated by that of a boy in the foreground, who is also pushing a large chunk of food towards his open mouth. If the identification is correct, Gascoigne was satirising the haughty aristocrat as coarse and infantile.

If so, it may not be entirely a coincidence that a bearded male figure leans towards the gluttonous child and is shown pouring wine from a flagon. The thin, stylized jet of liquid makes it look very much as if the man is symbolically pissing in the boy's direction. This may be reading too much into the scene, but sly humour like this would be perfectly in keeping with Gascoigne's temperament. If the resemblance was intentional (and in the original the illustration is far too small to be absolutely sure) it was a private joke on the poet's part, but no more than that.

Philip Sidney's revenge on Gascoigne was much less ambiguous and, in the long run, devastatingly effective. He wiped him from the record of contemporary English poetry. He also retaliated against his writing in other ways.

The Posies of George Gascoigne Esquire was Gascoigne's banned book under a new title, with the original sequencing of its contents jumbled up. It also contained new material, including *Certayne notes of Instruction concerning the making of verse or ryme in English*. This was the first essay on English prosody ever published and supplies a practical discussion of the mechanics of writing a poem. A good poem, Gascoigne argues, should begin with 'some fine invention' – meaning some clever and original idea, not a cliché. The poet should try not to be obscure, keep to the same metre, understand the importance of ordering words according to stress, avoid words of many syllables and favour monosyllables and beware rhyme for the sake of it. The poet should also avoid too much repetition, eschew strange words, keep to ordinary English and not set the adjective after the noun, and take care with the placing of caesuras (or pauses). Finally, a poet should possess an accurate understanding of the structure of metrical forms.

In general terms, *Certayne notes* forms part of that wider movement, exemplified by William Tyndale's translation of the New Testament, Thomas Wilson's *The Arte of Rhetorique* (1553) and Roger Ascham's *The Scholemaster* (1570), which resisted foreign syntax and words ('inkhorn terms') and promoted the value of ordinary, everyday English. Manifesto writers are usually driven by a burning passion to explain, persuade and convert the reader to their great literary cause. Gascoigne's essay has an altogether more relaxed tone. 'Certayne' simply means 'some', modestly indicating that it does not pretend to be a comprehensive guide. It is written in a casual, genial, chatty style: 'I write moved by good will, and not to show my skill'. In fact it very probably *was* written casually, in a single draft. Section 16 breezily begins, 'I had forgotten a notable kind of rhyme, called riding rhyme…' Gascoigne is not bothered by formal elegance but just pops his digression in as it stands. He does not bother to go back, rewrite the essay, and locate it where it more properly belongs, in section 14.

Gascoigne's essay excited the sixteenth century scholar Gabriel Harvey more than anything else the poet wrote, if we measure that emotion by quantities of marginal jottings. In that, Harvey was four centuries ahead of his time. Only in recent years has *Certayne notes* attracted a substantial quantity of academic commentary.

For centuries it lay in the shadows of a more famous work. Philip Sidney's *Defence of Poesie*, also known by the title *An Apology for Poetry*, is the best known work of literary criticism of the Elizabethan age. This is partly due to the massive public relations campaign orchestrated by the Earl of Leicester after his nephew's early death in the Low Countries, and partly due to a later cultural ignorance of the Latin writings of the age. For example, Henry Dethick's *Oratio in laudem Poëseos* [*Speech in Praise of Poetry*] is probably a work of the 1570s but in common with most Elizabethan criticism has lacked recognition by virtue of having been written in Latin.

What has never been acknowledged is that *The Defence of Poesie* is almost certainly an attempt to denigrate Gascoigne, without ever actually mentioning him by name. *Certayne notes* is dedicated to an Edouardo Donati, who is almost certainly bogus. Sidney's essay begins with a mention of a different Edward, 'the right vertuous *Edward Wotton*' – who very definitely *did* exist – and *John Pietro Pugliano* – a famous Italian equestrian master, whose student Sidney was. A *genuine* Edward and a prestigious Italian. Coincidence? Possibly. But possibly also an aristocratic squashing of the upstart Gascoigne.

The Defence of Poesie is a classic which scholars tend to approach very deferentially and quite uncritically, from a kneeling position. It was probably written some five years after Gascoigne died. It makes the exaggerated and silly claim that poetry 'from almost the highest estimation of learning is fallen to be the laughing-stocke of children.'[5] This is the sixteenth century equivalent of an editorial in a populist newspaper, whipping itself into a froth of outrage. Sidney demands to know 'why *England* (the Mother of excellent mindes) should bee growne so hard a step-mother to Poets'. The very earth itself laments the fact 'That Poesie…embraced in all other places, should onely finde in our time a hard welcome in England.'[6]

Sidney then constructs a highly contentious English poetic tradition to prove his point. He makes the patronising observation that '*Chaucer*, undoubtedly, did excellently in hys *Troylus and Cresseid*…Yet had he great wants, fitte to be forgiven in so reverent antiquity.'[7] He admires the anthology *The Mirrour for Magistrates* (1559). He gushes over the Earl of Surrey's lyrics, finding in them 'many things tasting of a noble birth, and worthy of a noble minde.' He approves of *The Shepherd's Calendar* (1579), which Spenser dedicated to Sidney, but ticks the poet off for the 'framing of his stile to an old rustick language'. Apart from these writers, says Sidney, there is no modern English poet of worth.

The claim is ludicrous. Sidney ignores Wyatt. He disdains to mention Tottel's hugely popular and influential *Songes and Sonettes*. And most of all, of course, he excludes the most popular and outstanding poet of the 1570s, George Gascoigne. When Sidney says of poetry, 'base men with servile wits undertake it: who think it enough if they can be rewarded of the Printer'[8] it sounds very much like a dig at Gascoigne.

160

Sidney asserts that the reason why 'Poesie...is not esteemed in *Englande* is the fault of Poet-apes, not Poets.' That is hysterical abuse, not criticism. Sidney in reality was an excruciating snob. His drooling over the Earl of Surrey's 'noble birth' and his lyrics 'worthy of a noble minde' are absolutely characteristic of his narrow-minded pomposity. When *The Copy of a Letter* appeared, attacking his uncle the Earl of Leicester, Philip Sidney penned a passionate response. It revealed a great deal about him. As Elizabeth Jenkins laconically observes,

> None of the accusations is answered, however, except the one to which Sidney devotes the greater part of the paper, that Leicester's father, Sidney's grandfather, John Duke of Northumberland, was of ignoble lineage. This roused Sidney beyond any charges of murder, treason, lechery, robbery, cruelty, greed and cowardice brought against his uncle. To say that the Duke of Northumberland was not a gentleman born![9]

Sidney, I believe, had read *Certayne notes*, and *The Defence of Poesie* is a calculated retort to it. His intention was both to erase Gascoigne from the record of previous literary achievement and to obliterate his short, straightforward essay on the mechanics of poetry by substituting a longer essay weighted down with learning, name-dropping and dogmatic assertions. It is strange therefore to see *The Defence of Poesie* regarded as some kind of impartial and objective assessment of the true state of verse at this period. The distinguished Sidney scholar John Buxton writes:

> in the 1560s and 1570s Turberville, Gascoigne, Breton, and Whetstone published poems; but even by the time when Sidney was writing his *Apologie*, in the early 1580s, he felt compelled to admit that he found 'the very true cause of our wanting estimation is want of desert; taking upon as to be Poets in despight of *Pallas*.' To Sidney and his friends about this time English literature seemed to be in a state of decay.[10]

This dresses up Sidney's personal prejudices as a compulsion to tell the truth about the sorry state of English poetry. It uncritically recycles his version of recent literary history.

Of the four writers mentioned by Buxton, the outstanding success story was Gascoigne's. His *Hundreth Sundry Flowers* (1573) was the admired bestseller of the time. For years afterwards, many poets wanted to write like Gascoigne and his reputation endured to the end of the century. Puttenham's *The Arte of English Poesie* (1589) identified ten poets 'who have written excellently well'. The list included Sidney and Gascoigne. That same year Thomas Nashe wrote that 'Master Gascoigne is not to bee abridged of his deserved esteeme, who first beat the path to that perfection which our best poets have aspired to since his departure.' Nine years later, in *Palladis Tamia*, Francis Meres, drew up a list of fourteen poets 'the most passionate among us to bewaile and bemoane the perplexities of Love'. His list included Sidney, Spenser, Shakespeare and Gascoigne. Gascoigne remained popular until the end of Elizabeth's reign, judging by Sir John Davies's satire of 1597, which poked fun at a flashy young man about town:

> He weares a hat of the flat-crowne block,
> The treble ruffes, long cloake, and doublet French;
> He takes tobacco, and doth weare a lock,
> And wastes more time in dressing than a wench:
> Yet this new fangled youth, made for these times,
> Doth above all praise old George Gascoine's rimes.

John Buxton goes on to agree with the assessment that Gascoigne 'was a naturally gifted poet who had not studied his art with the diligence needed to become a great poet'.[11] Thus, by a curious sleight of hand, the man who wrote the first essay on prosody ever written in English and who demonstrated an acute self-consciousness about the art of writing poetry, gets wrapped over the knuckles for not properly studying his art.

As a prig, Sidney, who abhorred 'scurrility, unworthy of any chast eares', was no doubt appalled by Gascoigne's bawdy innuendo.[12] His temperament was the opposite of that of Shakespeare, whose sensibility meshed with Gascoigne's word-play, punning and sly mix of obscenity and high-minded Petrarchan sentiment. Sidney sneered at plays which were 'neither right Tragedies, nor right Comedies;

mingling Kings and Clownes'.[13] There was nothing in his essay for a playwright like Shakespeare.

Philip Sidney's air-brushing of Gascoigne from the record of sixteenth century literature conceivably extended to the writer's drama. Sidney sweepingly condemns all English tragedy and comedy for 'observing rules neyther of honest civilitie nor skilfull Poetrie' except *Gorboduc* (adding 'of those that I have seene').[14] He makes no mention of *Jocasta* or *Supposes* even though one of his biographers believes Sidney probably saw both plays. His attack on 'mongrell Tragy-comedie'[15] could possibly have been a barbed attack on Gascoigne's 1576 play *The Glass of Government*. But while finding himself unable to mention George Gascoigne's diverse achievements even once, Sidney twice mentions the utterly forgotten Scottish writer George Buchanan (1506-82), heaping glowing praises on his 'piercing' wit and expressing 'divine admiration' for his tragedies.[16] Buchanan wrote in Latin and was certainly highly regarded in the sixteenth century, but posterity's verdict has been brutal: 'an intellectual mediocrity'.[17]

*

Sidney's poetic practice also seems like a calculated attempt to spurn Gascoigne and all he stands for. His 'Certaine sonnets' have a variety of line-lengths, rhyme schemes and stanza forms and ostentatiously shun Gascoigne's strict definition of the form.

The basic foundation of *Certayne notes* is the recommendation that the 'making of a delectable poem' requires that it be grounded 'upon some fine invention'.[18] But as G.W. Pigman notes, 'The first sonnet of Sidney's *Astrophil and Stella* reads like a refutation of Gascoigne's advice in [his opening] paragraph.'[19] A conscious and deliberate refutation, one might add. Sidney complains that he studied 'inventions fine' and they were no help at all. He takes Gascoigne's advice and it gets him nowhere. His muse tells him he is a 'Foole'.

Sidney's sister Mary, who was also at Kenilworth, collaborated in the project of erasing Gascoigne's achievement. Her version of Psalm 130 has been seen as stemming from 'a determination to respond to Gascoigne's stanzaic virtuosity.' She borrowed a pair of his rhymes and much else, in order to re-write Gascoigne and produce a new and

163

superior version of his poem. In Roy T. Eriksen's words, 'The influence of Gascoigne's earlier attempt is felt almost throughout [her] psalm, in her choice of stanza, metaphors, and of rhymes, but not so much in terms of plagiarism as in terms of a pervasive desire to outwit her precursor at his own game.'[20]

*

In expunging Gascoigne from the record of English literary achievement in *The Defence of Poesie*, Sidney was stunningly successful. A large part of that success, however, derived from what happened after Sidney's death in the Netherlands in 1586. The reality was that Sidney died in a pointless military skirmish, because of his own stupidity and vanity in not wearing leg armour. He died a slow, painful death after the amputation of one leg. But those un-heroic aspects were removed from the record. Instead, Sidney was transformed into a legendary figure, worthy of a massive state funeral. In Alan Stewart's words, 'That funeral procession has been marching across the English imagination for the last 400 years.'[21] The Earl of Leicester orchestrated one of the greatest publicity campaigns in history, to promote his dead nephew as 'a great national hero, courtier, soldier and poet, who epitomised the ideals of Elizabethan chivalry, passionate Protestantism and an ineffable sense of Englishness.'[22]

Sidney's writings were elevated to the status of classics. His plodding romance *The Arcadia* was acclaimed, whereas Gascoigne's lively, complex prose fiction *The Adventures of Master F.J.* – arguably the first English novel, and 150 years ahead of the great eighteenth century pioneers of the form – sank into complete obscurity. *The Defence of Poesie* was read with reverence and admiration, while *Certayne notes of Instruction concerning the making of verse or ryme in English* was forgotten. Sidney's sonnet sequence *Astrophil and Stella* became part of the canon of classic English literature. Gascoigne's versatile sonnet sequences, hugely influential on Shakespeare, and his sparkling narrative verse in *A Hundreth Sundry Flowers*, were ignored and neglected. In the seventeenth century, seven separate editions of Sidney's *Works* were published; Gascoigne's writing merely gathered dust.

The memorial to George Gascoigne (with a wrong year of birth) put up in the 1930s close to the site of his home in Walthamstow.

By the twentieth century, the distinction between the age of Shakespeare, Spenser and Sidney and what came before it had become colour-coded. Their era was 'golden', and what came before was grey or colourless. In C.S. Lewis's killer phrase, it was the 'drab age', its 'Drab poetry' self-evidently inferior to the later 'Golden poetry'. Lewis did, however, generously permit Gascoigne just a dash of colour, identifying him as 'one in whom we see the Golden quality coming to birth'.[23]

Only in recent decades have these complacent judgements been eroded. Gascoigne's astonishingly versatile range of writing has begun to be revalued, attracting a growing quantity of academic commentary. After four centuries, an authoritative edition of *A Hundreth Sundry Flowers* has finally appeared. His novel and poems have recently become available in paperback editions. The tide has slowly begun to turn.

In the words of Michael Schmidt, '[Gascoigne's] neglect is one of the not uncommon outrages in English poetry: Donne and Herbert were overlooked and misvalued for centuries...Gascoigne for centuries has been more of a footnote than part of the living text. He deserves as much celebrity at least as Surrey, as Ralegh – maybe even as Sidney.'[24]

It is strange to think that the origins of that neglect are most likely

165

to be found in the mutual hostility of the two men at Kenilworth Castle in July 1575. The only occasion on which the two men are known to have been in the same place at the same time is on that year's royal progress. And here, too, admirers of Sidney have erected the mythology of a sophisticated twenty-year-old in the presence of bumbling simpletons. Since Sidney witnessed the reception for Henry III at Venice in 1574, which included water pageants, ceremonial speeches and a tragedy by Frangipani, Buxton conjectures that

> The *Princely Pleasures* cannot but have seemed naïve and provincial after this, with the jog-trot verses of Gascoigne, Hunnis, and Ferrers instead of sonnet, capitolo, and canzone; with a Coventry play, 'Good bangz a both sidez', instead of a tragedy on the classical model... No doubt Sidney, like the Queen, laughed at the clowns; but perhaps, remembering Venice and his foreign friends, he winced a little.[25]

But perhaps he didn't. After all, the sort of writing put on at Kenilworth had been commissioned by his uncle. And there were, in fact, no clowns. The country wedding ceremony was not intended to be a comedy, and it is only regarded as humorous because Patten subjects it to withering scorn, partly for his own satirical purposes.

Three years later, Sidney produced his own entertainment for the Queen. And what did this super-sophisticated young man come up with? Well, actually, lines like:

> Two thousand sheepe I have as white as milke,
> Though not so white as thy lovely face,
> The pasture rich, the wooll as soft as silke...[26]

A perfect example, in fact, of what Gascoigne cautioned against – the *trita et obvia*, or familiar, tired old cliché.[27]

18　The Protheus anomaly

In the long run, the person most significantly affected by Kenilworth was surely William Shakespeare. Everyone who writes about Shakespeare's life wonders *how* a glover's son from Stratford managed to turn himself into a leading London playwright. But no one ever asks *why*. What motivated Shakespeare to leave his home, his wife and his young children? What made him dream of becoming an actor or a writer of plays?

As a fifteen year old he might, in theory, have been to Worcester to attend one of the last ever performances of the Mystery plays, put on there by the craft gilds. Nearer home, in Stratford, there were local entertainments. In 1583 Stratford corporation paid 13s. 4d. 'to Davi Jones and his company for his pastime at Whitsuntide'. In 1583-4 professional travelling players performed in the Gild Hall and possibly also in the inn-yards of Bridge Street. But none of those shows can possibly have matched what the boy Shakespeare saw at Kenilworth. The Stratford players may have been just as professional, but nothing they put on could have equalled the stunning backdrop of Kenilworth Castle and its massive artificial lake.

The impact on the boy Shakespeare was surely enormous. Kenilworth was not just an extended entertainment but the most stunning theatrical display of Elizabeth's reign, in a fabulous setting. If anything fired Shakespeare's imagination and made him want to become involved in theatre and entertainment, it was surely this experience. To a child it must indeed have seemed like 'a midsummer night's dream'. A popular BBC TV four-part life of the bard, 'In Search of Shakespeare', didn't even mention Kenilworth. Yet the reality is that the extravaganza staged by Robert Dudley for Elizabeth was surely the transforming experience of William Shakespeare's early years. The Kenilworth experience unquestionably had a profound impact on Shakespeare's writing. It connects intriguingly with his still imperfectly understood decision to become a playwright. Beyond any doubt, I think, Shakespeare had a continuing fascination with the greatest event in the years of his mundane provincial upbringing. Kenilworth castle was also rooted in the English history that he would later dramatise, being at times home to King John,

Henry V and Henry VIII.

The so-called 'lost years' of Shakespeare are those between 1585, when his children Hamnet and Judith were born and he is presumed to have been in Stratford upon Avon, and 1592, when, in a passage which alludes to a line in *Henry VI, Part Three*, he was famously attacked as 'an upstart crow...in his own conceit the only Shakescene in a country.' No one knows where Shakespeare was during those seven years, or how he made the transition to actor and playwright.

One plausible seventeenth century tradition is that 'he had been in his younger yeares a Schoolmaster in the Countrey'. More recently there has been a revival of the theory that Shakespeare was employed by the Hoghton family at Lea Hall in Lancashire and that the 'will*iam* Shakeshafte' [sic] mentioned in a will of 1581 is the future playwright.[1]

The distinguished scholar S. Schoenbaum was sceptical of this notion, remarking, 'if Shakespeare was at seventeen in Hoghton's service, he would have had to be back in Stratford to woo, impregnate, and marry Anne Hathaway before his nineteenth birthday, not – on the face of it – the most plausible of scenarios.'[2] Mark Eccles was sceptical on different grounds: 'Since dozens of Shakeshaftes lived in Lancashire and Cheshire, there is no real evidence to support the theory that William Shakeshafte was William Shakespeare.'[3]

It has further been suggested that in Shakespeare's early plays, images of mountains, the sea and an estuary landscape derive from his knowledge of the Lancashire coast. In support of the Hoghton family theory, Park Honan quotes from *Henry VI, Part Three*:

Why, then, I do but dream on sovereignty
Like one that stands upon a promontory
And spies a far-off shore where he would tread,
Wishing his foot were equal with his eye,
And chides the sea that sunders him from thence,
Saying he'll lade it dry to have his way –
(3.2.134-9)

Honan comments, 'These topographical images correspond with

nothing in Warwickshire's landscape.'⁴

I don't think that's true. Substitute 'lake' for 'sea' and we are back at Kenilworth Castle in July 1575. The child Shakespeare is once again on that promontory to the west of the castle. He is staring across the waters of the Great Mere, which must indeed have seemed like a great sea to a small boy who had never seen a stretch of water wider than the River Avon before.

In the passage in question Richard of Gloucester is dreaming of being king. In portraying Richard's dream, Shakespeare is, perhaps, remembering his own boyish dream of greatness. He dreamed of becoming an actor, one of those magical figures who literally walked on water (albeit supported by hidden bulrushes), or who rode on the back of a gigantic dolphin, or who materialised out of the night on a magic floating island. All that stood between him and them was water – lots of it. He'd 'lade it dry to have his way'.

The word 'lade' means 'drain'. It expresses Richard's intense, gigantic ambition. In July 1575 Shakespeare, too, would have happily emptied the Great Mere if it would have allowed him to walk through the watery space between him and the actors and become a part of their magical profession. That drastic option proved unnecessary, though the Great Mere was a body of water that could indeed be drained, and was, some forty years after Shakespeare's death.

This, at any rate, seems to me a speculative reading which is just as plausible as the theory that it refers to the Lancashire coast. This is what writers do: they draw on their own experience, but they imaginatively transform it.

The *Henry VI* trilogy was written at the very start of Shakespeare's career (around 1590-2), probably in the order Part Two, Three and One. I don't think it is entirely a coincidence that the two occasions on which Shakespeare directly mentions Kenilworth Castle are in *Henry VI, Part Two*:

My gracious lord, retire to Killingworth (4.4.39)

Therefore away with us to Killingworth. (4.4.44)

The ninth scene of Act IV is actually set at Kenilworth Castle. It was a conscious or unconscious tribute by Shakespeare to a place where

169

his own destiny had been forged. At the very start of his career as a dramatist, Kenilworth Castle was on his mind.

*

A Midsummer Night's Dream reprises some of the central aspects of the Kenilworth entertainments. The opening lines of the play focus on desire which is frustrated and put off to another day. Theseus presents Hermia with the stark choice of marriage

> Or on Diana's altar to protest
> For aye austerity and single life.
> (1.1.89-90)

Even the mighty Theseus is made to wait and grumbles about 'how slow / This old moon wanes! She lingers my desires'. (1.1.3-4) Demetrius pursues Hermia but is rejected by her. Helena pursues Demetrius and is equally rejected. And the workings-out of the human drama in the foreground are mirrored by the 'moonlight revels' (2.1.141) of the fairies. In fact Puck is almost like a version of Gascoigne's wild man of the woods – an elemental force of nature, emerging from the trees to do his master's bidding.

A Midsummer Night's Dream is one of the few plays which Shakespeare wrote which did not overtly draw on another, already existing narrative. This reinforces the probability that he drew on his own experience and memories for a play which often seems to echo what occurred at Kenilworth. The entertainment planned by Theseus matches the ambition of Leicester:

> A fortnight hold we this solemnity
> In nightly revels and new jollity.
> (5.1. 359-60)

The solemn theme of marriage is burlesqued by the 'lamentable comedy' of Peter Quince and his associates, just as the coarse, brash country wedding seemed to William Patten to present an unintended parody of Leicester's courtship of Elizabeth.

*

Modern biographers of Shakespeare sense that the question of how he became an actor and playwright is connected in some way with the theatrical troupes which visited and performed in Stratford-upon-Avon. There are numerous theories, but no one has yet come up with the missing link which would authoritatively associate him with a particular acting company at a period in the 1580s.

Of particular interest is the fact that between December 1586 and December 1587, five companies of players passed through Stratford. One of these companies, its members wearing the badge of a bear and a ragged staff, was Leicester's. It was not their first visit to the town. Mark Eccles records that, 'The Earl of Leicester's men, led by James Burbage, were at Stratford in 1573, probably in September, on their way from Nottingham to Bristol. "Master Bayly," Roger Sadler, paid their reward and was repaid by the chamberlains.'[5] Stratford seemed to warm to them: 'In 1576-77 Leicester's players were given fifteen shillings and Worcester's only three shillings fourpence.'[6]

Leicester's players obtained their patronage from Lord Robert Dudley in 1559, some five years before he was made an Earl. It is not known at what point James Burbage joined the players but by 1572 he was their leader. Burbage (born around 1531) was originally apprenticed as a joiner (or craftsman-carpenter) before turning actor and, in the wake of Kenilworth, a theatrical entrepreneur. He and his son Richard were to become close associates of Shakespeare.

Edmond Malone, the great eighteenth century editor of Shakespeare, spent a lifetime brooding about how that shift from provincial Stratford to London was effected. The truth eluded him, as it has eluded everyone, but in the end he wearily concluded:

It is, I think, much more probable, that his own lively disposition made him acquainted with some of the principal performers who visited Stratford, the elder Burbage, or Knell, or Bentley; and that there he first determined to engage in that profession. Lord Leicester's servants, among whom was one of the performers just mentioned. James Burbage, the father of the celebrated tragedian [i.e. Richard Burbage], had been honoured with a royal licence in 1574. With this company, therefore, or the Queen's, or Lord

171

Warwick's comedians, it is reasonable to suppose, that he agreed to enrol himself, and that with one or the other of them he first visited the metropolis.[7]

But was it simply a hypothetical 'lively disposition' which drew Shakespeare to become acquainted with one or more of the players? There is a more straightforward possibility. James Burbage was one of the performers at Kenilworth Castle in July 1575 and at the age of 22 or 23, Shakespeare had the opportunity to come face to face with one of the actors who had so enraptured him as a boy. The childish fantasies of an eleven year old staring from a promontory in Warwickshire now had the possibility of becoming true.

Who actually performed in the masques and pageants at Kenilworth? For his explosive Zabeta play, Gascoigne explained that it was *'prepared and redy (every Actor in his garment) two or three dayes together'*, but who those actors were we can only guess. We know that on different days John Badger played the part of Hercules, Henry Goldyngham rode the giant dolphin and Gascoigne dressed up as a savage man and as Sylvanus. William Hunnis, George Ferrers and Richard Mulcaster were also active participants in the entertainments. We can guess that even the elderly William Patten may have been enrolled in some minor capacity. But that makes seven at most. Entertainments as lavish and spectacular as those put on at Kenilworth are hardly likely to have relied on just seven men for their presentation. Probably Gascoigne was the only member of the team to have had any personal experience of acting on a stage, and that was nine years earlier. They were all, at best, amateurs.

Burbage's presence at the Kenilworth entertainment is never discussed, but it seems inconceivable that professional players - Leicester's Men - were not involved. The royal patent of 10 May 1574, which licensed them, names five players: James Burbage, John Perkyn, John Lanham, William Johnson and Robert Wilson.

Probably the most professional entertainment put on at Kenilworth was the one about which we know the least, namely the two-hour play staged on the night of Sunday 17 July, after the banquet. Presumably it was performed in the Great Hall. A play lasting two hours sounds like something much more than a masque or a series of symbolic recitations. The obvious candidates for putting on such a

The Great Hall

show are James Burbage and the rest of Leicester's men. Gascoigne was clearly not involved, nor, apparently, were any of the other members of the writing team. The absence of this play text from Gascoigne's anthology of Kenilworth scripts is eloquent. A man with a shrewd entrepreneurial sense like James Burbage is unlikely to have wanted to hand it over for another man's book. Besides, the play may have been required for future performances, in which case it would not have been very smart to divulge its contents.

Peter Ackroyd notes that as Shakespeare's father began to accumulate property in Stratford-upon-Avon, he rented a house 'to one William Burbage, who may or may not have been related to the London acting family. Ordinary life is filled with coincidence.'[8] Of more relevance than that interesting but perhaps remote possibility is the nature of Stratford-upon-Avon itself. To visit it and walk its streets is to appreciate just what a tiny place it was in Shakespeare's lifetime. The pattern of streets established around the beginning of the thirteenth century – three running parallel to the river, three more cutting across them – still exists today. The claustrophobic interior of John Shakespeare's home and workplace on Henley Street was replicated in the world outside. In the late 1560s Stratford consisted of less than 240 households. It was surely a world like a modern soap opera, where everyone knows everyone else and is always bumping into each other. Even much later, when Shakespeare owned New Place, his parents lived nearby, as did each of his two married daughters and their husbands.

When the Earl of Leicester's men arrived in Stratford, Shakespeare had ample opportunity to seek them out and talk to a man like Burbage. According to one tantalising anecdote, Shakespeare 'lived in Shoreditch', which is where Burbage established his pioneering 'Theatre'. A connection between James Burbage and William Shakespeare, forged in Stratford-upon-Avon, involving the shared experience of Kenilworth, is, at the very least, an interesting possibility. It also solves one enigmatic anomaly about the dolphin episode in *A Midsummer Night's Dream*. We can be confident that Shakespeare read *The princelye pleasures at the Courte at Kenelwoorth* but he almost certainly never saw a copy of *A Letter*. Yet he refers, as Patten does, to *Arion* on the dolphin's back, not, as Gascoigne has it, Protheus.

Of the two accounts, it is more likely that the obsessive, note-taking Patten's is the most accurate one. It is improbable that the boy Shakespeare actually knew who Henry Goldyngham was supposed to represent. This suggests he must have talked about the episode to someone who was actually there that July evening and who remembered exactly who it was. Someone, perhaps, in a profession which relied on the gift of a very accurate memory.

Who could that person have been?

James Burbage is the obvious candidate.

174

19 'counterfeit supposes'

Modern biographers of Shakespeare believe that by the age of 23 or 24 he had probably started acting in a troupe. By the time he was 28 he was well enough known as a playwright to be attacked as an 'upstart crow'.

This abusive image referred both to the feathered hats that actors wore and the popular Renaissance image of the crow as a thief. In other words, Shakespeare was a plagiarist, a user of other people's lines. The charge, though largely meaningless at a time when neither romantic notions of 'originality' nor legal copyright existed, was not without foundation. Shakespeare was a great pilferer of other writers' work but he was a creative plagiarist. He copied – but in the process of copying he reinvented.

There was a book published in 1587, at the very moment Shakespeare's theatrical career was taking off. He dipped into it time and time again. It was a book which meant a lot to him. He was always taking things from it. If you open this book today you can sometimes get a strange shock of recognition. You might almost be reading Shakespeare:

> The common speech is, spend and God will send,
> But what sends he? A bottle and a bag,
> A staff, a wallet and a woeful end,
> For such as list in bravery so to brag.
> Then if thou covet coin enough to spend,
> Learn first to spare thy budget at the brink,
> So shall the bottom be the faster bound.
> But he that list with lavish hand to link
> In like expense a penny with a pound,
> May chance at last to sit aside and shrink
> His harebrained head without dame dainty's door.

It's a lively dramatic monologue. It continues at the same racy, conversational pace. It could almost be by Shakespeare but it was probably written about a decade before the Kenilworth revels. And we can be reasonably certain that Shakespeare didn't read it until

1587 at the earliest, which is when *The Whole woorkes of George Gascoigne Esquyre: Newlye compiled into one Volume* was published. It came out, by accident or design, in the year of the tenth anniversary of Gascoigne's death.

The volume consisted of the contents of *The Posies of George Gascoigne Esquire*, dispersed into three sections, together with the satire *The Steele Glas* (in a new printing), *The Complaint of Philomene* and *The princelye pleasures at the Courte at Kenelwoorth*. The title was misleading, as editions claiming to be complete works so often are. This *Whole woorkes of George Gascoigne Esquyre* did not include his play *The Glass of Government*, his anonymous hunting book *The Noble Arte of Venerie*, his lively pamphlet on the sacking of Antwerp in 1576 or his two theological works.

Even if he had never met James Burbage or talked to him about the Kenilworth entertainments, this book would have attracted Shakespeare's eye because of its account of *The princelye pleasures*. But I think it was more than just the text of the scripts put before the Queen that mattered to Shakespeare. It was that Shakespeare felt a strong personal association with Gascoigne. He may very well have seen him acting at Kenilworth. Gascoigne was special. He was part of the magic of Kenilworth.

*

The most famous Gascoigne of early Tudor England appears in one of the best-known scenes of Shakespeare's drama. At the climax of *Henry IV, Part Two* Falstaff's affectionate, inappropriate familiarity is brusquely cut short by his former comrade-in-delinquency, the newly crowned King Henry V:

> I know thee not, old man. Fall to thy prayers.
> How ill white hairs becomes a fool and jester!
> (5.5.47-8)

The other central figure on stage with Falstaff at this moment is a man called Gascoigne. Shakespeare never names him: in the play he is simply identified as 'the Lord Chief Justice' but everyone in the audience knew who he was.

Lord Chief Justice Gascoigne, or Sir William Gascoigne as the

176

history books call him, was popularly supposed to have quarrelled with Henry, Prince of Wales. Henry struck Sir William, who had him arrested and imprisoned. In the pre-Shakespeare play *The Famous Victories of Henry V* Gascoigne is given 'a boxe on the eare'.[1] The story is briefly alluded to in Shakespeare's *Henry IV, Part One* when the king tells the prince 'Thy place in Council thou hast rudely lost' (3.2.32).

At the start of *Henry IV, Part Two* the Chief Justice is merely a rather dull, sober figure of authority and an easy foil for the quick-witted and engaging rogue Falstaff. But at the end of the play the tables are well and truly turned. When the formerly-disgraced Henry becomes king he confronts his old persecutor. The dramatic tension is intense. Surely Justice Gascoigne is about to lose his job, be imprisoned, or suffer something worse? But the Lord Chief Justice is coolly unperturbed by the abrupt change in Henry's fortunes. Gascoigne makes a solemn speech about the impartiality of the law. No one is above it, he tells the new king. When the Prince hit him he was in reality lashing out at the king himself, whose authority the Lord Chief Justice embodied. His imprisonment was a just punishment. The repentant, transformed Henry accepts this slice of judicial wisdom and invites the judge to continue in his post. It is Falstaff, not Gascoigne, who is rejected.

In reality the story was apocryphal, even historically ludicrous. No sane person would have dared to lay a finger on the heir to the throne. But Shakespeare made good use of the story to promote the idea of the impartiality and objectivity of the law and Henry's exemplary moral transformation, giving a dramatic twist to what was really just Tudor propaganda. It may also have been another private tribute to the impact made by that other Gascoigne. Lord Chief Justice Gascoigne was someone from whom Bedfordshire's George Gascoigne was directly descended.

It is, I believe, no coincidence that Shakespeare refers to Stamford in a discussion about passing time and death in this same play, *Henry IV, Part Two*. Stamford was where Gascoigne died, and the play was evidently composed in 1597, exactly two decades after Gascoigne's untimely end.

This was the year the theatres were closed by the Privy Council from July to October, in retaliation for the staging of Ben Jonson and

Thomas Nashe's 'very seditious and sclanderous' *Isle of Dogs*.[2] Shakespeare's own career was now being affected by the kind of state censorship which had impinged upon Gascoigne's.

The twentieth anniversary of the poet's death and the reality of censorship silencing artistic endeavour (whether by the confiscation of books or the forcible closure of theatre) conceivably put Gascoigne into Shakespeare's mind at this time. The Lord Chief Justice in *Henry IV, Part Two* was, arguably, a surrogate of the poet himself: a Gascoigne not afraid to offend authority, a Gascoigne with a core of sturdy integrity, a wholly admirable Gascoigne. What is new about Sir William Gascoigne in Shakespeare's play is the importance given to him. He becomes a pivotal figure in the drama. That prominence is lacking in Shakespeare's sources or in other dramas about the reign.

Henry IV, Part Two is a death-haunted play. In the first scene of Act Three the old king broods about passing time and change ('Tis not ten years gone, / Since Richard and Northumberland, great friends, / Did feast together, and in two years after / Were they at wars. It is but eight years since, / This Percy was the man nearest my soul'). (3.1.57-60) This leads on to the scene in which Justice Shallow and Justice Silence reminisce about the good old days when they were young. Shallow remembers a fight behind Gascoigne's old Alma Mater, Gray's Inn. He thinks about how many of his old acquaintances are dead. The scene continues:

> *Silence.* We shall all follow, cousin.
> *Shallow.* Certain, 'tis certain, very sure, very sure. Death, as the Psalmist saith, is certain to all, all shall die. How a good yoke of bullocks at Stamford fair?
> *Silence.* By my troth, I was not there.
> *Shallow.* Death is certain. Is old Double of your town living yet?
> *Silence.* Dead, sir.

Their conversation is rambling, inconsequential and comic. The sudden reference to Stamford fair seems quite arbitrary and pointless. *What's the price of two bullocks at Stamford fair?* Shallow asks. *Don't know. Wasn't there,* Silence replies.

It's like a dialogue between a pair of drunks, the continuity slurred, going off at tangents. For his dramatic purpose, Shakespeare might

178

have chosen any fair. But to the playwright it perhaps had a personal connection with death. Stamford was where George Gascoigne died. Michael Billington has described *Henry IV Part Two* as 'a play about death, disease and decay' ('First Night', *Guardian*, 18 August 2007) and Gascoigne died in his early forties after a long, lingering unidentified illness, in the autumn of 1577. Stamford saw the end of a censored, silenced poet and of the man who was at the centre of the Kenilworth revels. In that sense he was perhaps nothing less than Shakespeare's 'old Double' himself. And it may not be entirely a coincidence that Gascoigne's poem 'The greene Knights farewell to Fansie', which reads like a farewell both to life and to writing, includes the memory of the time he spent 'feeding bullocks fat, when pryce at markets fell'.

*

Though George Gascoigne is today chiefly remembered as a poet and a proto-novelist, he was also a playwright. What Shakespeare took from Gascoigne for his plays is a topic which has largely gone unexplored because few scholars nowadays read his work. A rare exception is Roger Prior, who has located over thirty borrowings from Gascoigne in both *Romeo and Juliet* and *A Midsummer Night's Dream*, concluding that Gascoigne's 1572 masque for Viscount Montague was an important source for both plays.[3] He believes these borrowings indicate that the plays were written as a pair and at much the same time, with *A Midsummer Night's Dream* probably written first.

However, Shakespeare's greatest dramatic use of Gascoigne was unquestionably in *The Taming of the Shrew*, which substantially drew on the poet's play *Supposes* and showed a close aquaintanceship with his writing.

In a satirical poem written during the 1560s, Gascoigne attacked 'vain ambition' and other evils of the age, adding:

Thus is the stage stakt [staked] out, where all these parts be plaied,
And I the prologue should pronounce, but that I am afraide.[4]

The metaphor is that of the popular drama of Gascoigne's childhood, where the stage was literally 'staked out' on a temporary basis in a town square or a village green.

Sometimes mystery plays, miracle plays and moralities included a Prologue in which a confiding angel or some other spokesman for the dramatist pointed out the meaning of the play and the appropriate conclusions to be drawn from it. But why should Gascoigne be 'afraid' and fall silent?

One reason would have been the perils of attempting satire in a Tudor state which employed censorship and could punish dssenting opinions with bans, book burning, imprisonment, amputation or even execution. It is likely that Gascoigne was at court for the Christmas entertainments in December 1559, when a play was put on for Elizabeth which enraged her. What the 'matter' was which upset the Queen we don't know, though probably it touched either on religion or her unmarried status. The players were sharply commanded to stop, the play was abandoned and masquers rushed on to the stage and began a dance.

Gascoigne claims to be frightened because the modern world has become like a play:

First *Cayphas* playes the priest, and *Herode* sits as king,
Pylate the Judge, *Judas* the Jurour verdicte in doth bring.

This describes a scene from an old mystery play, namely the trial of Christ. But it is also by implication the condition of corrupt contemporary justice.

Tudor society, in its immorality, has become identical to the world of the old moralities, with its stock figures like the Vice, Pride, Wantonness, Riot and Revel. A weary disgust saturates the poem's throwaway conclusion:

When all is done and past, was no part plaide but one,
For every player plaid the foole, till all be spent and gone.

The poem indicates that Gascoigne had theatre on his mind when he renewed his association with the Inns of Court in the mid-1560s, after his marriage. But by this time the plays of his childhood had almost completely vanished. The Mystery plays, rooted in the Bible, and dramatizing such matters as the Nativity, the Passion and the Resurrection, and the Miracle plays, which were concerned with the lives of the Saints, had been methodically suppressed. Such drama belonged to the old culture of traditional Catholicism; the reformed Church of England had no need of it. At the same time the popular shows put on in halls or town squares by travelling players as yet lacked the sophistication and resources which would develop out of the first purpose-built commercial theatres in London from the late 1570s.

It was therefore only natural that when George Gascoigne turned his own hand to playwriting he wrote inside that third contemporary English theatrical tradition which had developed inside the universities and the Inns of Court. It consisted of gentlemen amateurs putting on plays for their peers in the great halls of those institutions. The association between the inns and drama is not perhaps surprising since law was, and remains, an immensely theatrical enterprise.

Whether at the universities or the Inns, plays were usually full-length five act productions, often drawn from Roman, Greek or Italian theatre. At Oxford and Cambridge plays were as likely to be performed in Latin as in English but at the London law schools there was more enthusiasm for drama in the vernacular. For the legal community at Gray's Inn, the long, grey, cold dreary heart of a winter in Elizabethan London was briefly enlivened by the music and spectacle of the Christmas revels. 'Revels' formed a central aspect of Inn life and the term encompassed everything from grand formal banquets given by Readers at their installation to music and dancing and spectacular masques and plays. Each Inn had its Master of Revels, who organised entertainments from a period which began shortly before Christmas and continued until Candlemas Night (2 February) and sometimes later.

In 1566 or 1567 – the exact year is uncertain - these midwinter revels were dominated by one man: George Gascoigne. He worked with other law students to put on two plays, one a solemn tragedy, the other a slapstick comedy. But though these entertainments were collaborations which drew in scores of Gray's Inn members, the dominant and controlling figure was Gascoigne.

The tragedy was *Jocasta*, which Gascoigne described as 'A tragedie written in Greke by *Euripedes*, translated and digested into Acte by

George Gascoigne, and Francis Kinwelmershe.' In fact Euripedes wrote no play with that title. Gascoigne's *Jocasta* is a version of Euripedes' *Phoenissae*, otherwise known as *The Phoenecian Women*.

By 'digested into Acte' Gascoigne acknowledged that the original free-flowing eight scene drama had been recast into five acts, to conform to orthodox Renaissance dramatic theory. Kinwelmersh, himself a poet, had probably known Gascoigne back in the 1550s, during the poet's first stint as a student of law. Gascoigne was characteristically ingenuous in suggesting that he and Kinwelmersh had translated the play from the original Greek. This was a cheeky bluff. What they had actually done was to translate the play from an Italian adaptation, *Giocasta*, by Lodovico Dolce, published in Venice in 1549.

It seems likely that Dolce himself translated the play into Italian not from the original Greek but from an existing Latin translation. The Gascoigne/Kinwelmersh *Jocasta* is not, therefore, an exact translation of the Euripides play but rather a distorted, imaginative adaptation subject to such variables as Dolce's own unreliable text and Gascoigne and Kinwelmersh's sometimes shaky grasp both of Italian and some aspects of the original play. 'Go to the land of Thesbrotia', commands Queen Jocasta's brother, Creon, to which his son Meneceus replies, 'Where Dodona doth sit in sacred chair?' 'Even there my child,' Creon solemnly replies.[5] Sadly for George bluff-your-way-in-Greek Gascoigne, Dodona was not a person but a city.

Ironically, in the light of what later happened at Kenilworth, the play engaged obliquely with the Queen's failure to marry and produce a male heir. *Jocasta* was highly topical. Its theme of a disputed succession spreading a vast circle of disaster was an idea very acceptable to the ruling Elizabethan elite and to its sons at Gray's Inn. The issue of the succession dominated parliamentary proceedings between September 1566 and January 1567. If Gascoigne was hoping to benefit from this parliamentary storm – and it would have been entirely in character for him to want to do so – then *Jocasta* was probably composed in the autumn of 1566 and performed early in 1567.

But *Jocasta* was also written very much with one eye on the great theatrical hit of the decade – Thomas Norton and Thomas Sackville's *Gorboduc*. This was an original play about a British king who divided his realm between his two sons. The younger brother killed the elder. Out of revenge, the Queen killed her surviving son. The common people rose up in rebellion and slew their King and Queen. The nobles annihilated the rebels but then fell out among themselves. Civil war raged and for many years the realm became a waste land.

The *Phoenissae* was a good choice for competing with *Gorboduc*, in so far as it was also a play full of solemn, wise sayings. Both dramas were played before an audience largely comprised of lawyers and legal trainees, and each play enshrined in a ceremonial way the ideal majesty and spectacle of the law and the law courts.

Jocasta is a play in slow motion. Its five acts basically consist of lots of majestic, stately entrances, long solemn speeches, and slow, stately exits. Human destinies and lives may be at stake but there is no hurry. *Jocasta* is a sententious play, with constant appeals to authority. A typical example is: 'wise is he, that doth obey the Gods'.[6] Sententiousness carries an essentially conservative and unthreatening message. In the closing words of Oedipus: 'every man must beare with quiet minde, / The fate that heavens have earst [previously] to him assignde'.[7]

Gascoigne's intention in *Jocasta* was clearly to surpass *Gorboduc*. His choice of Greek play was canny, as the *Phoenissae* has the biggest cast of any Greek tragedy. *Jocasta* has speaking parts for 17 actors, non-speaking roles for 80 identified figures and other parts for miscellanous 'ladyes and dames'. Even allowing for doubling-up, this was, by any theatrical standards and particularly those of 1566/7, a massive cast, unequalled by any other Tudor drama. Its dumb shows used a chariot, a spectacular wheeled stage prop and even special effects involving fire and moving scenery.

But dazzling as this all must have been, it did not in the end make *Jocasta* a successful play. As a tragedy it is not rooted in individual psychology and the characters are too stereotypical; they lack individuality. Their world is one of curses, inescapable destiny and doom. There is no real room for human freedom or choice. Its popularity was restricted to its time and it probably had at most only one more performance. When Robert Dudley paid an official visit to the University of Oxford in 1569 the entertainments included 'a playe or shew of the destruction of Thebes, and the contention between Eteocles and Polynices for the government thereof'.[8] E.K. Chambers believed this might have been *Jocasta*.[9] It is likely that Dudley was also in the audience at Gray's Inn for the play's premiere. If so, he was one of the very few people who ever saw both performances. It may well have been one of the determining factors in making him choose Gascoigne for a starring role at Kenilworth.

The beginnings of popular commercial theatre in the late 1570s saw English drama take a different path. *Jocasta* fails because action and spectacle are divorced from the dialogue. The high drama of the individual dumb shows is followed by the anti-climax of each slow-moving act. The speeches, though poetically charged, are essentially static and sometimes far too long (in Act II, Jocasta takes 83 lines to tell Eteocles to cast aside ambition). The action – the fight between Eteocles and Polynices, the death of Jocasta – is never seen, merely reported at second hand.

Whereas *Jocasta* was a solemn and stately production which would have been watched with silent and respectful awe, Gascoigne's second play was the exact opposite. *Supposes* is a boisterous, racy comedy about disguised identities. The play is in the spirit of the election of lords of misrule and the traditional pranks of their followers on Candlemas Night, 2 February, which is a possible occasion for its performance. It also has historical significance as the first English comedy in prose.

Attending the performance of *Jocasta* would have been like being in church or at a coronation, requiring a deferential attention. But *Supposes* was fun. It positively encouraged an active response from its audience. The plot hinges on a young nobleman, Erostrato, swapping his name and social position with his man Dulippo, in order to find employment as a servant in the household of Damon and thereby woo his daughter, Polynesta.

Shakespeare read *Jocasta*, finding little there he could use apart from some rich phraseology. But *Supposes* excited and impressed him for its dramatic possibilities. He borrowed from its plot, characters and text in writing *The Taming of the Shrew*. Shakespeare's Lucentio and his servant Tranio are versions of Gascoigne's Erostrato and Dulippo, and Lucentio's wooing of Bianca replicates Erostrato's pursuit of Polynesta. Likewise Shakespeare's Baptista is based on Damon and old Gremio is a version of Gascoigne's Cleander.

The play was Gascoigne's unaided translation of Ludovico Ariosto's *I Suppositi*, which was first written in prose for the carnival season in Ferrara. *I Suppositi* is set in that city around the year 1500. Although Gascoigne retained the Ferrara setting he cut the play's references to specific locations in the city.

Ariosto was an ex-law student and the play's provocatively barbed comments about lawyers and legal chicanery made it an attractive choice for Gascoigne to put before a Gray's Inn crowd. There are jokes about drinking, whoring, and preferring sex to studying books. Young Erostrato's scorn for the aged barrister Cleander – 'the silly doctor with the side bon[n]et, the doting foole'[10] – may involve an in-joke about the formal garb of the Gray's Inn elders. The 'Master Doctor' is portrayed as an ageing bumbler who, 'old as he is, and as many subtilties as he hath learned in the law' is no match for his much younger rival in love.[11] *Supposes* invited a response from its witty, cynical sophisticated metropolitan audience and no doubt got one – laughter, catcalls, applause.

Gascoigne made very minor adjustments to the cast list. He defined Litio as an innkeeper. He slightly changed the names of most of the characters and gave the name 'Petrucio' to one of the un-named servants of the Sienese man. This was subsequently borrowed by Shakespeare, who used it for the hero of *The Taming of the Shrew*. Shakespeare also borrowed 'Litio' for Hortensio's bogus identity as a lute teacher.

Gascoigne's Prologue milks the word 'suppose' for all it is worth and offers a parody of a lawyer's nitpicking, pedantic argumentation. Just as Ariosto himself performed the role for the first Italian performance, there can be little doubt that Gascoigne also appropriated this speech for himself. As if addressing a judge or jury, the speaker steps out on to the stage and introduces the play. 'I *suppose*', the speaker remarks, 'you are assembled here *supposing* to reap the fruit of my travails' [labours]. 'To be plain,' he continues – in a speech which quickly becomes far from plain, about a play where all is confusion – 'I mean presently to present you with a comedy called *Suppose*'. Gascoigne then lets rip:

the very name whereof may peradventure drive into every one of your heads a sundry *Suppose*, to *suppose* the meaning of our

supposes. Some percase will *suppose* we mean to occupy your ears
with sophistical handling of subtle *Suppositions*. Some other will
suppose we go about to decipher unto you some quaint conceits,
which hitherto have been only *supposed* as it were in shadows: and
some I see smiling as though they *supposed* we would trouble you
with the vain *suppose* of some wanton *Suppose*.[12] (my italics)

This is comic overload – a device to elicit groans, hoots, applause,
catcalls and laughter from an audience of young men all too well
acquainted with the sophistry of a barrister's special pleading.

Anyone knowing the original Italian would have laughed that extra
bit louder, detecting in Gascoigne's vague mention of 'shadows'
(meaning pictures) an echo of Ariosto's specific allusion to Giulio
Romano's *I Modi* ('The Positions'), a notorious series of sixteen
explicit drawings depicting couples having sex, which were
subsequently scandalously reproduced in engravings by Marcantonio
Raimondi. As for the 'vain suppose of some wanton Suppose': that
was a muted echo of Ariosto's reference to the Elephanti, a legendary
collection of ancient pornography.

Having apparently exhausted the comic possibilities of repetition,
Gascoigne adopts a plain speaking idiom and goes on to summarise
the plot of the play in a single sentence:

But understand, this our Suppose is nothing else but a mistaking or
imagination of one thing for an other: for you shall see the master
supposed for the servant, the servant for the master: the freeman for
a slave, and the bondslave for a freeman: the stranger for a well
knowen friend, and the familiar for a stranger.

The play is fast-moving, funny and effective, and of Gascoigne's
three plays, *Supposes* is the one which remains eminently stageable.
The problem for any modern audience, however, is that many would
be likely to feel they had seen it all before. This is the consequence of
the enormous impact *Supposes* had on Shakespeare. The modern
cultural hegemony of Shakespeare means that his creative asset-
stripping makes Gascoigne seem reminiscent of him rather than the
other way round. Shakespeare himself briefly signalled his debt to
Gascoigne in Tranio's remark that 'supposed Lucentio / Must get a

father, called supposed Vincentio' (2.1.400-1) and Lucentio informing his new father-in-law that 'counterfeit supposes bleared thine eye' (5.1.106). Shakespeare's blank verse is a richer instrument than Gascoigne's racy vernacular prose. *The Taming of the Shrew* is also a more complex play. It gives us two plots, *Supposes* only one. Gascoigne's main plot becomes Shakespeare's back story.

The Taming of the Shrew is one of Shakespeare's earliest plays, written when he was still very much under Gascoigne's spell. We do not know where Shakespeare was on 8 January 1582, but it is improbable that he was in the audience for the performance of *Supposes* put on that day at Trinity College, Oxford. It is a play which Shakespeare came across at the very beginning of his career as a dramatist, possibly before he had ever written a play of his own. Damon's description of his daughter as 'a collop of my own flesh' (*Supposes*, 3.3.63) is echoed by Joan of Arc's father in *Henry VI, Part One*: 'God knows thou art a collop of my flesh' (5.4.8), just as Vincentio's abusive 'crack-hemp' (glossed as 'a rogue that deserves to be hanged') (*The Taming of the Shrew*, 5.1.40) seems to originate in a half-remembered conflation of Gascoigne's 'crack-halter' (1.4.4) and 'hempstring' (4.2.19).

Supposes was also a play which Shakespeare either remembered very clearly in later years or went back to and re-read. He obviously appreciated the dramatic potential of the scene in which Philogano, Litio and the Ferrarese bang on the door of Erostrato's house and have difficulty in getting anyone to open the door:

FERRARESE: Lo you, sir, here is your son Erostrato's house. I will knock.
PHILOGANO: Yea, I pray you, knock.
FERRARESE: They hear not.
PHILOGANO: Knock again
FERRARESE: I think they be on sleep.
LITIO: If this gate were your grandfather's soul, you could not knock more softly. Let me come. Ho! Ho! Is there anybody within?
DALIO: What devil of hell is there? I think he will break the gates in pieces.[13]

This scene is recycled in *The Taming of the Shrew* (1.2.5-42 and

5.1.7-14). It surely also supplies the germ of the famous knocking-on-the-gate episode in Act Two, Scene Three, of *Macbeth*.

But something went wrong for Gascoigne the playright. After these two plays, nothing happened. Neither drama was put on at court. No one sought Gascoigne's services. No patrons appeared on the scene for him to dedicate his writings to. George Gascoigne remained where he had been a decade earlier: an outsider at court, a man on the margins of the cliques that controlled the state and the royal household.

It is an odd and unexplained fact that the fruits of comedy and acting – laughter and applause – are associated by Gascoigne with humiliation. One poem describes how the speaker survives misfortune and betrayal and vows 'to clap my hands, / And laugh at them which laught at me: lo thus my fancy stands'.[14]

Even more searing are the last two lines of 'And if I did what then?' The poem ends with a vision of men who have been deceived and betrayed by their mistresses. The abandoned lover is tossed by time 'on the shelf' (meaning a sandbank):

And when they stick on sands,
That every man may see:
Then will I laugh and clap my hands,
As they do now at me.[15]

Something bitterly personal seems to be swirling around below the surface of these lines, linking Gascoigne's private life with his brief involvement with the world of theatre. After what on the face of it were two dazzling shows, Gascoigne gave up theatrical production. Gray's Inn asked for no more revels penned by Gascoigne.

Perhaps the actors let Gascoigne down; perhaps, as Richard Madox grumbled when *Supposes* was re-staged at Trinity College, Oxford, the play was 'handeled...indifferently'.[16] Possibly the playwright was invited on stage, only to be mocked and jeered at.

Gascoigne wrote one more play in his lifetime, *The Glass of Government*. It was never performed in Gascoigne's lifetime, nor has it been since. Nor is it ever likely to be. It is a seriously flawed work, which is more mental theatre than something viable for the stage.

The title means 'the mirror (or shining example) of wise

authority/self-restraint and good behaviour' and the play contrasts the educational fortunes of the youngest and oldest sons from two close and wealthy families. The two younger sons Phylotimus and Phylomusus, both aged nineteen, are diligent, virtuous and hard-working. Their older brothers, Phylosarchus and Phylautus, are twenty, and far more interested in pleasure and entertainment than sober and industrious study. A schoolmaster named Gnomaticus attempts to inculcate all four brothers with the finest teachings and moral examples. But the two older brothers become involved with a whore named Lamia and her associates Dick Drum, Pandarina and Eccho. At the end of the play Phylosarchus and Dick Drum are executed for carrying out a robbery and Phylautus is banished for fornication and given a severe whipping.

Gascoigne's only practical experience of what an audience wanted was before a Gray's Inn crowd. But what entertained law students, well used to lengthy disquisitions, nit-picking arguments and solemn citations of legal authority, was not what amused the majority who lived their lives outside this narrow world.

In *The Glass of Government* none of the brothers are rounded, individual characters and it is hard to care about any of them. The two younger brothers are nauseatingly virtuous prigs and the fate of the licentious older brothers is likely to leave the reader unmoved. The play, which is firmly on the side of good behaviour, is more likely to provoke yawns than laughter or tears. The language of the play really only comes alive when it captures the reality of everyday Tudor life, as in Dick Drum's grumble that his coat is so old and 'hath cleft so long to my shoulders that a louse can not well climb the cliffs thereof without a pitchfork in her hand'.[17] But moments like that are rare. Much commoner are Gnomaticus's ponderous recommendations of the importance of being acceptable to God, pleasing to the world, profitable to oneself and respectful to one's parents.

Ronald C. Johnson has suggested that in its treatment of the prodigal son theme, *The Glass of Government* had an indirect influence on *All's Well That Ends Well*.[18] Shakespeare's comic character Parolles (who in some ways is the ancestor of Falstaff) is at one point called 'Good Tom Drum' (V.iii. 315), and elsewhere there is a reference to 'John Drum's entertainment' (III.vi. 36), which may conceivably echo Gascoigne's Dick Drum.

The Glass of Government, completed in the spring of 1575, seems to have been the first thing Gascoigne wrote after the banning of *A Hundreth Sundry Flowers* and it looks suspiciously like an attempt to prove that he was morally rehabilitated. It worked in so far as the play's publisher, Christopher Barker, commissioned him to produce *The Noble Arte of Venerie or Hunting*. And then a second commission came his way: the Earl of Leicester contacted him about some entertainments he was planning to stage at Kenilworth Castle later in the year...

20   The secret voice of Shakespeare

Gascoigne's most obvious creative impact on Shakespeare is on his sonnets. Take the beginning of Sonnet 106, for example:

> When in the chronicle of wasted time
> I see descriptions of the fairest wights,   [individuals]
> And beauty making beautiful old rhyme,
> In praise of ladies dead, and lovely knights;

This basically rewrites the opening lines of Gascoigne's poem 'The lover encouraged by former examples, determineth to make vertue of necessitie':

> When I record within my musing mind,
> The noble names of wightes bewicht in love:
> Such solace for my selfe therein I find,
> As nothing may my fixed fansie move:[1]

Gascoigne's 48-line poem rattles through great lovers of the past – King David, Solomon, Holofernes, Sampson, Hercules and Ovid – and the women they were in thrall to, drawing the conclusion that if 'lust of love' controlled men of such stature, then 'I hold me well content, / To live in love, and never to repent.'

Gascoigne's poem makes a simple point. To be trapped by desire for a faithless woman is to be no different to the great lovers of the past; it is simply part of the (male) human condition and has to be accepted. Shakespeare's argument is different and more compact: the beauty of knights and their ladies celebrated in ancient literature prefigures the beauty of the person the sonnet is addressed to, but not even those writers would have been able adequately to celebrate a beauty that dumbfounds all who witness it.

It's obvious that Shakespeare read and was profoundly influenced by *Certayne notes of Instruction concerning the making of verse or ryme in English*. As Katherine Duncan-Jones notes, 'The building blocks of *Shakespeare's Sonnets* are units of fourteen pentameter lines rhyming according to the 'English', or 'Surreyan', form of the sonnet, as defined by Gascoigne in 1575... [Gascoigne's definition] correctly describes the rhyme-scheme Shakespeare uses: abab, cdcd, efef, gg.'[2] Duncan-Jones believes Shakespeare may also have been influenced by an earlier passage in *Certayne notes*, in which he cautioned against cliché:

> If I should undertake to wryte in prayse of a gentlewoman, I would neither praise hir chrystal eye, nor hir cherrie lippe, &c. For these things are *trita et obvia*. But I would either finde some supernaturall cause whereby my penne might walke in the superlative degree, or els I would undertake to aunswere for any imperfection that shee hath, and thereupon rayse the prayse of hir commendacion.[3]

This advice surely informs Sonnet 130 ('My mistress' eyes are nothing like the sun'). It also lies behind that comic moment in *A Midsummer Night's Dream* when Demetrius wakes and gazes on Helena:

> O Helen, goddess, nymph, perfect, divine –
> To what, my love, shall I compare thine eyne?
> Crystal is muddy! O, how ripe in show
> Thy lips – those kissing cherries – tempting grow!
> (3.2.137-40)

The influence of Gascoigne's theory and practise of the sonnet on Shakespeare did not end there. *Shakespeare's Sonnets* conforms to Gascoigne's recommendation that 'the more monosyllables that you use...the lesse you shall smell of the Inkhorne'.[4] It has been estimated that around ten per cent of lines in Shakespeare's sonnets are entirely monosyllabic.[5] And a complaint levelled by Don Paterson against one of Gascoigne's sonnets – 'a fine poem, but it finishes on line 12 – a good example of superfluous couplet syndrome'[6] – parallels John Berryman's grumble about Shakespeare's sonnets: 'their chief defect [is] a certain indifference to how things wind up, so that most of the couplets are weak.'

Did Shakespeare's publisher, Thomas Thorpe, know of Shakespeare's affection for Gascoigne? If he did, and if he owned or had seen a copy of the poet's banned book *A Hundreth Sundry Flowers*, it would supply a solution to one of the greatest riddles attached to *Shakespeare's Sonnets*.

Notoriously, 'T.T.' prefaced his edition with a cryptic dedication 'TO. THE. ONLIE.BEGETTER.OF. THESE.INSVING. SONNETS. M^r.W.H. ALL. HAPPINESSE. AND. THAT. ETERNITIE. PROMISED. BY. OVR. EVER-LIVING. POET. WISHETH. THE. WELL-WISHING. ADVENTVRER. IN. SETTING. FORTH.'

The identity of 'Mr W.H.' has vexed scholars and readers for centuries. But as Park Honan has pointed out, both Shakespeare and his publisher seem to have deliberately set out to tease: 'Shakespeare writes with a sense that sonnets are indeed toys, little games in which a mystifying poet (aided, if possible, by a publisher's mystifications) pretends to unlock autobiographical secrets...'[8] Thorpe himself seems to have been something of a prankster, once publishing a book with a preface but no main text, 'perhaps as a Jonsonian joke'.[9]

The outstanding example of this kind of tongue-in-cheek mystery-making is to be found in Gascoigne's first book, *A Hundreth Sundry Flowers* (1573). The novel it contains is prefaced by a cryptic introduction. Its very first line features an address from 'H.W. to the Reader', who goes on to explain how the book's contents were received from 'Master *G.T.*', who later sent him a letter about obtaining the narrative of amorous adventures from 'your friend and myne Master *F.J.*'

In fact these mysterious figures were figments of Gascoigne's imagination, used to create the sense that the material was about real people. The trick worked and people rushed to buy the book and read all about a sex scandal at a grand country residence, involving – but everyone could guess for themselves at which particular home the tale was set and just who that raunchy, promiscuous married woman was.

We don't know if Thomas Thorpe had a copy of the book (which was later suppressed) or if he knew about this publishing sensation some thirty years before *Shakespeare's Sonnets*. But if he did, it is highly likely that the mysterious 'Mr W.H.' had no existence at all and was simply invented to create a sense of mystery. Indeed, 'Mr W.H.' was simply Gascoigne's 'H.W.' reversed, with a laconic disdain for the stupider kind of reader that Gascoigne himself would have appreciated, had he still been around to enjoy the joke. After the furore over *A Hundreth Sundry Flowers*, Gascoigne grumbled that too many of his readers were either humourless and literal-minded, exceptionally dim, or pedantic nitpickers. He sarcastically called them 'curious Carpers, ignorant Readers, and grave Philosophers'.[10]

Gascoigne was alert to the punning possibilities of individual letters, basing a dazzling poem around a *'comparison betwene two letters'* – the letter 'G' (which stands for gold, 'good thinges' and, of course, Gascoigne) and the letter 'B' (which represents not only the surname of a love-rival, Boyes, but also 'bawdy, braynsicke' and other 'bad' things). Alluding to the cross-shaped board used to teach Tudor children the letters of the alphabet, Gascoigne writes:

> Of all the letters in the christs crosse rowe,
> I feare (my sweete) thou lovest *B.* the best,
> And though there may be good letters many mo,
> As *A.O.G.N.C.S.* and the rest,
> Yet such a liking bearest thou to *B.*
> That fewe or none thou thinckest like it to be.

Gascoigne dryly adds that the letter B spells 'worse than may be tolde' (he probably has in mind the word 'buggers', which he puns on in a different poem). This punning is echoed in *Twelfth Night*, when Shakespeare invites the audience to laugh at Malvolio's obtuse wonder at Olivia's handwriting: 'her very C's, her U's, and her T's, and thus makes she her great P's' (2.5.88-9) – in other words (in other letters) her cunt and her great pisses.

Thomas Thorpe, as a prankster, may well have had *Twelfth Night* in mind in constructing his enigmatic dedication. 'To the onlie begetter of these insuing sonnets Mr W.H. all happiness...' carries an echo of Maria's bogus letter made to mock and fool Malvolio: 'To the unknown beloved, this, and my good wishes.' (2.5.92-3) The letter is in the form of a teasing riddle. Malvolio grasps that the line '*M.O.A.I.* doth sway my life.' (2.5.109) is in some kind of mysterious way a representation of 'Malvolio'. But, unlike '*A.O.G.N.C.S*' (which can be re-arranged to spell 'GASCON' – an acceptable Tudor spelling of 'Gascoigne' – there is no way that '*M.O.A.I.*' can ever spell 'Malvolio'. It is incomplete; moreover, the handwriting is a worthless

194

imitation. Shakespeare echoes George Gascoigne; Thorpe echoes both writers. Wheels within wheels.

If Thorpe had Gascoigne's book in mind, this might also help to make sense of the enigmatic reference to 'THE WELL-WISHING ADVENTURER'. His use of the word 'adventurer' seems to refer to himself as the publisher, and carries the sense of 'to adventure' in the sense of 'to take a risk'. Gascoigne's 'H.W.' uses the word in the same sense, explaining that 'the worke (for I thought it worthy to be published) I have entreated my friend *A.B.* to emprint… This I have adventured, for thy contentation (learned Reader). And further I have presumed of my selfe to christen it by the name of *A hundreth sundrie Flowers*: In which poeticall posie are setforth manie trifling fantasies, humorall passions, and straunge effects of a Lover.'[11]

'A.B.' was an entirely fictitious printer. And what 'H.W.' was adventuring, first of all, was a narrative entitled – that word 'adventure' again - *A Discourse of the Adventures Passed by Master F.J.*

Gascoigne's novel is about the triangular relationship between a married woman who sleeps with both 'F.J.' and another, unidentified lover, just as *Shakespeare's Sonnets* centre on the poet's infatuation with both a handsome young man and a promiscuous woman. Both works give the appearance of being about real people and events, but the information which might allow us to put names to these figures simply isn't there. In Gascoigne's case, the willingness of readers to fall into the trap he had set them misfired, drawing the attention of the censors to his scandalous book and in so doing effectively destroying his career.

Shakespeare clearly understood how Gascoigne's writing career had been blighted by censorship. Sonnet 66 reads as follows:

Tyr'd with all these for restfull death I cry,
As to behold desert a begger borne,
And needie Nothing trimd in jollitie,
And purest faith unhappily forsworne,
And gilded honour shamefully misplast,
And maiden virtue rudely strumpeted,
And right perfection wrongfully disgrac'd,
And strength by limping sway disabled,

And arte made tung-tide by authoritie,
And Folly (Doctor-like) controuling skill,
And simple-Truth miscaled Simplicitie,
And captive-good attending Captaine ill.
　　Tyr'd with all these, from these would I be gone,
　　Save that to dye, I leave my love alone.

No one has ever noticed that what is striking about this sonnet is just how much it owes to George Gascoigne.

Less than a year after the Kenilworth extravaganza, Gascoigne published a satire entitled *The Steele Glas*. Its central conceit is the contrast between the truthful reflections to be seen in the old-fashioned English steel mirror and the vanity and pretension shown by modern Venetian glass mirrors.

One stanza in particular illustrates how Gascoigne's ghostly presence is everywhere in sonnet 66:

But now (aye me) the glasing crystal glass　　[glazing]
Doth make us think that realms and town are rich
Where favour sways the sentence of the law,
Where all is fish that cometh to the net,
Where mighty power doth over rule the right,
Where injuries do foster secret grudge,
Where bloody sword makes every booty prize,
Where banqueting is compted comely cost,　　[counted]
Where officers grow rich by princes pens,
Where purchase comes by couyn and deceit,　[coin / fabrication]
And no man dreads but he that cannot shift,
Nor none serve God, but only tongtide men.[12]

The technique of repeated words or phrases at the beginning of a sequence of lines is one for which the technical term is anaphora. It produces an insistent, thumping, assertive effect, reminiscent of a preacher repetitiously hammering home a point to his congregation. The analogy is apt in so far as both *The Steele Glas* and sonnet 66 involve a moral denunciation of their age.

Helen Vendler notes in this Shakespeare sonnet a 'generalizing lack of specificity',[13] something which owes everything to the template

The promontory west of the castle, still clearly defined by the lines of the hedgerows, with Purlieu Lane cutting across it from the bottom right-hand corner. From here Shakespeare would have had a good view of the giant mermaid and dolphin on 18 July 1575.

which shapes it, which is guilty of the same vice. Or as Colin Burrow puts it, sonnet 66 reads 'like a survey of abstract ills'[14] – which is largely what *The Steele Glas* amounts to.

Shakespeare's inventory of abuses is different to Gascoigne's but there is some overlap. Gascoigne attacks extravagant banquets; Shakespeare attacks worthless people in ostentatious clothes. Gascoigne attacks mighty power over-ruling right; Shakespeare supplies four variations on this theme as he attacks folly controlling skill, art censored by authority, strength disabled by weak authority and the enslavement of good by what is bad. Gascoigne attacks secret grudges, Shakespeare attacks the slander of perfection. Gascoigne gives us men punished for unbending principle; Shakespeare denounces undeserving honour, truth described as stupidity and vows broken or betrayed.

There are differences. Shakespeare mentions women and the poor; Gascoigne mentions neither (though Shakespeare's 'needie Nothing' is probably an echo of Gascoigne's 'needy lacke' which is found in the second stanza after the one quoted above).

In its final two lines Gascoigne's stanza alludes to the Day of Judgement and religious persecution, evidently humouring his patron, Lord Grey, who belonged to the austere, fundamentalist wing of Protestantism. The obscure line 'Where all is fish that cometh to the

197

net' is perhaps a reference to Christ as the fisher of men, signifying that nowadays the Lord would simply fail to find any good men. In the margin of the line in the first edition is the gloss: 'common woe'.

Gascoigne draws on his own experiences to attack judicial corruption, corrupt officers of the state and false 'purchase' (perhaps a dodgy land deal – something Gascoigne had much experience of, both as perpetrator and victim).

Shakespeare's description of 'captive-good attending Captaine ill' may conceivably be a distant echo of Gascoigne's experiences in the Low Countries, which the poet himself alludes to in his reference to a bloody sword and booty. It is reasonable to assume that Shakespeare had read Gascoigne's long poem about his experiences in the Low Countries, '*The fruites of Warre...*' and understood that Captain Gascoigne had both been taken prisoner and accused of treachery. John Kerrigan glosses 'captive' as in one sense a noun signifying 'prisoner-of-war'.[15] By the time *Shakespeare's Sonnets* were published the rank of captain had long since become associated with beggars and confidence tricksters making bogus claims of military service.

The dimensions of Shakespeare's debt to Gascoigne in sonnet 66 are very substantial. Few if any of the other sonnets so nakedly expose their origin in someone else' work. Knowledge of this debt enables us to understand that sonnet 66 was a five-finger language exercise for Shakespeare, not an outpouring of his soul. Secondly, it clarifies the meaning of a line that has long perplexed scholars.

The ninth line of sonnet 66 picks up Gascoigne's own use of the word 'tongtide' and re-applies it to the fate of the poet. Gascoigne's first book was banned. So was his second. He was effectively silenced as a creative writer. The reference to 'arte made tung-tide by authoritie' is not, as every commentator asserts, a vague, general reference to censorship. On the contrary, it transmits Shakespeare's very acute sense of what happened to the career of his old Kenilworth hero, George Gascoigne.

21   Elsinore's ghosts

Shakespeare shunned writing about London and contemporary Tudor life. James Shapiro believes that 'Shakespeare's choice of subject matter suggests that from his early twenties, and perhaps from his childhood, he was the kind of writer who dreamed and wrote of kings and queens, war and empire, heroism and nobility, and stranger shores.'[1]

It's not unreasonable to root this other-worldiness in Shakespeare's experiences at Kenilworth. He arrived there from the dreariest of backgrounds: Stratford-upon-Avon was, after all, 'a drab backwater, devoid of high culture. There was little touring theatre, few books, hardly any musical instruments, no paintings to speak of, the aesthetic monotony broken only by painted cloths that adorned interiors…'[2] The Kenilworth revels marked Shakespeare for life. This should not surprise us. Stanley Wells cites the case of Robert Willis, born the same year as Shakespeare, who never forgot the impact made upon him when his father took him as a small boy to see players perform 'the Mayor's play' in Gloucester. This must have been a very much smaller and simpler instance of theatricality than was on display at Kenilworth but the memory of it endured for a lifetime:

After describing the play in well-remembered detail, Willis wrote some seventy years later that the sight 'took such impression in me that when I came towards man's estate   it   was   as   fresh   in   my memory as if I had seen it newly acted.'[3]

It is not unknown for childhood experience – even a single event – to shape an artist's later output. The themes and obsessions of Alfred Hitchcock's films are plainly rooted in his childhood years, in particular the traumatic experience of being locked up in a police cell. J. G. Ballard's fictions of apocalypse, desolation and violence are an imaginative response to childhood years spent in a wartime Japanese internment camp. For twentieth century artists, the shaping experience is often a dark and disturbing one. An art rooted in a life transformed by happiness and wonder is harder for us to envisage but that, I think, was what Kenilworth amounted to for Shakespeare.

The theatricality of the Kenilworth entertainments was unique: day after day of astonishing entertainment, combining spoken language, song and music, in a fabulous setting. If he was present, the lake would have been the greatest stretch of water the provincial boy from Stratford had ever seen. It served, like the lavishly modernized castle and the surrounding forest, as a giant stage for a sequence of dazzling spectacles. There were masques, speeches, songs and entertainment involving both professionals and amateurs. There were special effects ranging from fireworks to barges shaped like dolphins and mermaids. There were royal hunts and bear-baiting. Kenilworth was both an example of the power of living theatre to dazzle and enthral and a resource on which to draw. It was unforgettable. A London theatre could never hope to match Kenilworth in scale but it could mimic its magic in other ways. And if Kenilworth Castle is the place where Shakespeare's theatrical career was first conceived, its ghostly contours may also lie behind what is arguably his greatest play. It is a striking coincidence that *Hamlet* should be set inside a great castle. And in *Hamlet*, as at Kenilworth, the celebrations turn sour and the relationship of a royal couple becomes increasingly fraught, exploding in a final crisis. The trigger of that crisis, both at Kenilworth and in *Hamlet*, is a play which causes offence.

'Elsinore', in its pronunciation, has parallels with 'Kenilworth'. The two place names are each trisyllabic. At the level of language and speech, the one reverberates off the other. The sixteenth century spellings (like the modern equivalents) include an identical sequencing of three consonants and a vowel: 'l', 'n', 'o' and 'r' – eLseNOuR, kiLLiNgwORth. Just as at Kenilworth in July 1575, Elsinore is a place where players come, to entertain a royal couple.

In *Hamlet* Claudius, it emerges, has committed murder in order to obtain the hand of his Queen. Likewise the Earl of Leicester was a man suspected of murder in his efforts to secure the hand of Elizabeth. Kenilworth in the summer of 1575 marked both the climax and the bitter termination of that ambition. As in *Hamlet*, a play brought everything crashing down. Hamlet's remark to the First Player, 'I heard thee speak me a speech once – but it was never acted, or, if it was, not above once' (2.2.372-73) sounds like a muddy echo of the mysteries surrounding what occurred on Wednesday 20 July 1575 when Gascoigne's untitled play of two acts and seven scenes was abruptly aborted.

Elsinore in *Hamlet* clearly has nothing at all to do with the actual castle of that name in Denmark, which Shakespeare had no personal knowledge of. The play's description of the castle is perfunctory, its architecture and lay-out sketchy in the extreme. It is a castle of the mind, not a precisely defined location. Elsinore in fact seems like a dark, monstrous echo of those July days at Kenilworth.

Kenilworth was a castle beside water, its walls dropping away into the tranquil surface of the Great Mere. Elsinore is a haunted castle, where a ghost might lure you 'to the dreadful summit of the cliff / That beetles o'er his base into the sea' (1.4.70-71). It's a place of coldness and desolation, where the past comes back in a disturbing form to haunt and perplex the present. *Hamlet* begins on the battlements of a castle; the ghost's appearance makes Horatio think of 'stars with trains of fire and dews of blood' (1.1.116). He is referring to strange portents which preceded the death of Julius Caesar but he might just as well be describing fireworks – specifically, rockets shooting across the sky and shedding sparks.

Hamlet is commonly regarded as Shakespeare's greatest and most compelling play but it also acknowledged as his most enigmatic and difficult text. All the indications are that Shakespeare himself found it a troubling work, hard to cast into a final, stageable form. This is often lost sight of because virtually all modern editions of *Hamlet* are synthetic texts, made up from a merging of the second published edition of the play and the First Folio text.

There seem to have been at least four versions of *Hamlet* in circulation in the playwright's lifetime. The first was the lost play which scholars now refer to as the *Ur-Hamlet*. This was a tragedy staged in the 1580s, involving a ghost and a character named Hamlet. It has traditionally been attributed to Thomas Kyd but the authorship is unknown. The second text, perhaps radically abridged from a much longer manuscript, was the promptbook of Shakespeare's play (i.e. the script actually used by the Chamberlain's Men at The Globe). Some scholars believe there was another, shorter promptbook, used for a touring production. If so, the second promptbook, like the first, is lost to us; in Shapiro's words, 'the two most valuable scripts for understanding how *Hamlet* was actually performed no longer exist'.[4] The third text is the published *Hamlet* known as the First Quarto or Q1 (1603). Its status is enigmatic, though it is commonly regarded as an unauthorized reconstruction of the play in performance, derived from the memory of an actor who had participated in it. The fourth text is the Second Quarto or Q2 (1604), a version of the play far too long ever to have been performed on a Tudor stage; Shapiro calls it 'Shakespeare's dark first draft'.[5] The scholarly consensus is that this reproduces, not always accurately, Shakespeare's manuscript of *Hamlet*. The situation was then further complicated after Shakespeare's death by the publication of the First Folio *Hamlet*, which is a comprehensively revised text, significantly different to Q2 and sometimes agreeing with Q1. Whether or not Shakespeare was responsible for the large number of revisions made to the First Folio text remains a matter of scholarly debate. What we are left with are three distinctly different printed texts of *Hamlet*, none of which reproduces the text which audiences at the Globe actually witnessed in performance.[6]

Shakespeare's restless engagement with the script of *Hamlet* doubtless partly reflected the reality that plays were fluid forms, reshaped and revised in rehearsal and after initial performance. But in the case of this particular play the radical variations in textual possibility seem likely to have been a symptom of its troublingly personal elements. Every biographer is alert to the coincidence of the death of Shakespeare's only son Hamnet in 1596 and the composition of *Hamlet* some three to five years later. Stephen Greenblatt notes that 'in the loose orthography of the time, the names [Hamnet and Hamlet] were virtually interchangeable...the coincidence of the names - the act of writing his own son's name again and again – may well have reopened a deep wound, a wound that had never properly healed.'[7]

What has not been noticed, however, is that Hamnet Shakespeare died at the same age that his father would have been if he witnessed the entertainments at Kenilworth. In the summer of his eleventh year, William Shakespeare, I believe, had a life transforming experience at a castle; in the summer of his eleventh year, Hamnet Shakespeare died. Exactly twenty-one years separated those two crucial summers. Elizabethans were notoriously lax about identifying their ages; like the spelling of their surname it wasn't regarded as a matter of much significance – except when they reached the age of twenty-one. Twenty-one was the legal age distinguishing between a minor and an adult; it was the age at which a first born son might inherit a dead father's wealth. All kinds of symmetries reverberated between the life of William Shakespeare and the time of his son's dying.

Significantly, *Hamlet* is a play of *doublings*, both of fathers and sons (Fortinbras and Fortinbras, Hamlet and Hamlet) and of characters (Cornelius and Voltemand, the two ambassadors, the indistinguishable Rosencrantz and Guildenstern). Doubling was, in any case, an essential aspect of an actor's profession. Q1 has twenty-six speaking parts, Q2 and F thirty-one. Thompson and Taylor calculate that, using doubling, all three texts can be performed by just eleven actors.[8] Polonius, for example, can double as the Gravedigger. Claudius sometimes doubles as the Ghost. If this latter procedure is adopted it gives extra edge to Hamlet's barbed remark about his 'uncle-father' (2.2.313) A different kind of doubling is at work when Polonius says he was once an actor and 'did enact Julius Caesar...Brutus killed me' (3.2.99-100). Shakespeare's *Julius Caesar* was probably performed in the twelve months preceding the staging of *Hamlet*; regular theatregoers would have appreciated the in-joke that John Heminges, playing Polonius, had previously played Caesar, with Richard Burbage, now playing Hamlet, in the role of Brutus. A very similar kind of in-joke involving doubling occurs in Tarantino's *Kill Bill*. In Volume 1, The Bride overcomes martial arts expert Johnny Mo; in Volume 2 we learn from a flashback that she learned her fighting abilities from Pai Mei. Both parts are played by the same actor: Gordon Liu teaches her the skills which enable her to defeat Gordon Liu.

Hamlet is, in the words of Frank Kermode, 'obsessed with doubles of all kinds'.[9] *Hamlet* itself doubles a lost play which had a ghost and a hero named Hamlet. Doubling is rooted in the very language of the play: 'Thanks, Rosencrantz, and gentle Guildenstern. / Thanks, Guildenstern, and gentle Rosencrantz.' (2.2.33-34) Hamlet addresses the King as if he was his mother; when the King corrects him, Hamlet sarcastically replies: 'My mother. Father and mother is man and wife. / Man and wife is one flesh. So – my mother.' (4.3.49-50) It's a play of multiple and receding perspectives, all blurring into one. That blurring is evident even in the versions of the text. Where the Second Quarto has 'heated visage' (3.4.48), the First Folio has 'tristfull visage' – but whether or not 'Heaven's face' (i.e. the sky) is flushed and angry or pale and sad at Gertrude's hasty remarriage hardly seems to matter: both seem equally valid.

As many scholars have noted, in *Hamlet* Shakespeare makes striking use of the obscure literary device known as hendiadys – the pairing of words to communicate a single idea (as in 'the dead waste and middle of the night'). Frank Kermode connects this with the play's preoccupation with memory and identity and also with the enigmatic poem 'Let the bird of loudest lay', written around the same time. This poem (better known by its traditional and non-Shakespearean title 'The Phoenix and the Turtle') is about sinister portents of 'the fever's end', of a 'priest in surplice white' at a funeral, of mourners, lamentation, death, the union of two selves, a funerary urn and two selves 'Leaving no posterity'. It's impossible to reduce this notoriously opaque poem to autobiography; equally, it's hard not to see the material as rooted in Shakespeare's loss of his only son and heir.

What hendiadys does, usually, is connect two, sometimes three, nouns which would not conventionally be associated. A good example is Rosencrantz's phrase 'the strength and armour of the mind' (3.3.12) The meaning of things is both deepened (since 'armour' has all kinds of reverberations in relation to the plot of *Hamlet*) and blurred. Quite distinct matters – the tangible and material (armour) – are merged with the intangible and elusive (the inner life of the mind). This literary device is not associated with any particular character; rather it becomes an aspect of the world of the play, which vibrates with levelling echoes. A labyrinth of doublings is alive with other sorts of multiplicity. It is even embodied in the textual ambiguity of the play – the radical variations of Q1, Q2 and F, which give us not one *Hamlet* but three.

Even the play *Hamlet* itself is doubled by a play-within-the-play, which in turn, in its dumb-show, doubles itself. The idea that Kenilworth castle nests inside the castle of Elsinore is therefore perhaps not so outlandish. Castles and acting, as at Kenilworth in 1575, are intertwined. A player in the royal castle of Elsinore performs a monologue which describes the collapse of Ilium, the royal castle at Troy. *Hamlet*, with its topical allusion to competition from the children's companies (in the Folio text) is rooted in the commercial world of early seventeenth century London theatre. But Elsinore expresses a much older theatrical tradition, of the sort found at Kenilworth castle, involving aristocratic patronage. Thompson and Taylor make the point that when Hamlet insists the players be treated well,

a stress is placed on the quality of the hospitality offered to the visiting players, suggesting a nostalgic, almost feudal relationship between the players and their aristocratic patrons, unlike the more commercial or professional one evoked by the earlier references to the contemporary London theatres.[10]

The player's visible emotion causes Hamlet to reflect on the curious nature of the profession. An actor can whip himself into a frenzy about fictitious events, whereas he, Hamlet, suppresses his true feelings about what's happening around him. But Hamlet, too, is just an actor. 'Real' emotion recedes and becomes elusive.

That Shakespeare's writing articulated a crisis in his own life at this time is signified by what one might call the lack of professionalism of *Hamlet*. Q2 and F are the longest texts in the entire body of Shakespeare's work. Each has been estimated to require four hours of stage time and *Hamlet* is almost always cut in performance. But five years before the play was composed the Lord Chamberlain had decreed that plays must begin at 2 p.m. and end 'between four and five'. It seems likely that the radically shortened Q1 more truly reflects the practical performance realities of the staging of *Hamlet* even though it does not accurately transmit the text. But why would Shakespeare, an experienced professional, waste everyone's time by writing a script which was far too long to be realistically performed?

Not only did the script seem to run away with him but ultimately it didn't make sense; *Hamlet* is, notoriously, a play full of riddles, contradictions and inconsistencies. James Shapiro argues that F represents Shakespeare's attempt to bring coherence to the text, concluding that 'The Hamlet of the revised version is no longer adrift, no longer finds himself in a world where action feels arbitrary and meaningless.'[11] But the First Folio text was almost as long as Q2 and equally impossible to stage.

Further evidence that *Hamlet* draws on Shakespeare's own childhood is suggested by the uncanny coincidence that four years after the Kenilworth entertainments, in December 1579, a girl named

Katherine Hamlett drowned in the river Avon, about a mile from Stratford. Katherine Duncan-Jones believes this is a matter 'that cannot be ignored',[12] finding in it an analogue for Shakespeare's representation of the death of Ophelia. In short, all kinds of very personal materials were swirling around in Shakespeare's imagination as he composed *Hamlet* and at their core, perhaps, was the playwright's bitter sense that Kenilworth had changed his life – but not necessarily for the better. He was a wealthy and successful dramatist and theatrical entrepreneur – but he was most probably far from home when his son fell sick and he may well not have been present either for the death or the burial. When, in the very first scene of *Hamlet*, Francisco says ' 'Tis bitter cold / And I am sick at heart' (1.1.6-7), he introduces a matter which, like so much else in the play, is never explained. Frank Kermode puts it well when he refers to 'Francisco's heartsickness (of which we don't know, and never will know, the cause: it belongs to the play rather than to this transient character)'.[13]

The notion that *Hamlet* is a play which obliquely alludes to episodes in Shakespeare's life and career is reinforced by Polonius's critical concentration on the word 'beautified' ('that's an ill phrase, a vile phrase, "beautified" is a vile phrase' (2.2.109-10).This has been interpreted, not implausibly, as an allusion to Shakespeare's 'offence at the description of him in Greene's *Groats-worth of Wit* (1592) as "an upstart Crow, beautified with our feathers".'[14] But, assuming that this passage was included in the performed text, the allusion surely meant nothing to the theatre audience. It was, at best, understood only by Shakespeare's closest associates. And though the allusion indicates that Greene's insult still rankled, Shakespeare puts the criticism of the word 'beautified' not in the mouth of Hamlet but in that of the pompous and pedantic Polonius. He makes a joke out of it.

There may also be echoes of another theatrical event, from the following year. In 1593 Christopher Marlowe was stabbed to death in Deptford. The official version was that the killing was the consequence of a quarrel about the bill or 'recknynge'. Touchstone's reference to 'a great reckoning in a little room' in Act 3 Scene 3 of *As You Like It* is widely interpreted as an oblique reference to the killing. Marlowe's fate was perhaps still on Shakespeare's mind when he wrote *Hamlet* soon afterwards. The word 'reckoning' is used again, in connection with a murder. The ghost describes the scene in the garden and protests about the purgatorial consequences of such a violent end:

Cut off even in the blossoms of my sin,
Unhouseled, disappointed, unaneled,
No reckoning made but sent to my account
With all my imperfections on my head.
O horrible, O horrible, most horrible!
(1.5.76-80)

Even more strikingly, imagery linking a bill or *reckoning* and a fatal blow from a stiletto or dagger is present in Hamlet's famous speech about suicide (3.1.74-75). When Hamlet refers to making a 'quietus' he means 'pay his complete account (i.e. end his life); *quietus est* (Latin) was a phrase used to confirm that a bill or debt had been paid.'[15]

The thought of a reckoning in connection with a violent murder is repeated in Hamlet's later reflection that the murderous Claudius

...took my father grossly full of bread
With all his crimes broad blown, as flush as May,
And how his audit stands who knows, save heaven,
But in our circumstance and course of thought
'Tis heavy with him.
(3.3.80-84)

The audit – the rendering of accounts – is likely to be substantial for someone who dies, as Hamlet's father and Christopher Marlowe did, suddenly, with no chance to atone for a lifetime's sins. *Unhouseled* (i.e. without having taken the sacrament), *disappointed* (unprepared for death), *unaneled* (not anointed): 'Taken together, these three adjectives emphasize that the Ghost has been deprived of the 'last rites' due to a dying Christian.'[16]

The king was killed in a garden; Marlowe after coming indoors from an afternoon spent in one. We might recall that Marlowe was killed after supper, when he would *literally* have been 'full of bread'. Whether or not the allusion was a conscious one on Shakespeare's part is impossible to say. It may not have been, and in any case it served no dramatic function and would have been lost on a contemporary audience. But that Marlowe's violent end was on his mind during the writing of this passage is reinforced by the choice of figurative language – not just that invocation of an *audit* but also the thought of someone being murdered with their crimes (or sins) 'broad blown, as flush as May'. That was the month of Marlowe's killing: 30 May 1593, to be precise.

*

Hamlet's famous speech on the subject of self-destruction can be traced back to George Gascoigne's writing. It reprises sonnet 66, which is also about a yearning for 'restful death'. It inventories the troubles of a life but in a manner oddly improbable for a prince. The heir to a throne is hardly likely to suffer

Th'oppressor's wrong, the proud man's contumely,
The pangs of despised love, the law's delay,
The insolence of office and the spurns
That patient merit of th'unworthy takes
(3.1.70-74)

The literary device used in this monologue is, as in sonnet 66 and as in the lines of Gascoigne which it creatively recycles, anaphora. The speech moves to the drum beat of the definite article, thumping repeatedly, sometimes employing hendiadys: the question, the slings and arrows, the heartache and the thousand natural shocks, the rub, the respect, the whips and scorns of time – and so on, ending with: the dread, the undiscovered country, the will, the native hue of resolution, the pale cast of thought, the name of action.

That Gascoigne and his work should have been on Shakespeare's mind is logical enough if *Hamlet* is, in part, a 'doubling' or creative rewriting of events at Kenilworth a quarter of a century earlier. The play at one point references a royal progress, darkly scrutinising it. What was a royal progress? It was, literally, *a progression* - the passage of sovereign and court around a large swathe of the kingdom. It was an enormous undertaking, involving movement from one private residence to the next. These were the homes of the ruling class, who occupied the finest habitations in the land. At their best they were mansions and castles. In Elizabeth's reign the most spectacular of them all was Kenilworth Castle, which by July 1575 had been reconstructed as a royal playground. The two forms of play on offer were hunting and theatre, and it was the second one which dominated Elizabeth's nineteen days there.

Even the royal hunting trips were framed by theatre. Kenilworth Castle and its environs became a vast stage, manipulated by the Magus-like Leicester for a dual purpose: marriage and foreign intervention. It marked the most spectacular and theatrical moment of any of Elizabeth's royal progresses during her long reign. But *Hamlet* scorns that historical reality. Gascoigne had celebrated and memorialized *The Princelye Pleasures at the Courte at Kenelwoorth* but Hamlet literally reduces the concept of a royal progress, regarding it with disgust and contempt. Polonius's corpse and the thought of worms feasting on it, inspires Hamlet to give Claudius a philosophy lesson. A worm can eat a king, a fish can eat the same worm, a man can eat that fish. Baffled, the King asks Hamlet what he means. 'Nothing but to show you how a king may go a progress through the guts of a beggar' is the jeering reply (4.3.29-30).

The notion of massive royal grandeur reduced absurdly in size and transformed into something both disgusting and little is repeated in the scene with the Gravedigger, where Hamlet invites Horatio to share the thought that 'the noble dust' of Alexander the Great may have ended up 'stopping a bung-hole' (5.1.193-4). Dust serving as the stopper for the mouth of the hole in a barrel is a death-haunted image which brings to mind a buried corpse, its mouth packed with dirt.

Critics have often noted two very personal echoes in this famous scene. The Gravedigger's reference to a tanner's corpse lasting longer than others before it rots is a mordant reminder that Shakespeare's father was a whittawer – a skilled glover whose trade involved tanning animal skins. When Shakespeare wrote these lines his father was evidently in poor health. John Shakespeare died in September 1601, by which time, most scholars agree, *Hamlet* was already written. The gravedigger's reference to Adam and heraldry (5.1.31-33), described by Thompson and Taylor as 'somewhat gratuitous'[17], is also commonly viewed as a private allusion to the repeated efforts of John Shakespeare to acquire a coat of arms. The playwright successfully assisted his father in that ambition in October 1596 but it was a bitter victory. Hamnet Shakespeare, the only male heir, had died just two months earlier.

There may be another dimension of allusion in this scene. Discovering it involves identifying both the time the play was written and the recognition that in certain key aspects *Hamlet* is rooted in what happened at Kenilworth castle in July 1575, and in Shakespeare's presence there. No one knows exactly when *Hamlet* was written but the scholarly consensus is that the manuscript was probably completed between late 1599 and the spring of 1601.[18] If *Hamlet* was written in 1600 then it may add a personal dimension to the moment when the Gravedigger holds out the skull of the old King's jester, Yorick, remarking 'Here's a skull now hath lien you i'th'earth three and twenty years' (5.1.163-4). That is an oddly precise figure. Elsewhere in this play of indecision and imprecision Shakespeare deals in round numbers – thirty years, a thousand times, two thousands souls, twenty thousand ducats, forty thousand brothers, threescore thousand crowns, millions of acres. Consistency, accuracy and precision in numbering do not greatly trouble him. So why twenty-three years? Why not twenty years, say? Dramatically it would be of no consequence at all. It's a striking fact that in the year 1600 what the Gravedigger says about Yorick could also have been said about the remains of George Gascoigne, who died exactly 23 years earlier, in 1577.

Just a coincidence? Possibly. And yet Yorick is remembered as *a performer*, which is what Gascoigne was at Kenilworth. And he is remembered in two contrasting ways, just as Gascoigne was. The Gravedigger remembers him with contempt and loathing. Yorick was, he says, a whoreson mad fellow, a mad rogue – in short, a crazy, malicious son of a whore. Once the jester even poured a flagon of wine over his head. But Hamlet has warmer memories; he recalls him with affection as 'A fellow of infinite jest, of most excellent fancy'. (5.1.174-5) The word 'fancy', meaning invention or creative imagination, is a key one in Gascoigne's *oeuvre*. One of his greatest poems is 'The greene Knights farewell to Fansie', which adopts the posture of a man ruefully looking back over his life and bidding farewell to it. This man is also a successful writer. It's not hard to believe that Shakespeare read it (or more likely re-read it) while he was composing *Hamlet*. Indeed, the third stanza, which bids farewell to 'The glosse of gorgeous courtes', contains the line

To lie along in Ladies lappes, to lispe and make it nice:

Hamlet, of course, accuses Ophelia of lisping (3.1.143) and asks, 'Lady, shall I lie in your lap?' (3.2.108) He also accuses her of 'paintings...God hath given you one face and you make yourself another' (3.1.141-3). This theme is reiterated in the Gravedigger scene : 'Now get you to my lady's table and tell her, let her paint an inch thick, to this favour she must come' (5.1.182-4). Such remarks echo Gascoigne's attack on the painted ladies of the court and his denunciation of 'The painted pale, the (too much) red made white'.[19] This poem, in which Gascoigne mocks made-up court ladies, asserting that the nutbrown complexion of a country girl is far preferable, was one Shakespeare knew and liked enough to steal from at the very beginning of his career. The adjectives in 'glitt'ring golden towers' (*Lucrece*, 945) are blatantly pilfered from 'glittring golden gite' [gown] in the Gascoigne poem.

The Gravedigger twice condemns Yorick for being 'mad'. In 'The greene Knights farewell to Fansie' Gascoigne ruefully confesses to the same sin. As a younger man he wore flowers in his hat 'full harebrayndly' (i.e. as madly as March hare; in other words literally, as a wild young man about town, and metaphorically, as a poet). He was once even a 'madde' musician. That this persona was not fictitious is indicated by the Cambridge scholar, Gabriel Harvey, who grumbled that one of Gascoigne's great failings was 'levity'.[20] Many years after Gascoigne was dead was dead, Harvey wrote a poem imagining him in heaven, just as carefree, boisterous and disrespectful as he was in life:

Me thinkes thou sckornist seignores,
   And gibist at thrise mightye peeres,
And maakst a ieste of monumentes,
   And caarest not for a thousand yeeres.[21]

That word *jest* again.

211

To say this is not to say that we should interpret Yorick as a literal representation of Gascoigne. If Gascoigne ever articulated them, Shakespeare himself can hardly ever have been in a position to hear 'flashes of merriment, that were wont to set the table on a roar' (5.1.180-1). But Yorick is nevertheless of the same mould as Gascoigne: a performer associated with mockery, wit, jests and song. A performer, moreover, who is a little wild, a little crazy and over-exuberant, just as Gascoigne was when he broke the branch and almost caused Elizabeth I to come crashing down off her horse.

Hamlet remembers Yorick as someone who 'hath bore me on his back a thousand times' (5.1.175-6). Figuratively, of course, that's what Gascoigne was – a support. His writing supplied templates to be used, whether those of plot (as in the lifting of material from *Supposes* for *The Taming of the Shrew*), critical theory (as in his definition of the sonnet) or language (numerous creative plagiarisms of language and phrasing). In addition, the players at Elsinore employ a dumb show, which by 1600 was an archaic device. It's possible that Shakespeare had in mind Gascoigne's collaborative tragedy *Jocasta* (1566/7), which has five dumb shows and is written in the same stilted, overwrought style as the speech about Pyrrhus which Hamlet recites and which is then continued by the First Player (2.2.388ff). Whatever support Shakespeare derived from Gascoigne's work is surely rooted in childhood experience: what applies to Yorick and Hamlet also applies to Gascoigne and Shakespeare.

Hamlet himself at times doubles his creator. He thinks like a playwright. He tells Horatio that before he could 'make a prologue to my brains / They had begun the play' (5.2.30-31), referring to the King's plot to use Rosencrantz and Guildenstern to have him executed in England. In the face of adversity Hamlet does what Shakespeare evidently did with *Hamlet*: he rewrites the text and changes its meaning: 'I sat me down, / Devised a new commission, wrote it fair – ' (5.2.31-32) Hamlet enjoys performing and takes pleasure in extracting the comic potential of language, mocking Osric with consciously overwrought diction.

It's curious that the Gravedigger complains that Yorick once poured 'a flagon of Rhenish' over his head (5.1.170). If Katherine Duncan-Jones is correct in suggesting that one of Gascoigne's illustrations in *The Noble Arte of Venerie* is intended as a satirical depiction of Sir

Philip Sidney, then it's a striking coincidence that a bearded male figure who resembles Gascoigne should be shown tipping wine from a flagon in the direction of a Sidney lookalike. Is the Gravedigger's complaint a sardonic allusion on Shakespeare's part to an incident which actually occurred at Kenilworth Castle a quarter of a century earlier? Impossible to say, of course, though as Thompson and Taylor observe, the Gravedigger's anecdote makes little dramatic sense: 'This may seem an odd thing for the King's jester to do to a gravedigger.'[22]

*

Shakespeare's knowledge of what occurred at Kenilworth Castle in July 1575 derived from three sources. Firstly, published accounts. For reasons explained earlier I think it most unlikely that Shakespeare ever encountered *A Letter*; the only text he is likely to have known is Gascoigne's very selective selection of scripts and commentary. That would have provided him with little insight into the complex events which unfolded at Kenilworth Castle that July.

Secondly, as this book contends, there was his personal experience as an eye-witness. As the child of a commoner, this is likely only to have been, most of the time, a long-distance experience. He saw what anyone might see – fireworks, masques on the Great Mere, public entertainments in the castle's outer court. It is impossible to conceive of him ever being permitted into the privileged interior of the castle. A more interesting possibility is that he got close to the entertainments at those moments when the Queen entered the castle. It is conceivable that children, who posed no kind of security threat, were allowed nearer than adults. If Shakespeare was present, he was surely there on Monday 18 July, when the giant dolphin appeared. He may very likely have been there from the first day, Saturday 9 July. He was surely present for at least one of the fireworks displays, held on 9, 10 and 14 July. On 20 July the entertainments programme was abruptly terminated. Later the weather turned bad. Probably most people from the outlying areas drifted back home, including the child from Stratford and whoever was with him – Uncle Henry, perhaps; his brother, Gilbert.

Finally, Shakespeare may have been able to draw on the memories of others present. The most obvious candidate is James Burbage. In the year following the great royal entertainment at Kenilworth, Burbage built The Theatre in London. It was, as Stanley Wells notes, 'the turning point' in the history of early modern drama: 'Named after the amphitheatres of ancient Rome, it formed the prototype for London theatres for the next sixty and more years. Even more importantly, its construction was to provide the catalyst for an explosion in dramatic writing.'[23] Burbage is an elusive figure, particularly in his early years. He was one of Leicester's Men and 'possibly its head'.[24] This troupe consisted of at least five players and surely performed at the castle in July 1575. It is intriguing that shortly afterwards, in April 1576, Burbage focused his attention on building The Theatre in Shoreditch. It may simply have been that the vast crowds who turned up to watch the royal entertainments gave him a fresh sense of the commercial possibilities that a fixed theatre offered. Or perhaps any displeasure on Leicester's part at the failure of the entertainments to win over Elizabeth extended to Burbage, too. It was, after all, a play which detonated the collapse of the programme, and Leicester's patronage of Gascoigne ended as quickly as it had begun. Leicester's Men were surely involved in Gascoigne's aborted two act play, which would have featured impressive special effects. James Burbage would almost certainly have been involved in a double capacity as both actor and joiner, together, perhaps, with his younger brother or half-brother Robert, a professional carpenter.

Shakespeare's early career as an actor and playwright is known to have brought him into contact with Burbage, and the entrepreneur's son Richard later became one of the Globe's leading actors and one of Shakespeare's closest associates. The scholarly consensus is that Richard Burbage was the originator of the role of Hamlet. If Burbage's family saw him perform before Elizabeth in July 1575 then his son Richard (born c.1567) may have been there too. It's a startling possibility: the eight-year-old Richard Burbage, the eleven-year-old William Shakespeare, together with James Burbage: three of the key figures in early modern English drama, each present at Kenilworth castle, and all their lives, in their different ways, transformed by that event. And if George Gascoigne was the kind of man who went round emptying flagons of wine over other people's heads – in the case of Philip Sidney doubtless it would have been a careless *accident* – then

James Burbage may have witnessed it.

But though Hamlet remembers Yorick with affection, the remembrance is also connected to disgust: 'and now how abhorred in my imagination it is. My gorge rises at it.' (5.1.176-7) That sense of disgust suffuses the play.

*

Some critics are perplexed by Hamlet's remark that 'this goodly frame, the earth, seems to me a sterile promontory'. (2.2.264-5) Bernard Lott calls it a 'strange image...it is hard to see the full force of the word *promontory* here'.[25] In citing this passage, which he describes as 'superbly crafted oration'[26], it's noticeable that Frank Kermode omits the words 'seems to me a sterile promontory', replacing them with ellipses; it seems unwittingly to acknowledge Lott's point that the metaphor isn't quite appropriate.

Lott himself, puzzled, suggests that 'It may refer to a sandy headland sticking out into the sea, away from the fertile plains. The *promontory* may be an image of life thrusting out into the great seas of eternity.' He adds, 'It is as likely to be a reference to the physical surroundings of the theatre of Shakespeare's day, the stage jutting out into the audience area...' Well, maybe. But I'm inclined to think Shakespeare's mind had drifted back to Warwickshire at this point. That word *promontory* had very precise associations for Shakespeare.

By the time he wrote *Hamlet*, Shakespeare was a successful and accomplished playwright, an actor and a theatrical entrepreneur. He'd long since made that crossing of the Mere and joined the troupe. But the distant boyhood dream had turned sour. After about 1600 Shakespeare's attitude to the theatre changed. Acting became for him, Anne Righter argues, 'a symbol of disorder, of futility and pride'[27]: 'It is difficult not to feel, however, that some obscure but quite personal disgust with the London theatre and with the practice of the actor's and the dramatist's craft...lies behind this change.'[28]

Hamlet's description of the sky as a 'brave o'erhanging firmament, this majestical roof fretted with golden fire' (2.2.293-4) may well be a literal reference to gilt decorative work at the Globe, but it also carries a fading image of that tremendous firework display at Kenilworth. Now, says Hamlet bitterly, that vision 'appears no other thing to me than a foul and pestilent congregation of vapours'. (2.2. 295-6) The acrid stench of smoke from the massive display of fireworks perhaps merges here in the playwright's memory with the mists and fogs of the Mere, the moats and the marshland and ditches which surrounded Kenilworth. The promontory on which he had stood as a child, watching the distant players, the giant dolphin and the fireworks, was no longer a place of enchanted memory. For Shakespeare at the turn of the century, as for so many others before him who were also present at Kenilworth Castle in July 1575, that extraordinary experience seems to have ended in disappointment and disillusion. *Hamlet* reprises, in a distorted, fictional form, what happened at Kenilworth in July 1575, but it replicates it in a bitter, concentrated, parodic fashion. Leicester was a rumoured murderer; Claudius really is one. The offensive play at Kenilworth made Elizabeth angry but nothing worse than that; the offensive play at Elsinore results, directly or indirectly, in six deaths. At Kenilworth one of the most memorable moments was Arion singing sweetly from a dolphin's back; *Hamlet* contains six songs but five of the songs are sung by the deranged Ophelia and the sixth by the Gravedigger.

Even as Hamlet expresses his disgust he is aware of Rosencrantz laughing. When asked why, Rosencrantz replies, 'To think, my lord, if you delight not in man what Lenten entertainment the players shall receive from you; we coted them on the way and hither are they coming to offer you service.' (2.2.281-4)

What we get in this part of *Hamlet* is a sequence running from the word 'promontory' through imagery of fireworks and an allusion to the structure of the Globe theatre to a troupe of actors arriving at a great castle to entertain a king and queen. Elsinore, then, is grounded in Shakespeare's childhood experience of the great entertainments at Kenilworth and in its impact upon his later life. But Rosencrantz's laughter is also, in part, Shakespeare's own. It signals his detachment as an artist. And his complex response to the Kenilworth experience continued through his later career.

22 'this bare island'

In *Richard III*, the play's eponymous villain recalls how

> When last I was at Exeter,
> The Mayor in courtesy showed me the castle,
> And called it 'Rougement', at which name I started,
> Because a bard of Ireland told me once
> I should not live longer after I saw Richmond.
> (4.2.103-7)

The Mayor pronounces 'Rougemont' to sound like 'Richmond' and the bard's prediction duly comes true. A visit to a castle changes everything. For Shakespeare, if he was at Kenilworth in July 1575, it was arguably the same: a transfiguring experience. And if 'Rougement' signifies a private dimension of meaning to Richard, so too did 'Elsinore' to Shakespeare.

Richard III is not the only Shakespeare play that connects a castle with prediction and life transformation. 'Good sir, why do you start and seem to fear / Things that do sound so fair?' Banquo asks, after the three witches have each made an accurate prediction, prefaced by 'All hail Macbeth'. That intoxicating vision of 'the all-hail hereafter' (1.5.53) is the engine of the play, driving the ambition of Macbeth and his wife. The monosyllabic word 'hail' recurs and reverberates in the text with the same thudding intensity as the bell that rings out before Duncan's murder and the knocking at the castle entrance that comes after it. It also shuts down the drama, with order restored. 'Hail, king, for so thou art,' cries Macduff to Malcolm. 'Hail, King of Scotland.' 'Hail, King of Scotland,' echo the other figures in that final scene (5.9.21, 26).

It is worth noting that when Elizabeth approached Kenilworth Castle at around eight o'clock on the evening of Saturday 9 July 1575 she was met in the park by ten sibyls. One of these pagan prophets stepped forward to greet her:

> All hayle, all hayle, thrice happy prince,
> I am Sibilla she
> Of future chaunce, and after happ,

217

foreshewing what shalbe.[1]

It is certainly possible that Shakespeare personally witnessed Elizabeth's arrival at Kenilworth. There is little doubt, I think, that the recurring salutation 'hail' in *Macbeth* originates in that moment outside Kenilworth castle. The sibyls would have been boys or men dressed as women; Banquo's observation that 'you should be women, / And yet your beards forbid me to interpret / That you are so' (1.3.43-5) may be a laconic nod to Jacobean stage convention; it might equally allude to the Kenilworth tableau. It is also not entirely out of the question that the role of chief sibyl was played by the bearded George Gascoigne, keen to put himself before the Queen at every available opportunity.

Macbeth, like *Hamlet*, seems to replicate in various direct and indirect ways the Kenilworth events. Some are so general that they might not be specific allusions, but all, intentionally or not, duplicate some aspects of them. In *Macbeth* a royal visitor, the sovereign, arrives at a castle in high summer. It may even be evening, since the stage direction calls for 'Torches'. There is the music of 'Hautboys', just as there was on 9 July 1575. The castle architecture is vague but we hear of jutties, friezes, buttresses, a hall, 'the palace gate' (3.1.48) and battlements. The only route into the castle that we hear about is 'the south entry' (2.2.69). Elizabeth I's grand, formal admission to Kenilworth Castle was made through the south entry. Duncan's host, Macbeth, is a murderer (the same accusation having been levelled against Robert Dudley). The royal visit involves 'carousing' (2.3.20) until the early hours. A royal banquet is convulsively terminated 'With most admired disorder' (3.4.110) ('admired' in the sense of 'astonishing'). A 'crew of wretched souls' (4.3.141) is cured of the King's Evil, just as Elizabeth supposedly cured nine commoners at Kenilworth Castle on 18 July 1575. Macbeth boasts that 'our castle's strength / Will laugh a siege to scorn' (5.5.2-3); Kenilworth Castle proved impregnable after the longest siege in English history. At the climax of the play Macbeth cries out, 'They have tied me to a stake; I cannot fly, / But bear-like I must fight the course' (5.7.1-2) Bear-baiting was a common entertainment in Shakespeare's London, of course, but the first time he ever witnessed it may have been on Thursday 14 July 1575, when thirteen bears were brought out to fight

218

dogs in the outer court at Kenilworth; a muzzled bear and stake was, of course, the badge of Robert Dudley and his family.

Two dramatic moments in *Macbeth* are unquestionably rooted in the writing of George Gascoigne. As noted in Chapter 19 above, the prolonged knocking at the castle entrance scene owes its origins to *Supposes*. More explicitly, although never previously noticed, Gascoigne's never-performed play *The Glass of Government* lingered in Shakespeare's memory. Lady Macbeth's famous cry, 'all the perfumes of Arabia will not sweeten this little hand' (5.1.42-3) is creatively plagiarised from Act 3 Scene 4 of Gascoigne's play, where the gullible Phylosarchus extravagantly praises the whore Lamia, who he believes to be respectably virtuous: 'the sweetness of her heavenly breath, surpasseth the spiceries of *Arabia*'.

Apart from those two examples, the images of fishing, tidal flow and a sand-bank present in Macbeth's guilty, turbulent thoughts of murder and its consequences 'upon this bank and shoal of time' (1.7.6) sound like an echo of Gascoigne's 'tides of turning time' which 'toss...fishers on the shelf' so that they 'stick on sands, / That every man may see'. [2]

If William Shakespeare was present at Kenilworth Castle in July 1575, what did the experience mean to him? If he was there, it seems probable that he witnessed the Queen's arrival on 9 July and the subsequent fireworks display. He was surely present on Monday 18 July to see the giant dolphin. If so, he was likely there the next day, to see the Coventry play. The following day it was effectively all over. How many days he was there, or if he was present at all, is forever outside our knowledge. If Shakespeare *was* there, then his response was surely one of wonder and amazement – a sense of the way in which ordinary life can be transformed by the magic of theatrical spectacle. Its effect was to make a glover's son want to participate in that world of spectacle. Later, when he had achieved that ambition, Kenilworth remained a defining experience. He honoured it in his writing. In a very different arena to that of a castle and an enormous lake, it helped to shape his sense of theatre. It was always on his mind – as was that central figure at Kenilworth, the poet, dramatist and amateur performer George Gascoigne. It was a resource which intertwined with both his developing career as a dramatist and his life experiences.

219

If this interpretation is correct, then Kenilworth is where it all began. It would make sense for the events of thirty years before to feed into Shakespeare's imagination, since *Macbeth* is a play interested in origins. Banquo is excited by the possibility that the witches genuinely possess the power to 'look into the seeds of time / And say which grain will grow and which will not' (1.3.56-7) Their prophecies excite in Lady Macbeth the feeling of 'The future in the instant' (1.5.56). But the future which grows out of a seed of time may be a bleak one. By Act Four a desperate and hysterical Macbeth is demanding more insights into the future, even if the price to be paid is that 'castles topple on their warders' heads... though the treasure / Of nature's germen tumble altogether / Even till destruction sicken' (4.1.55,57-9) The warder of a castle is its guardian or keeper; a role which is implicitly Macbeth's. Seed ('germen') is associated with gluttony and illness. Out of a seed of time can grow a future which is sickening and destructive.

The Kenilworth revels were the grain from which Shakespeare's life in the theatre grew. They may also have shaped his sense of the tragic, in so far as *Hamlet* both echoes and darkly inverts them. It is hard not to see the death of Shakespeare's son Hamnet as being connected with that tragic sense, casting a private shadow over Shakespeare's theatrical representations of childhood, fathers and sons, and the theme of inheritance. Stephen Greenblatt quotes Polixenes' warm speech about his son in *The Winter's Tale* - 'He's all my exercise, my mirth, my matter' (1.2.166) – and suggests that 'Perhaps...Shakespeare found himself thinking back to his son.' (p. 291) If the playwright *was* thinking of the dead Hamnet then it is interesting that the boy 'makes a July's day short as December' (1.2.169). July, month of the Kenilworth revels, is associated with pleasure, with the speedy passage of time and, I think, with the revels of Christmas. Leontes, gazing on his own son, is reminded of his own childhood. In his imagination he 'did recoil / Twenty-three years, and saw myself unbreech'd, / In my green velvet coat'. (1.2.154-6) *Twenty-three*: that number which, as I have argued in the previous chapter, was associated in the first year of the new century with Shakespeare's memories of George Gascoigne at Kenilworth.

Gascoigne seems present in the play which Shakespeare probably wrote immediately after *Hamlet*, a ramshackle comedy first published under the title *A Most pleasant and conceited Comedy, of Sir John Falstaff, and the merry Wives of Windsor* (1602). This play itself doubles, or ludicrously inverts, *Hamlet*. As G.R. Hibbard notes, it is a revenge play - but a farcical one: 'Placed in a bourgeois setting, inspired by trivial motives, and seen from a middle-class point of view, revenge becomes a subject for comedy not tragedy.'[3]

But even this anarchic comedy seems to contain muted echoes of what happened at Kenilworth. 'Robert Shallow esquire' (1.1.3), who is obsessed with emphasizing his status as a gentleman 'in any bill, warrant, quittance, or obligation' (1.1.7-9) sounds oddly like George Gascoigne esquire, who also evinced a haughty sense of his place in the social pecking order which he was keen to insist on in all his titles other than his transgressive, anonymous publications.

Justice Shallow represents that sturdy figure of judicial integrity, Lord Chief Justice Gascoigne, transfigured into farce. It's interesting, too, that Shallow's status as a gentleman is confirmed by his family coat of arms, distinguished by a dozen white luces. This has traditionally been regarded as an allusion to the Lucy family of Charlecote, near Stratford-upon-Avon, and connected to the legend of Shakespeare the deer poacher. It seems just as pertinent to note that a luce (or pike) featured prominently in the Gascoigne coat of arms.

The figure of Herne the Hunter (4.4.26-36) may be another muted representation of Gascoigne, a dramatic variation on the almost-catastrophic wild man of the woods episode. Herne is a spectre and a performer, made farcical by Falstaff's impersonation. 'Am I a woodman, ha?' asks Falstaff (5.5.27), unconsciously echoing Gascoigne's self-definition as a 'woodman' in 'Gascoignes wodmanship' a long poem which frames his life as a sequence of misadventures.[4]

It's also significant that *The Merry Wives of Windsor* is set in the environs of a great royal castle and pays homage to a 'radiant queen' (5.5.46). The play's Fairy Queen is implicitly Elizabeth I. But though the instruction is given, 'Search Windsor Castle, elves, within and out' (5.5.56) the play remains outside the castle; the closest we get to it is Page's mention of the castle ditch (5.2.1) If *The Merry Wives* reprises *Hamlet* as a low-life comedy, it similarly holds the Kenilworth experience at a distance, muting it and mocking it.

Stephen Greenblatt's observation that when Polixenes reminisces about his son 'the words fit the play, but they also fit the playwright'[5] is one that can be applied elsewhere. I have argued earlier that at some deep, private level the death of his only male heir Hamnet aged eleven in the summer of 1596 was associated by Shakespeare with his own eleventh summer at Kenilworth in 1575. Twenty-one years – the age at which Hamnet would have become Shakespeare's legal heir – separated those two summers. In *King Lear* a personal sense of loss informed by those overlapping realities is, I believe, expressed in Edgar's reply to Lear's question 'What has thou been?' (11.75) Edgar, masquerading as Tom o'Bedlam, makes a speech purporting to summarize his life. It is an outpouring of disgust which climaxes incoherently in what seems like either free-associating words and images or fragments of meaning which can't be connected to make sense.

Still through the hawthorn blows the cold wind. Heigh no nonny.
Dolphin, my boy, my boy! Cease, let him trot by.
(*King Lear*, 11.88-90)

Editors always struggle to make sense of these lines. One explanation is that Shakespeare is quoting from a lost ballad about a horse named Dauphin (conventionally spelled 'Dolphin' at this period). Well, maybe. But childhood – boyhood – is part of the context here. Just moments before Edgar has quoted from the nursery rhyme 'Pillicock sat on pillicock's hill'. There is nonsense and absurdity here but also, as in the childish rhyme, a deeper meaning. Edgar mimics a mind at the end of its tether: the words he speaks signify the collapse of rationality and order in an irrational and disordered world. Dramatically it is important that his speech appears opaque and its fragmented content impossible to connect.

Of course a ballad may one day turn up about a horse named Dauphin. But even if one did it would make no difference to the probability that 'Dolphin' is a glancing allusion to the Kenilworth revels and the giant dolphin. At a time when spelling was not yet formally enshrined in dictionaries, 'dolphin' and 'dauphin' were as interchangeable as 'Hamnet' and 'Hamlet'. 'Dolphin, my boy, my boy!' can be read as a private howl of grief for a vanished, life-transforming moment in Shakespeare's eleventh year and,

222

simultaneously, for the loss of eleven-year-old Hamnet. Where there was once the warmth of summer, now 'blows the cold wind'.

Pillicock, pillicock sat on a hill,
If he's not gone - he sits there still.

'Pillilock' was an affectionate term for a boy. The couplet is about human identity and the passage of time: Lear was once the ruler of his land and if he hadn't given it up, he still would be. Partly it is about the absurdity of language and meaning: these two rhyming lines make something out of nothing. If someone hasn't gone, then they are still there. It's a comically obvious observation but at the same time it bears the tragic sense of life. Everybody is 'gone' one day; everybody dies. Edmund calls out, 'Quickly send, / Be brief in't, to th' castle' (24.240-1) but it is too late. In this, the bleakest of all Shakespeare's plays, a castle is a place of death; the site of an event that breaks a father's heart and kills him.

*

The Kenilworth experience haunted Shakespeare to the end. Its lineaments are imprinted on what is probably his last full-length play, *The Tempest*. This has conventionally been perceived as Shakespeare's farewell to the theatre; in Stephen Greenblatt's words, 'it has the air of a farewell, a valediction to theatrical magic, a retirement.'[6] It's interesting to note that Prospero has been marooned on his island for twelve years. That seems to match the time span between the dismantling of the Theatre in Shoreditch at the end of December 1598, its subsequent reassembly as The Globe in Southwark in 1599, and the period that *The Tempest* was written – evidently between the later months of 1610 and 1 November 1611, when it was performed at Whitehall before King James.[7] Prospero's domain is inherently theatrical and the parallels between the island and the stage merge at the climax of the play, when he steps forward to beg for liberation via the applause of the audience.

Whereas *Hamlet* refracted the Kenilworth experience darkly and bitterly, *The Tempest* returns to the more benign engagement of *A Midsummer Night's Dream*. And like that earlier play *The Tempest* focuses on the two aspects of Kenilworth which appear to have made the deepest impression upon the child Shakespeare – the fireworks and the dolphin episode. Interestingly, like *A Midsummer Night's Dream, The Tempest* has no source for its plot. Shakespeare drew on his own imagination and memory rather than creatively plagiarising and rewriting existing texts. At the end of the play Prospero promises to tell

> the story of my life,
> And the particular accidents gone by
> Since I came to this isle
> (5.1.305-7)

That telling remains offstage and in the future. And in so far as Prospero can be identified with his creator that story was never recorded. Shakespeare's own biography is assembled out of scrappy, miscellaneous materials ranging from church registers and legal documents to anecdotes which have no firmer status than gossip. Is it reasonable to identify Shakespeare with Prospero? Stephen Greenblatt asserts, to my mind plausibly, that it is. He says that 'the figure of the princely magician suggests that Shakespeare understood what it meant to be Shakespeare'.[8] In that sense what Prospero calls in the play's Epilogue 'this bare island' is also the stage he stands on.

But perhaps it's also the source of Shakespeare's first involvement in theatre. If he was there as a child, Shakespeare witnessed the Kenilworth spectacle from the shoreline of the Great Mere. The castle was, quite literally, an island, surrounded by an expanse of water and Prospero's magical island bears a number of striking similarities to the Kenilworth entertainments. The title of Shakespeare's play refers to the synthetic storm which Ariel creates at Prospero's bidding, and its manifestation greatly resembles a fireworks display:

I flamed amazement. Sometimes I'd divide
And burn in many places – on the topmast,
The yards and bowsprit would I flame distinctly,
Then meet and join. Jove's lightning, the precursors
O'th'dreadful thunderclaps, more momentary
And sight-outrunning were not; the fire and cracks

224

Of sulphurous roaring, the most mighty Neptune
Seem to besiege and make his bold waves tremble,
Yea, his dread trident shake.
(1.2.198-206)

Ariel's illusion has all the appearance of fireworks, sounds like fireworks and smells like fireworks. Moreover this display is associated with water. The verb 'to besiege' is also revealing, since what is usually *literally* laid siege to is a castle.

   A far more striking form of enchantment which the visitors experience on Prospero's magic island is music. Ariel plays on a tabor and pipe as well as singing four songs which have a hypnotic effect on their listeners. As Caliban explains, 'The isle is full of noises, / Sounds and sweet airs that give delight and hurt not.' (3.2.135-6) Partly this is Shakespeare exploiting the resources of an indoor theatre: 'At the Blackfriars, Shakespeare had access to instrumentalists and boy singers who could create a magical island out of sheer sound.'[9] But it also seems to hark back to what happened on 18 July 1575 when Arion sang from the giant dolphin. That memory was first mediated in *A Midsummer Night's Dream* as a memory shared by Oberon and Puck, characters who prefigure Prospero and Ariel. In *The Tempest* the memory of enchanting instruments and song is articulated by Caliban, who speaks of its marvellous hypnotic effects, 'that when I waked / I cried to dream again.' (3.2.142-3) And if Arion's song imprinted itself upon the memory of the young William Shakespeare, it is worth recalling that it also made an enormous impact on the otherwise sour, sly, malicious and elderly William Patten. Patten, quite out of character, made no mention of the mishap with the mask. Instead he heaped his praises on the singer ('a skilful artist...his parts so sweétly sorted') and his 'delectabl', 'melodious' and 'deliçioously deliverd' song:

every instrument again in hiz kind so excellently tunabl: and this in the éening of the day, resoounding from the callm waters... the hole [h]armony conveyd in tyme, tune, & temper thus incomparably melodious

Or as Gonzalo would say: 'Marvellous sweet music!' (3.3.19)

The source of the musical sweetness at Kenilworth was a figure named Arion; in *The Tempest* the name is Ariel.

At Kenilworth the theme of the necessity of marriage was to have been reiterated by Gascoigne's short play at Wedgnock Park, in which the *dramatis personae* consisted of Diana, goddess of chastity and three attendant nymphs, Mercury the messenger of Jove, and Iris the messenger of Juno. It included special effects: Mercury descending in a cloud and Iris coming 'downe from the Rainebowe sent by *Juno*'. *The Tempest* reprises this with a masque involving Iris, Juno and Ceres. But the masque is abruptly terminated, as in *Hamlet*, this time by Prospero who '*starts suddenly and speaks; after which, to a strange hollow and confused noise, they heavily vanish.*' (4.1). Prospero has just remembered Caliban and his confederates in mischief, who are on their way to kill him.

The threat is contained, just as those who have intruded into the island are controlled by Prospero's 'charm' (5.1.17) – a double-edged word, which also applies to the manipulative powers exercised by a playwright on his audience. The abandonment of Prospero's magical power has long been interpreted as a metaphor for Shakespeare's retirement from the theatre. That farewell to his 'rough magic' (5.1.50) seems also to invoke the distant memory of the Kenilworth revels: 'thunder' (5.1.44) and 'fire' (5.1. 45) are associated with the shaking of a 'strong-based promontory' (5.1.46). The connection between the promontory and noise is underlined by the Folio spelling ('strong bass'd') and it leads on to 'heavenly music' (5.1.52). 'I'll break my staff', Prospero promises (5.1.54) – a loss of power which remotely echoes that moment when George Gascoigne disrupted his performance at Kenilworth by breaking the branch he was holding.

If the Kenilworth revels and theatre were inextricably associated in Shakespeare's imagination, what then of Shakespeare's last dramatic writing? If, as is possible, *The Two Gentlemen of Verona* was his first play, then his last one, *The Two Noble Kinsmen*, 'the title of which it perhaps echoes'[10] is where we might expect to find some final traces of that connection. It is a play with theatre on its mind: the cryptic remark that 'Our losses fall so thick' in the final line of the Prologue is commonly interpreted as a reference to the burning down of The Globe on 29 June 1613. It is also a play in which one of the central characters is haunted by the death of an eleven year old child. Emilia looks back to her own eleventh year, when her great friend Flavina died. Her powerful remembrance of their innocent love is defined as a 'rehearsal' (1.3.78), a word which means narrative or story but also evokes theatricality. Noting just how passionate the expression of those memories is, Hippolyta observes 'You're out of breath!' (1.3.82)

Many critics have interpreted *The Two Noble Kinsmen* (probably written 1613-14) as a melancholy, death-haunted play. Bones, skulls and unburied cadavers trouble the play's characters, which may owe something to revenge tragedy and the success of John Webster, and might equally be rooted in personal obsessions. Lois Potter has interestingly connected the inscription carved on Shakespeare's grave, with its curse on 'he y^t moves my bones', with the Prologue's anxiety about respecting Chaucer's bones. As she suggests, what the play and the inscription have in common is 'a fear not only of physical exposure but also of literary desecration'.[11]

If such personal and private matter can be detected in the play, then it should not be a surprise that it briefly reprises material from two plays where the Kenilworth connection is strong. The country entertainment on offer in Act Three, prefaced by a long-winded speech by the schoolmaster, is a piece of comic theatre reminiscent of the show put on by Peter Quince and his associates in *A Midsummer Night's Dream*. That echoed the local entertainment put on for the Queen in the outer courtyard at Kenilworth, slyly mocked in *A Letter* and snobbishly ignored by Gascoigne.

More directly, the madness of the jailer's daughter replicates that of Ophelia. Her songs, which sound nonsensical but contain significant private meaning, are heard by her wooer in a location which bears a striking resemblance to Kenilworth Castle:

 the great lake that lies behind the palace,
From the far shore, thick set with reeds and sedges (4.1.53-4)

Having identified the source of the singing, the wooer describes the jailer's daughter as

    like the fair nymph
That feeds the lake with waters, or as Iris

Newly dropped down from heaven. (4.1.86-8)

At Kenilworth there was both a Lady of the Lake (who would have been played by a boy, just as the jailer's daughter would have been in *The Two Noble Kinsmen*) and, in Gascoigne's aborted play, Iris mechanically descending 'downe from the Rainebowe'. The jailer's daughter throws herself into the lake but she is spared Ophelia's fate by the intervention of the wooer.

In the following scene that magical word 'promontory' makes its final appearance in Shakespeare's writing. Gazing at a portrait of Arcite, Emilia impulsively praises his good looks. In exaggerated language (and only moments before changing her mind and deciding that Palamon is better looking), she praises his brow:

> Fame and Honour,
> Methinks, from hence, as from a promontory
> Pointed in heaven, should clap their wings and sing,
> To all the under-world, the loves and fights
> Of gods and such men near 'em. (4.2.21-4)

Here, a promontory is like a stage. It is a place where performers look down on those below and narrate in song tales of love and fighting involving gods and men. This passage involves, I think, the simultaneous evocation of both that promontory by Kenilworth Castle and Shakespeare's subsequent dramatic career: a chain of associations linking a heavenly promontory, song and theatrical performance. It is divine and heavenly but it is also inextricably connected to 'the under-world' of men.

The triumphant performance of Fame and Honour who 'should clap their wings and sing' sounds like a distant echo of Gascoigne's 'Then will I laugh and clappe my hands'.[12] The triumph of love is framed in theatrical imagery. But moments later all this is reversed. Emilia turns her attention to Palamon's picture and changes her mind. She praises 'this brown manly face! Oh Love, this only, /From this hour, is complexion! (4.2.41-3). Or as Gascoigne put it, 'A lovely nutbrowne face is best of all.'[13]

23 Zabeta and the others

Though she continued to go on progresses almost to the end of her reign, Elizabeth I never went back to Kenilworth Castle. This was clearly a deliberate decision on her part.

Ten years after the extravaganza of July 1575, Leicester was still plaintively urging her to return, writing to her 'From your old lodging in the Castle of Kenilworth, where you are daily prayed for and most often wished to be.'[1] But Kenilworth was a place of unhappy memories. For the two leading figures there in July 1575, the great entertainment had turned into a fiasco. Elizabeth was enraged to be treated as an equal, not as a superior. She grew sick of the repeated hints and suggestions that she should marry her host. Gascoigne's play lecturing her on the inadequacies of the single woman was the last straw. Her final days were spent sulking in her room, and she left Kenilworth prematurely. The show put on for her may been the most spectacular of her reign, but it did not please her and she plainly had no desire to undergo a repeat performance.

For Robert Dudley, too, it ended in failure. He learned his lesson and never again solicited Elizabeth's hand in marriage. Instead he transferred his secret affections from Douglas Sheffield to Lettice Knollys. Those nineteen days of summer nevertheless seem to have possessed an intense emotional and sentimental attraction for him. He even tried to perpetuate its power after death, insisting that the contents of Kenilworth were 'all to remain to the said Castle and House, and not to be altered or removed'. Elizabeth Goldring persuasively argues that 'the deliberate fossilization of the castle and its picture collection suggests a desire to create a lasting memorial to the revels of 1575 which, for all their mishaps, nonetheless constituted Kenilworth's (and, to a certain extent, Leicester's) apotheosis.'[2]

*

After Kenilworth, the writing team dispersed, and fortune smiled on several of its members.

Three years after Kenilworth, Henry Goldyngham's services were required for another royal progress: he was commissioned to write a masque for the Queen's entry into Norwich. Goldyngham also wrote 'The Garden Plot', an allegorical poem of 164 verses dedicated to Elizabeth. It seems never to have been published. The surviving copy was evidently intended as a gift, since it is prepared for introducing illuminations, though in the event none were finished. Quite possibly Goldyngham died. After 1578 he drops out of sight as enigmatically as he first appeared. He may well have been snuffed out by the plague which accompanied the royal progress of that year.

The career of William Hunnis, Master of the Children of the Queen's Chapel, continued to flourish. In 1578 he published a volume of versified scripture, the title of which punned on his name: *A Hyve Full of Honye: Contayning the Firste Booke of Moses, called Genesis. Turned into English Meetre.* It bore the bear and ragged staff on the reverse of the title page and was dedicated to Leicester:

Your Honors Bountie towardes mee, more than I here confesse,
Compelleth mee in humble sort my dutie to expresse.[3]

In 1583 his verse translation of the penitential psalms was hugely successful, and by 1629 had run to ten editions. *Hunnies Recreations: conteining foure godlie discourses* came out in 1595, and he died two years later.

Richard Mulcaster's career also ripened. His first book, *Positions* (1581), outlined the first principles of education, and proposed, among other reforms, a standardization of textbooks. A sequel, *The First Part of the Elementarie which entreateth chefelie of the right writing of our English tung* (1582), was a book of educational psychology which campaigned for a standardized English. It was dedicated to Robert Dudley. Mulcaster wrote that he was 'exceedinglie indetted' to him for 'speciall goodnesse, and most favourable countenance these manie years.'[4] He was headmaster of St Paul's for 12 years and was also employed intermittently for dramatic productions as court. He died on 15 April 1611.

The Earl of Leicester's company of players died with Dudley. Some of the actors joined the household of his older brother, the Earl of Warwick. Others joined the Admiral's Men or Strange's Men. Perhaps none enjoyed quite such success as James Burbage. His recognition that it might be more profitable for actors to put on shows at a fixed location designed for that purpose, rather than simply travelling around performing in inn yards and halls, proved astonishingly prescient. One year after the Kenilworth 'The Theatre' was erected on vacant land half a mile outside the Bishopsgate entrance to the city of London. Burbage performed often at Court, helped his two sons to achieve affluence and success, and died aged about sixty-six, an accomplished theatrical entrepreneur and actor.

*

Others fared less well.

William Patten seems never again to have found state employment or the patronage of a nobleman. His career as a minor, marginal writer continued, with a number of pamphlets clearly designed to solicit rewards. *A moorning diti* [mourning ditty] *upon the decease of...Prins Henry Earl of Arundel* (1580), was a broadside elegy in 13 stanzas. Another broadside publication (1583), paraphrased Psalm 72, with a musical setting. In 1589 he published a pamphlet, which elegised in Latin verse Sir William Winter. Another Latin verse elegey, *Luctus consolatorius* (1591), was in memory of Sir Christopher Hatton. In 1598 he published a paraphrase of Psalm 21 in seven stanzas. William Patten died around 1600, by the standards of his age an exceptionally old man. He can never have known that his masterpiece was *A Letter* and that centuries later it would make his old adversary Robert Langham immortal.

Patten's envy of Gascoigne was misplaced. Although he had only written the offensive play about Zabeta at Dudley's bidding, George Gascoigne no longer enjoyed the Earl's patronage. This suggests that the Earl, rather unreasonably, held the poet responsible for Elizabeth's fury. Perhaps Philip Sidney accepted this version of events: his uncle had been humiliated, and all because of George Gascoigne. Certainly Leicester was a man always happy to blame others for his own mistakes. Years later, when Elizabeth flew into a rage with him for a serious misjudgement he'd made in the Low Countries, Dudley quite unreasonably blamed the messenger who'd brought her the bad news, telling him 'It hath not grieved me a little that by your means I have fallen into her Majesty's so deep

231

displeasure.'[5] The charge was ludicrous.

Having evidently lost Leicester's goodwill, Gascoigne went back to dedicating books to his most reliable patron, Arthur, Lord Grey of Wilton, and other influential figures such as the Earl of Bedford. His high profile at Kenilworth failed to give him any protection from the vengeful force of state censorship. On 13 August 1576 Gascoigne's publisher was obliged to hand over his remaining stock of *The Posies of George Gascoigne Esquire* to the ecclesiastical censors. The poet did, however, succeed in finding employment with Lord Burghley and Francis Walsingham, and briefly worked for them both as a government agent and messenger in Paris and Antwerp in the autumn of 1576. The following year later he fell ill and died, obscurely, in Stamford.

One of Gascoigne's associates in the entertainments at Kenilworth also seems to have been dying in the summer of 1577. John Badger of Oxford, who'd written and performed the Hercules speech to welcome the Queen, made his will on 15 July 1577. Since he'd graduated from Christ Church in 1553 he was probably, like Gascoigne, in his forties when he died.

*

Seven months after Gascoigne's death, Elizabeth I set out on a long, slow, meandering progress to Norwich. She was once again entertained by the Earl of Leicester, but it was a low key affair, compared to Kenilworth. At the Earl's Wanstead residence she watched a masque written by Philip Sidney. Sidney showed that he had learned the lesson of Kenilworth, and obliquely complimented Elizabeth in his reference to 'those that have long followed one (in truth) most excellent chace, do now at length perceive she could never be taken: but if that she stayd at any time near the pursuers, it was never meant to tarry with them, but only to take breath to fly further from them.'[6] His masque also briefly featured the tale of Sylvanus, but it was a different one from Gascoigne's; another way of erasing him from the record, perhaps.

In 1578, Robert Dudley married Lettice Knollys. If *The Copy of a Letter* is to be believed, the marriage was performed in secret at Kenilworth Castle. A ceremony was held at Dudley's Essex home,

Wanstead Hall, in September, in the presence of her father and a handful of other guests. Lettice was many months pregnant. Leicester's discarded mistress, Douglas Sheffield, was married off to Sir Edward Stafford. The two women were, in the jeering words of *The Copy of a Letter*, 'his Old and New Testaments'. Lettice's first pregnancy ended in a miscarriage. She later gave birth to a son but the child was not healthy and died in 1584.

Elizabeth I was kept in the dark about Leicester's marriage and did not find out until late June of the following year. The news sent her into a fury and she wanted to clap him in the Tower of London. It was pointed out to her that a perfectly lawful marriage was not a sufficient reason to take such a drastic step. Instead, she had to make do with putting him under house-arrest, banishing Lettice from the court and dispensing with the services of Leicester's sister, Lady Mary Sidney, who was one of her most loyal and long-serving ladies-in-waiting.

Ten years after the heavy-handed hints set out on the drawbridge at Kenilworth Castle, the Earl of Leicester finally received his commission in the Netherlands. In 1585 Elizabeth named him commander of an expedition to assist the rebellion in the Low Countries against Spain. His military efforts there were undistinguished, and he enraged Elizabeth by accepting the title of Supreme Governor of the United Provinces. Philip Sidney was killed and Leicester's military campaign was a failure. He was finally recalled in 1587.

Leicester continued to reside at Kenilworth, on and off, until his death. By his early fifties he was 'worn, dissipated, somewhat infirm'.[7] He died, childless, in 1588, a puffy, bloated, prematurely old man.

Elizabeth died on 24 March 1603, ending her reign, as Germaine Greer has eloquently put it, 'cruel, bald and rotten-toothed'.[8]

*

Popular modern biographies of Elizabeth I put forward a common view of her nineteen days at Kenilworth in concluding that the visit was a great success. This orthodox verdict is long overdue for substantial revision. There is no reason to believe that Elizabeth enjoyed her visit. If she found it memorable, it was for all the wrong reasons.

The royal progress to Kenilworth was not, at the time, regarded as a major event. Elizabeth Goldring's description of it as 'the first Elizabethan court festival to have been commemorated by multiple printed pamphlets' is, I think, very debatable.[9] There is hard proof of only two contemporary accounts and there is no evidence that either of them enjoyed a wide circulation. Indeed, without Wiliam Patten and George Gascoigne what happened at Kenilworth would have vanished from history. As it was, thanks to the presence of those two idiosyncratic, talented individuals, we have an extraordinary record of the royal visit. But they each had their own reasons for putting a spin on it.

Indeed, those July days were remembered almost by accident. The antiquarian John Strype was astonished to discover that 'of her most splendid reception by the earl of Leicester at Kenelworth-castle, I find not a word in our historians.'[10] George Gascoigne orchestrated the publication of the scripts because he was a keen marketer of his wares, not because they were especially memorable writings. In many ways Kenilworth marked the steep decline of his creative genius – it was the sixteenth century equivalent of a great novelist doing hackwork for Hollywood.

An accurate attribution of *A Letter* is also long overdue. The book should be seen for what it is – a satire as much as an impartial record of the proceedings. William Patten wrote *A Letter* out of malice and a powerful sense of grievance, not because he wished to celebrate the Earl of Leicester's generosity or the splendour of his entertainment.

A work entitled *The Pastime of the Progresse* never existed. To believe it did is to fall for the myth that Kenilworth mesmerized Tudor readers. It didn't. *A Letter* no sooner appeared than it disappeared, and Gascoigne's *The princelye pleasures at the Courte at Kenelwoorth* was published just once, in 1576, by which time interest in Kenilworth had long since ebbed away. Ironically, these two titles have assumed a significance in modern times which they never enjoyed in the lifetime of their authors.

Yet Kenilworth proved important in a way Robert Dudley could never have anticipated when he planned his great entertainment. The extraordinary concentration of writers and actors at the castle that July provided a unique moment in Tudor cultural history. Never again would Philip Sidney, William Patten, George Gascoigne, James Burbage and William Shakespeare be found together in the same small corner of Warwickshire. The ramifications of that assembly of talent would last for centuries.

*

In a tone of melancholy resignation, Prospero announces, as the Earl of Leicester might well have done on the morning of 27 July 1575,

> Our revels now are ended. These our actors,
> As I foretold you, were all spirits, and
> Are melted into air, into thin air:
> And, like the baseless fabric of this vision,
> The cloud-capp'd towers, the gorgeous palaces,
> The solemn temples, the great globe itself,
> Yea, all which it inherit, shall dissolve,
> And like this insubstantial pageant faded,
> Leave not a rack behind.
> (*The Tempest*, 4.1.148-156)

But even here, Shakespeare could not quite shake off the links with Kenilworth and Gascoigne, since this famous passage echoes a moment from Gascoigne's 1566 play *Jocasta*. At the end of the first act the Theban chorus reiterates the imagery of palatial splendour, towers and ultimate collapse:

> Thy gorgeous pompe, thy glorious high renoume [renown],
> Thy stately towers, and all shall fall a downe.[11]

That happened to Kenilworth Castle too, far faster than anyone could have imagined. During the English civil war it suddenly regained the strategic significance which a century earlier it had lost, and high explosive was used to render it useless to royalist forces. The stately towers were gutted, the defensive positions at the eastern end were destroyed, and one side of the great Keep was blasted away. The Great Mere, a central feature of the glittering entertainments of 1575, was drained and turned into pasture.

235

'The cloud-capp'd towers, the gorgeous palaces' were prefigured in another late play, which also conjured up the insubstantiality of things, placing it in a theatrical context. Mark Antony's vision of 'black vesper's pageants' (*Antony and Cleopatra*, 4.14.8) alludes to cloud and mist and the weird shapes they can assume at dusk. His short speech, beginning 'Sometimes we see a cloud that's dragonish' is about perception, imagination and performance. Clouds and mist can take on many forms – dragons, bears, lions, horses – but in the end 'The rack dislimns and makes it indistinct' (4.14.10). The cloudy image changes shape and obliterates itself.

The key word here is *pageants*. The speech is about death. Evening is on its way. Antony will die, and so too will his lover. Pageants – amateur open air performances in town streets or open spaces - were the form of entertainment Shakespeare had known in his childhood and youth, before the sophistication of commercial theatre at a fixed site. It is perhaps not only Antony's world that is coming to an end here; Shakespeare's life in the theatre was beginning to wind down. And here, too, Kenilworth in 1575 was on the playwright's mind, in the form of the 'blue promontory / With trees upon't that nod unto the world / And mock our eyes with air' (5-7) But now the promontory is no longer the enchanted place from which dolphins are seen and the magic of theatre unfolds before a child's eyes. Now it is a mere 'vapour' (4.14.3), a site of shifting possibilities, ending in emptiness and mockery, mere air.

Appendix One: The 19 days

(1) Saturday 9 July 1575

The Royal Progress halts at Long Itchington. The Earl of Leicester welcomes Elizabeth to the region, and gives her a suitably lavish dinner. A local prodigy, the 'great Chyld', is displayed. After dinner the royal party goes off hunting.

The royal party reaches the parkland south of Kenilworth Castle in the mid-evening. Ten sibyls appear out of an arbour and the chief prophetess makes a speech. Elizabeth enters the castle through a wide, towered gateway and passes across The Brays to the Gallery Tower, where six giant trumpeters blow a welcome fanfare. The figure of Hercules in the gateway makes a speech, then grants the Queen and her party entry to the castle.

The Queen rides across The Tiltyard to Mortimer's Tower and enters the outer court of the castle. A floating island lit by torches moves towards the castle. It carries the Lady of the Lake and two attendants. The Lady tells her tale to the Queen. Elizabeth then crosses the great drawbridge into the inner court, while music plays.

The Queen goes to her lodgings. Guns are fired to celebrate her arrival. The night climaxes with a grand fireworks display.

(2) Sunday 10 July

In the morning Elizabeth attends a service at St Nicholas Church, Kenilworth.

In the afternoon there is music and dancing for the ladies of the court and their partners. That night there is another fireworks display, which goes on until after midnight. It features fireworks which appear to travel underwater.

(3) Monday 11 July

Elizabeth stays indoors until 5 p.m. She then goes hunting. The hunted deer escapes into the Mere and is captured and killed.

On the way back to the castle the Queen is entertained by George Gascoigne, dressed as a wild man of the woods, and his partner, Echo. In snapping his oak branch, Gascoigne almost unseats Elizabeth from her horse.

(4) Tuesday 12 July

A day devoted to music and dancing. The first meeting of the Privy Council is held at the castle (Robert Dudley is not present). At dusk the Queen walks through Leicester's Gatehouse and out on to the bridge, where she stands and listens to musicians playing 'sundry kinds'of music from a barge anchored on the Great Mere. Afterwards she goes for a stroll in the parkland north of the castle.

(5) Wednesday 13 July

There is another deer hunt, and once again the deer flees into the water. It is captured by 'the watermen' who hold up the animal's head. The Queen spares the animal's life but orders that its ears be cut off.

(6) Thursday 14 July

Thirteen bears are assembled in the inner court and fighting dogs in the outer court. The bears are then brought out to fight them. The dogs go for the bears' throats, while the bears slash the dogs' scalps. After this an Italian acrobat puts on an indoor show in front of Elizabeth. The Privy Council holds its second meeting at the castle, with Robert Dudley present. That night there is a third fireworks display. It again features fireworks which appear to burn underwater. The displays are synchronized with a great peal of guns and last about two hours.

(7) Friday 15 July

The day is windy and wet. No entertainments are put on.

The Privy Council holds its third meeting at the castle. Neither Dudley nor his brother, the Earl of Warwick, are present.

(8) Saturday 16 July

The day is again windy and wet. No entertainments are put on. The Privy Council holds its fourth meeting at the castle. Robert Dudley and the Earl of Warwick are both present.

(9) Sunday 17 July

In the morning Elizabeth attends a service at St Nicholas Church, Kenilworth.

In the afternoon, a 'country wedding' is staged in the outer court, before a large crowd of local people. Men from Coventry arrive and ask permission to put on their traditional play about the Danes. Permission is granted but the crowd grows unruly. The wedding group marches out through Leicester's gatehouse, back into Kenilworth, and the Coventry play is cut short. Elizabeth goes off to join the dancing which is taking place among the guests inside the castle. After supper a play lasting more than two hours is performed. This is followed by a banquet of 300 dishes. Because of the lateness of the hour, a masque scheduled to be put on after the banquet is called off.

(10) Monday 18 July

It is hot and sunny and Elizabeth remains indoors for most of the day. Inside the castle she knights five gentlemen: Thomas Cecil, Henry Cobham, Thomas Stanhope, Arthur Bassett, and Thomas Tresham. She also touches nine commoners, miraculously curing them of 'the king's evil'. The Privy Council holds its fifth meeting at the castle, with the Earls of Leicester and Warwick both present.

At 5 p.m. Elizabeth goes to The Chase and hunts deer with dogs. On her way back to the castle she is greeted by the god Triton, blowing a trumpet disguised as a giant whelk shell. He is in a boat shaped like a gigantic mermaid.

The Queen pauses on the bridge leading to Leicester's gatehouse while Triton tells her the tale of the cruel knight, Sir Bruce, and the Lady of the Lake. The Lady and her two attendants move across the surface of the water and present Elizabeth with the gift of Arion, on a giant dolphin. Arion sings a song, thanking the Queen for liberating the Lady.

(11) Tuesday 19 July

The Coventry play is performed a second time, this time in full. The Queen laughs out loud and is evidently very pleased with it. She rewards the men from Coventry with two deer and five marks. The Privy Council holds its sixth meeting at the castle.

(12) Wednesday 20 July

Gascoigne's play about Zabeta is cancelled. Supper at 'a fair pavilion' at Wedgnock Park is cancelled. There is 'earnest talk and appointment of removing.' The Privy Council holds its seventh meeting at the castle.

(13) Thursday 21 July
The actors wait to perform Gascoigne's play. Elizabeth remains indoors.

(14) Friday 22 July
The actors wait to perform Gascoigne's play. Elizabeth remains indoors. The Privy Council holds its eighth meeting at the castle.

(15) Saturday 23 July
Elizabeth remains indoors.

(16) Sunday 24 July
(In the morning Elizabeth attends a service at St Nicholas Church, Kenilworth?)

(17) Monday 25 July
Elizabeth remains indoors. The Privy Council holds its ninth meeting at the castle.

(18) Tuesday 26 July
Elizabeth remains indoors.

(19) Wednesday 27 July
Elizabeth departs from Kenilworth Castle, and goes hunting. She encounters Sylvanus (George Gascoigne), who runs alongside her horse and makes a speech. He leads her to Deep Desire. Musicians hidden behind a holly bush begin to play and Deep Desire sings a song of farewell.

Appendix Two: The hunting masque

Who list (by me) to learne, Assembly for to make,
    For Keysar, Kyng, or comely Queene, for Lord or Ladies sake:
  Or where, and in what sort it should prepared be,
Mark well my wordes, and thanke me then, for thankes I crave in fee.
  The place should first be pight, on pleasant gladsome greene,
Yet under shade of stately trees, where little sunne is seene:
  And neare some fountaine spring, whole chrystall running streames,
May helpe to coole the parching heate, ycaught by *Phoebus* beames,
  The place appointed thus, it neyther shall be clad,
With Arras nor with Tapystry, such paltrie were too bad:
  Ne yet those hote perfumes, whereof proude Courtes do smell,
May once presume in such a place, or Paradise to dwell.
  Away with fayned fresh, as broken boughes or leaves,
Away, away, with forced flowers, ygathered from their greaues:
  This place must of it selfe, afforde such sweete delight,
And eke such shewe, as better may content the greedie sight:
  Where sundry sortes of hewes, which growe upon the ground,
May seeme (indeede) such Tapystry, as we (by arte) have found.
  Where fresh and fragrant flowers, may skorne the courtiers cost,
Which daubes himselfe with Syvet, Muske, and many an ointment lost.
  Where sweetest singing byrdes, may make such melodye,
As *Pan*, nor yet *Apollos* arte, can sounde such harmenye.
  Where breath of westerne windes, may calmely yeld content,
Where casements neede not opened be, where ayre is never pent.
  Where shade may serve for shrine, and yet the Sunne at hande,
Where beautie neede not quake for colde, ne yet with Sunne be tande.
  In fine and to conclude, where pleasure dwels at large,
Which Princes seeke in Pallaces, with payne and costly charge.
  Then such a place once founde, the Butler first appears,
He shall be formost doctor there, and stande before his peares:
  And with him shall he bring, (if company be great)
Some wagons, cartes, some Mules or jades yladen till they sweate,
  With many a medicine made for common queynt diseases,
As thirstie throates, and typpling tongs, whome *Bacchus* pype appeases.
  These little pinching pots, which Pothecaries use,
Are all too fine, fye fye on such, they make men but to muse.

My Doctor brings his drugs, to counterpaise all quarrels,
In Kilderkins and Fyrkins full, in Bottles and in Barrels.
　　And yet therein he brings, (I would you wist it well,)
No rotten drammes, but noble wine, which makes mens hearts to swell.
　　And downe he doth dismount, his things for to addresse,
His flagons in the fountaine faire, are placed more and lesse.
　　Or if such fountaines fayle, My Doctor hath the skyll,
With sande and Campher for to coole, his potions at his will.
　　That doone: he spreades his cloth, upon the grassye banke,
And sets to shewe his Deintie Drinkes, to winne his Princes thanke.
　　Then cōmes the captaine Cooke, with many a warlike wight,
Which armor bring and weapons both, with hunger for to fight.
　　Yea some also set forth, upon a manlye mynde,
To make some meanes, a quarrel with, my Doctor for to fynde.
　　For whiles colde loynes of Veale, cold Capon, Beefe and Goose,
With Pygeon pyes, and Mutton colde, are set on hunger loose,
　　And make the forlorne hope, in doubt to scape full hard,
Then come to give a charge in flanke (else all the marte were marde,)
　　First Neates tongs poudred well, and Gambones of the Hogge,
Then Saussages and savery knackes, to set mens myndes on gogge.
　　And whiles they skyrmish thus, with fierce and furious fight,
My Doctor clearkly turned the Tappe, and goeth beyond them quite.
　　For when they be so trapt, enclosed round about,
No boote prevayles, but drinke like men, for that must helpe them out.
　　Then King or comely Queene, then Lorde and Lady looke,
To see which side will beare the bell, the Butler or the Cooke.
　　At last the Cooke takes flight, but Butlers still abyde,
And sound their Drummes and make retreate, with bottles by their side.
　　Herewith to stint all stryfe, the huntsmen come in hast,
They lycence crave of King or Queene, to see their battell plast.
　　Which graunted and obtaynde, they set on such as lyve,
And fiercely fight, till both be forst, all armour up to give.
　　And home they go dispoylde, like simple sakelesse men,
No remedie but trudge apace, they have no weapons then.
　　The field thus fought and done, the huntsmen come agayne,
Of whome some one upon his knee, shall tell the Prince full playne,
　　This little lesson here, which followeth next in place,
Forgive me (Queene) which am to bold, to speak unto yȯ grace.

My Liege forgive the boldnesse of your man,
Which comes to speake before your grace him call:
My skyll is small, yet must I as I can,
Presume to preach, before these Barons all,
And tell a tale, which may such mynds appal
As passe their dayes in slouthfull idlenesse,
The first foule nourse to worldly wickednesse.

Since golden time, (my liege) doth never stay,
But fleeth still about with restlesse wings,
Why doth your grace, let time then steale away,
Which is more worth, than all your wordly things?
Beleeve me (liege) believe me Queenes and Kings,
One only hour (once lost) yeldes more anoy,
Than twentie dayes can cure with myrth and joy.

And since your grace determined by decree,
To hunt this day, and recreate your mynde,
Why syt you thus and lose the game and glee
Which you might heare? Why ringeth not the winde,
With hornes and houndes, according to their kynde?
Why syt you thus (my liege) and never call,
Our houndes not us, to make you sport withall?

Perchance the fight, which sodenly you saw,
Erewhyles betweene, these overbragging bluddes,
Amasde your mynde, and for a whyle did draw
Your noble eyes, to settle on such suddes.
But peerelesse Prince, the moisture of such muddes,
Is much too grosse and homely for your grace,
Behold them not, their pleasures be but bale.

Behold us here, your true and trustie men,
Your huntes, your hyndes, your swaynes at all assayes,
Which ouerthrow them, (being three to tenne)
And now are prest, with bloudhounds and relayes,
With houndes of crye, and houndes well worthy prayse,
To rowze, to runne, to hunt and hale to death,

243

As great a Hart as ever yet bare breath.

This may be seene, (a Princes sport in deede)
And this your grace, shall see when pleaseth you:
So that voutsafe, (O noble Queene) with speede,
To mount on horse, that others may ensue,
Untill this Hart be rowzed and brought to view.
Then if you finde, that I have spoke amysse,
Correct me Queene: (till then) forgive me this.

Appendix Three: The huntsman's speech

Before the Queene, I come report to make
Then husht and peace, for noble Trystrams sake.
From out my horne, my fewmets first I drawe,
And them present, on leaves, by hunters lawe:
And thus I say: my liege, behold and see
In Hart of tenne, I hope he harbord bee.
For if you marke, his fewmets every point,
Ypou shall them finde, long, round, and well annoynt,
Knottie and great, withouten prickes or eares,
The moystnesse shewes, what benysone he beares.

Then if my Prince, demaund what head he beare,
I answere thus, with sober words and cheare:
My liege I went, this morning on my quest,
My hound did sticke, and seemde to scent some beast. (*nota bene*)
I held him short, and drawing after him,
I might behold, the Hart was feeding trym.
His head was high, and large in each degree,
Well palmed eke, and seemd full sound to be.
Of colour broune, he beareth eight and tenne,
Of stately heighth, and long he seemed then.

His beame seemd great, in good proportion led,
Well burred and round, well pearled, neare his head.
He seemed fayre, tweene blacke and berrie brounde
He seemes well fed, by all the signes I found.
For when I had, well marked him with eye,
I stept aside, to watch where he would lye.
And when I so had wayted full an houre,
That he might be, at layze and in his boure,
I cast about, to harbour him full sure.
My hound (by sent) bid me thereof assure.
Entring the thicke, these fewmets did I spy,
Which I tooke up, and layd my markes thereby.
In privie pathes I walkt, and (creeping throw)
I found the Slot, of other Harts ynow.

Both yong and olde, I founde of every syse,
But as for hym, I hope that still he lues:
So that your grace (by likelyhoode) may hym finde,
He harbord is, according to my mynde.

Then if she aske, what Slot or view I found,
I say, the Slot, or view, was long on ground,
The toes were great, the joyntbones round and short,
The thinne bones large, the demclawes close in port:
Short jointed was he, hollow footed eke,
In Hart to hunt, as any man can seeke.

Notes

The following abbreviations are used in the notes. Bibliographical information is confined to the bibliography.

BL	British Library, London
Flowers	George Gascoigne, *A Hundreth Sundrie Flowres*
Greenblatt	Stephen Greenblatt, *Will in the World: How Shakespeare Became Shakespeare*
Honan	Park Honan, *Shakespeare: A Life*
Jenkins	Elizabeth Jenkins, *Elizabeth and Leicester*
Kenilworth	Walter Scott, *Kenilworth: A Romance*
Kuin	R.J.P. Kuin, 'The Purloined *Letter*: Evidence and Probability Regarding Robert Langham's Authorship'
Laneham	Robert Laneham, *A Letter*
Letter	Robert Langham, *A Letter*
O'Kill	Brian O'Kill, 'The Printed Works of William Patten'
Princely Pleasures	John W. Cunliffe (ed), *George Gascoigne: The Glasse of Government, The Princely Pleasures at Kenelworth Castle, The Steele Glas and other poems and prose works*
PRO	Public Record Office, London
Prouty	C.T. Prouty, *George Gascoigne: Elizabethan Courtier, Soldier, and Poet*
Schoenbaum	S. Schoenbaum, *William Shakespeare: A Compact Documentary Life*
Scott	David Scott, 'William Patten and the Authorship of "Robert Laneham's *Letter*" (1575)'

1. The castle

1. The survey is reproduced as an appendix in *Robert Laneham's Letter*, 63-4.
2. See Richard K Morris, 'A Plan for Kenilworth Castle at Longleat', 34.
3. For the complete inventory see Elizabeth Goldring, 'The Earl of Leicester's Inventory of Kenilworth Castle, *c.*1578'.

2. The second visitor

1. *Reinventing Shakespeare*, 108.
2. *Kenilworth*, xxiii.
3. Ibid. xxix.
4. Ibid. 391.
5. Ibid. 168.

3. Elizabeth and Leicester

1. *Kenilworth*, 1.
2. *Elizabeth I: A Feminist Perspective*, 126.
3. Ibid. 1.
4. Ibid. 6.
5. Jenkins, 154.

4. 'a spy, an atheist and a godless person'

1. Eleanor Rosenberg, *Leicester: Patron of Letters*, xviii.
2. Ibid. 19.
3. I use Goldyngham's spelling of his name. See BL MSS Harley 6902.
4. Cited in Nichol, *The Lodger*, 157.
5. Cited in *Gascoigne's Princely Pleasures with the Masque intended to have been presented before Queen Elizabeth at Kenilworth Castle in 1575; with an introductory memoir and notes*, 99-100.
6. 2005 edition.
7. Ibid. 99.
8. PRO SP 12/86.
9. 'Phillip Sparrow' is a common abbreviation. The full title of this poem is 'He wrote (at his friends request) in prayse on a Gentlewoman, whose name was Phillip, as followeth'.

10. Frederick Gard Fleay, *A Biographical Chronicle of the English Drama 1559-1642*, Vol. 1. (1891), 241-2.

11. 'The greene Knights farewell to Fansie', 35.

12. Prouty's conclusion that *A Hundreth Sundry Flowers* was banned (Prouty, 79) has sometimes been challenged on the grounds of lack of evidence, since the records of the Stationers' Company July 1571 to July 1576 are missing, as are the records of the censors for this period. But it is plain that Prouty was right and that Gascoigne's Prefatory Letter in the *Posies* 'To the reverende Divines', which he dated 'this last day of Januarie. 1574' (old-style dating; actually 1575), is a response to censorship. His only possible motive in writing this letter and in restructuring the contents of *A Hundreth Sundry Flowers* for *The Posies of George Gascoigne Esquire* was to persuade the censors that the second edition was less offensive. In some ways it was, but on 13 August 1576 'by appointment of Q.M. Commissioners' (i.e. the censors), Gascoigne's publisher was obliged to return 'half a hundred of Gascoignes poesies' (cited *Flowers*, liii).

13. *Flowers*, 359.

14 Ibid. 423.

15 Prouty, 193.

5. The first day

1. MS. Pepys II.517 (Magdalene College, Cambridge). Cited in *Letter*, 6.

2. *The Progresses and Public Processions of Queen Elizabeth*, Vol. I, 93 [all references to Vol. I are to the Kenilworth facsicle].

3. Cited in Alan Stewart, *Philip Sidney: A Double Life*, 145.

4. *Letter*, 75-6.

5. *Princely Pleasures*, 92.

6. Ibid.

7. Quoted in *Gascoigne's Princely Pleasures with the Masque intended to have been presented before Queen Elizabeth at Kenilworth Castle in 1575; with an introductory memoir and notes*, 80.

8. *Princely Pleasures*, 92.

9. Ibid. 98.

10. *Letter*, 39.

11. *Princely Pleasures*, 92.

12. Ilana Nash, ' "A Subject without Subjection": Robert Dudley, Earl of Leicester, and *The Princely Pleasures at Kenelworth Castle*,' 92.

13. *Princely Pleasures*, 93.

14. *Letter*, 41.

15. *Princely Pleasures*, 95.

16. *Letter*, 41.

17. Op. cit., 100.

18. *Princely Pleasures*, 95.

19. For a full account of the inventory and its contents, see Goldring, 'The Earl of Leicester's Inventory of Kenilworth Castle, c.1578'.

20. *Letter*, 43.

6. The savage man

1. Laneham, 16.

2. Translated from the original Italian text in *Letter*, 124.

3. See 'a Sonet written in prayse of the brown beautie' in *Flowers*, 228.

4. Laneham, 17.

5. Ibid.

6. Ibid. 18.

7. Ibid.

8. Ibid.

9. *Princely Pleasures*, 102.

10. Ibid. 96.

11. Ibid. 97-100.

12. Laneham, 20-21.

13. *Princely Pleasures*, 96.

14. Ibid. 100-101.

15. *The Princelye Pleasures at the Courte at Kenelwoorth*, 30.

16. *Princely Pleasures*, 107.

17. Ibid.

18. Cited in *Letter*, 91.

7. The mermaid and the dolphin

1. *Princely Pleasures*, 102.

2. Laneham, 21.

3. Ibid.

4. Ibid. 22.

5. Ibid. 23.

6. Ibid. 24.

7 . Ibid.

8. Ibid.

9. *Princely Pleasures*, 95. Gascoigne's description applies to the display on the second night, but his memory is likely to have been at fault.

10. Ibid. 106.

11. Laneham, 26.

12. Ibid. 27.

13. Irene Potter describes it as 'local people performing a rather humorous version of an ancient country custom...in honour of its being St. Kenelm's day.' See *Queen Elizabeth I visits Kenilworth, 1575*, 32.

14. Laneham, 32.

15. Ibid. 33.

16. Ibid. 34.

17. For an account of possible editions which Captain Cox may have owned of each title, see *Letter*, Appendix G.

18. See *Ben Jonson: The Sad Shepherd, The Fall of Mortimer, Masques and Entertainments*, 781-6.

19. See Griffin, 'The Breaking of the Giants: Historical Drama in Coventry and London', 7.

20. Laneham, 38.

21. Ibid.

22. *Princely Pleasures*, 106.

23. Kuin points out that Arthur Bassett 'already appears as a knight on February 7th of this year, six months or so before his supposed elevation at Kenilworth.' See *Letter*, 101.

24. Laneham, 44-45.

25. *The Diary of Henry Machyn, Citizen and Merchant-Taylor of London, from A.D. 1550 to A.D. 1563*, edited by John Gough Nichols (London, 1848).

26. *Ungentle Shakespeare*, 12.   Her suggestion that Shakespeare read *A Letter* and Gascoigne's *Princely Pleasures* when he was a child is one I find unconvincing, as I am sceptical that copies of either work ever found their way to Stratford-upon-Avon in the 1570s. I also doubt if he read *A Letter* as an adult, since even the second edition was probably a rare and obscure book. Had Shakespeare done so, I would

have expected him to incorporate at least some of the author's unusual vocabulary into his plays.

27. *Shakespeare and the Idea of the Play*, 139.

28. Greenblatt, 48.

29. *Robert Laneham's Letter*, 1-2. In *The Winter's Tale* July is a month associated with happiness and carefree fun between a boy and his father (1.2.169)

30. Laneham, 41.

31. *Princely Pleasures*, 103.

32. Laneham, 42.

33. Greenblatt, 48.

34. *Princely Pleasures*, 104.

35. Laneham, 42.

36. Ibid.

37. *Princely Pleasures*, 104.

38. Greenblatt, 46.

39. BL MSS Harley 6395   This manuscript consists of 'Merry Passages & Jeasts' and includes a second unsourced story about Goldyngham, describing how he encouraged his wife to mount the horse of a nobleman who admired her, then slapped the horse, causing it to gallop off. Goldyngham ran after them, shouting with mock-indignation that the nobleman was running away with his wife. These anecdotes were collected by Sir Nicholas L'Estrange of Hunstanton, who died in 1669. Stephen Greenblatt erroneously describes L'Estrange's manuscript as 'an unpublished contemporary account of the festivities' (Greenblatt, 49).

40. *Princely Pleasures*, 106.

41. Laneham, 43.

42. *Princely Pleasures*, 105.

43. Laneham, 45.

44. See J.W. Binns, 'Shakespeare's Latin Citations: The Editorial Problem', 122.

8. The masque in The Chase

1. Edward Arber (ed), *Certayne Notes of Instruction in English Verse, The Steele Glas, The Complaynt of Philomene*, 20.

2. 'George Gascoigne and *The Noble Arte of Venerie*', 485.

3. *The Complete Poems of George Gascoigne*, Vol. I. xxv.

4. R.J.P. Kuin (*Letter*, 89) wrongly identifies the publisher as 'H. Bynneman'.

5. 'George Gascoigne, *The Noble Arte of Venerie*, and Queen Elizabeth at Kenilworth', 654.

6. Irene Potter, Op. Cit.

7. Cited in Alan Stewart, *Philip Sidney: A Double Life*, 149.

8. See *A Hundreth Sundrie Flowres*, 301-312.

9. 'George Gascoigne, *The Noble Arte of Venerie*, and Queen Elizabeth at Kenilworth'

10. For a lengthy analysis of these woodcuts, which argues that they 'create a symbolic narrative of courtly desire, assertion, and fulfillment', see Stephen Hamrick, ' "Set in portraiture": George Gascoigne, Queen Elizabeth, and Adapting the Royal Image', *Early Modern Literary Studies* 11.1 (May, 2005), 1-30.

11. 'George Gascoigne, *The Noble Arte of Venerie*, and Queen Elizabeth at Kenilworth'

9. Crisis

1. Laneham, 37.
2. Ibid. 38.
3. Ibid, 45.
4. *Princely Pleasures*, 106.
5. Ibid, 107.
6. Ibid.
7. Ibid. 120.
8. Laneham, 46.
9. *Princely Pleasures*, 120.
10. Jenkins, 198.
11. *Princely Pleasures*, 109.
12. Ibid. 114.
13. Ibid. 119.
14. Ibid.120.
15. Laneham, 46.
16. *Princely Pleasures*, 120.
17. Laneham, 56.
18. *Princely Pleasures*, 128.
19. Laneham, 45.

20. *Princely Pleasures*, 120.
21. Ibid.
22. Ibid.

10. Sylvanus
1. Laneham, 56.
2. *Princely Pleasures*, 121.
3. Ibid. 124.
4. Ibid. 121.
5. Ibid. 122.
6. Ibid. 122-3.
7. Ibid. 123.
8. Ibid.
9. Ibid. 124-5.
10. Ibid. 125.
11. Ibid. 127.
12. Ibid. 126.
13. Ibid. 127.
14. Ibid. 128-9.
15. Ibid. 130.
16. Ibid. 131.
17. Ibid.

11. The great hoax
1. *Ungentle Shakespeare*, 10. However, in his Oxford Shakespeare edition of the play, Peter Holland sceptically notes that eleven different weddings have been proposed as the occasion of the first performance of *A Midsummer Night's Dream* (112).
2. Laneham, p. 29.
3. Ibid. 40.
4. Ibid. 39.
5. Ibid. 30.
6. Ibid. 27.
7. Ibid. 46.
8. Ibid. 47.
9. See *Flowers*, 423, 439-54.
10. Laneham, 48.

11. Strype's *Survey of London*, cited in *The Progresses and Public Processions of Queen Elizabeth* Vol. II, 200.

12. Laneham, 76-7.

13. Ibid. 26.

14. Ibid. 79.

15. Ibid. 32

16. Ibid.

17. Ibid, 38-9.

18. Ibid. 77.

19. Ibid. 78.

20. Ibid. 77.

21. Ibid. 63-4.

22. Cited Scott, 299.

23. *Kenilworth*, 169.

24. Cited O'Kill, 35.

25. *Robert Laneham's Letter*, x.

26. See 'Note F – Robert Laneham' in *Kenilworth* (Collins' Clear-Type Press edition), 494.

27. *Kenilworth*, 168-9.

28. New STC 15190.5, commonly known as the A edition, and New STC 15191, known as B. Three copies of A are known to exist (at the Bodleian Library, Harvard and Emmanuel College, Cambridge), and fourteen of B. For an authoritative discussion of the problems and arguments surrounding these editions see 'Textual Introduction', *Letter*, 17-32.

29. Laneham, 24-5.

30. Ibid. 86.

31. Ibid. 84-5.

32. *Flowers*, 199.

12. Woodstock

1. Jenkins, 124.

2. Ibid. 125.

3. Cited ibid. 212.

4. My account of what happened at Woodstock is drawn from *The Queenes Majesties Entertainment at Woodstocke* (1585) and Gascoigne's 'The Tale of Hemetes the Heremyte' (in *Princely Pleasures*, 473-510).

13. A satirist unmasked

1. See O'Kill, 41-3.
2. *The Queen's Majesty's Entertainment at Woodstock 1575*, v-vi.
3. Greenblatt, 43.
4. *The Rise of the Common Player*, 143.
5. Ibid, 145.
6. Ibid, 143-4.
7. Cecil Papers 8/52.
8. O'Kill, 35.
9. Kuin, 124.
10. *Flowers*, xvii.
11. 'The Breaking of the Giants: Historical Drama in Coventry and London', 5.
12. *Philip Sidney: A Double Life*, 145. A fresh contribution to the debate has been announced for later in 2008 but remains unpublished as this book goes to press: Elizabeth Goldring, '"A mercer ye wot az we be": The Authorship of the Kenilworth *Letter* Reconsidered', *ELR: English Literary Renaissance,* 38.2 (2008), 1-25.

14. The mysterious *Pastime of the Progress*

1. See *1599: A Year in the Life of William Shakespeare*, 54 and 162.
2. *That Shakespeherian Rag*, 106.
3. Kuin, 123.
4. Ibid. 123-4.
5. Ibid. 124n.
6. *Flowers*, 144.
7. Ibid. 460.
8. Ibid. 458.
9. Cunliffe, *George Gascoigne: The Glasse of Government, The Princely Pleasures at Kenelworth Castle, The Steele Glas and other poems and prose works*, 437.
10. *Gascoigne's Princely Pleasures*, J.H. Burn edition, v-vi.

15. Subterranean textual blues

1. O'Kill, 38.
2. Ibid. 37.

3. Kuin, 127.
4. Laneham, 21-23.
5. O'Kill, 40.
6. Ibid. 39.
7. Laneham, 80-81.
8. O'Kill, 39-40.
9. *Princely Pleasures*, 95.
10. Kuin, 88
11. Ibid. 125.
12. Laneham, 83.
13. See *Acts of the Privy Council of England*, Vol. IX, 4-11.
14. Laneham, 83.
15. Kuin, 123.

16. Gaudina and Contarenus
1. Prouty, 223.

17. Philip Sidney's revenge
1. Cited in Alan Stewart, *Philip Sidney: A Double Life*, 127.
2. Ibid.
3. Katherine Duncan-Jones, *Sir Philip Sidney: Courtier Poet*, xii.
4. Ibid. 94.
5. *Defence of Poesie, Astrophil and Stella and other writings*, 84.
6. Ibid. 118.
7. Ibid. 120.
8. Ibid, 119.
9. Jenkins, 295.
10. *Sir Philip Sidney and the English Renaissance*, 14.
11. Ibid. 16.
12. *Defence of Poesie, Astrophil and Stella and other writings*, 123.
13. Ibid, 122.
14. Ibid, 121.
15. Ibid, 122.
16. Ibid, 118, 124.
17. T.C. Smout, *A History of the Scottish People*, 172.
18. *Flowers*, 454.

19. Ibid, 733.
20. Eriksen, 'George Gascoigne's and Mary Sidney's Versions of Psalm 130', 1-9.
21. *Philip Sidney: A Double Life*, 4.
22. Ibid, 2.
23. *English Literature Excluding Drama*, 268-9.
24. *Lives of the Poets*, 146.
25. *Sir Philip Sidney and the English Renaissance*, 81-2.
26. *Defence of Poesie, Astrophil and Stella and other writings*, 7.
27. *Flowers*, 455.

18. The Protheus anomaly

1. See E.A.J. Honigmann, *Shakespeare: the 'lost years'*.
2. Schoenbaum, 115.
3. *Shakespeare in Warwickshire*, 74.
4. Honan, 63.
5. Op Cit, 81.
6. Ibid.
7. Cited in Schoenbaum, 145-6.
8. *Shakespeare: The Biography*, 21.
9. Honan, 122.

19. 'counterfeit supposes'

1. Cited *The Second Part of King Henry IV*, xxxviii.
2. Cited ibid, xvii.
3. 'Gascoigne's *Posies* as a Shakespearean source', *Notes and Queries* (December 2000), 444-9. Interestingly, Prior shows that Shakespeare's eye wandered across to the poem which followed the Montague masque, 'The refusal of a lover', and used material from that, too. This confirms that Shakespeare's edition of Gascoigne was almost certainly the *Whole woorkes* of 1587 and not *A Hundreth Sundry Flowers*, where the poem is located (under a different title) much earlier in the volume than the masque. Shakespeare is unlikely to have been able to obtain a copy of the *Posies* more than a decade after it was suppressed.
4. *Flowers*, 281.
5. Ibid, 108.
6. Ibid, 107.

7. Ibid, 139.
8. Cited ibid, 513.
9. Cited ibid.
10. Ibid, 23.
11. Ibid, 29.
12. Ibid, 7.
13. Ibid, 38.
14. Ibid, 242.
15. Ibid, 215.
16. Cited ibid, 476.
17. *Princely Pleasures*, 62.
18. *George Gascoigne*, 157.

20. The secret voice of Shakespeare

1. *Flowers*, 260-2.
2. *Shakespeare's Sonnets*, 95-6.
3. *Flowers*, 455.
4. Ibid, 457-8.
5. Hyder Edward Rollins (ed), *A New Variorum Edition of Shakespeare: The Sonnets*, cited in *Berryman's Shakespeare*, 289.
6. *101 Sonnets from Shakespeare to Heaney*, 113.
7. *Berryman's Shakespeare*, 285.
8. Honan, 183.
9. Ibid, ,360.
10. *Flowers*, 365.
11. Ibid, 142.
12. *Certayne Notes of Instruction in English Verse, The Steele Glas, The Complaynt of Philomene*, 57.
13. *The Art of Shakespeare's Sonnets*, 310.
14. *The Oxford Shakespeare: The Complete Sonnets and Poems*, 512.
15. *The Sonnets and A Lover's Complaint*, 257.

21. Elsinore's ghosts

1. Shapiro, 308.
2. Ibid. 29.
3. *Shakespeare For All Time*, 8.
4. Shapiro, 354.

5. Ibid. 355.
6. For a detailed discussion of the status of the three texts see Appendix 2 of the Thompson and Taylor edition.
7. Greenblatt, 311.
8. Arden3 *Hamlet*, 559.
9. *Shakespeare's Language*, 100.
10. Arden3 *Hamlet* (2.2.461n).
11. Shapiro, 351.
12. *Ungentle Shakespeare*, 152.
13. *Shakespeare's Language*, 98.
14. Arden3 *Hamlet* (2.2.109-10n).
15. Ibid. (3.1.74n).
16. Ibid. (1.5.77n).
17. Arden3, 37.
18 For a detailed discussion of the dating of *Hamlet* see Thompson and Taylor, 36-59.
19. *Flowers*, 228.
20. Cited in Prouty, 278.
21. Ibid. 282.
22. Arden3 *Hamlet* (5.1.169-70n).
23. *Shakespeare For All Time*, 51.
24. Honan, 101.
25. New Swan *Hamlet* (ed Lott), 74.
26. *Shakespeare's Language*, 111.
27. *Shakespeare and the Idea of the Play*, 140.
28. Ibid. 155.

22. 'this bare island'

1. In his edition of *Macbeth* A.R. Braunmuller cites this version from the 1587 edition of Gascoigne's *Whole woorkes*, which is almost certainly the edition Shakespeare used.
2. *Flowers*, 215.
3. Penguin *Macbeth*, 26.
4. See *Flowers*, 312-16.
5. Greenblatt, 291.
6. Ibid, 373.
7. See Arden3 *Tempest*, 6.
8. Greenblatt, 377.

9. Arden3 *Tempest*, 19.

10. Arden3 *Two Noble Kinsmen*, 16. The play was co-authored with John Fletcher. Lois Potter argues against the theory of consecutive composition, suggesting that the collaboration involved 'minor adjustments and revisions that one writer may have made to another's work.' (25)

11. Ibid. 59.

12. *Flowers*, 215.

13. Ibid. 228.

23. Zabeta and the others

1. Quoted in Jenkins, 298.

2. 'Portraiture, Patronage, and the Progresses', 183.

3. Quoted in Eleanor Rosenberg, *Leicester: Patron of Letters*, 222.

4. Ibid. 294.

5. Quoted in Jenkins, 314.

6. *Defence of Poesie, Astrophil and Stella and other writings*, 12.

7. Jenkins, 303.

8. *Shakespeare*, 13.

9. 'Portraiture, Patronage, and the Progresses', 164n.

10. Quoted in John Nichols, *The Progresses and Public Processions of Queen Elizabeth*, Vol I, 93.

11. *Flowers*, 75.

Bibliography

Editions of *A Letter* cited

Robert Laneham (Ed. Frederick J. Furnivall), *Robert Laneham's Letter* (London: Kegan Paul, Trench, Trübner & Co, 1890)

- (Ed. with an Introduction by F.J. Furnivall), *Robert Laneham's Letter: Describing a Part of the Entertainment unto Queen Elizabeth at the Castle of Kenilworth in 1575* (London: Chatto & Windus, 1907)

- *A Letter [1575]* (Menston: Scolar Press, 1968) This is a facsimile edition of edition B (New STC 15191) held at the Huntington Library.

- Robert Langham (with Introduction, Notes and Commentary by R.J.P. Kuin), *A Letter* (Leiden: E.J. Brill, 1983) This text is based on edition A (New STC 15190.5), using the copy held at Emmanuel College, Cambridge.

Editions of George Gascoigne's works cited

The Noble Arte of Venerie and Hunting (London: Christopher Barker, 1575)

- Edited with an Introduction and Commentary by G.W. Pigman III), *A Hundreth Sundrie Flowres* (Oxford: Oxford University Press, 2000)

- *Gascoigne's Princely Pleasures with the Masque intended to have been presented before Queen Elizabeth at Kenilworth Castle in 1575; with an introductory memoir and notes* (London: J.H. Burn, 1821)

- *The Princelye Pleasures at the Courte at Kenelwoorth* (London: F. Marshall, 1821)

- Edited by Edward Arber, *Certayne Notes of Instruction in English Verse, The Steele Glas, The Complaynt of Philomene* preceded by George Whetstone's *A Remembrance of the well imployed Life, and godly end of George Gascoigne Esquire, etc.* (London: A. Constable & Co, 1901)

- Edited by John W. Cunliffe, *George Gascoigne: The Glasse of Government, The Princely Pleasures at Kenelworth Castle, The Steele Glas and other poems and prose works* (Cambridge: Cambridge University Press, 1910)

\- Edited, with a memoir and notes by William Carew Hazlitt, *The Complete Poems of George Gascoigne* (Roxburghe Library, 1869-70)

Editions of Shakespeare's poems cited
Shakespeare's Sonnets, edited with analytic commentary by Stephen Booth (New Haven and London: Yale Nota Bene, 2000)
\- *The Complete Sonnets and Poems*, edited by Colin Burrow (Oxford: Oxford University Press, 2002)
\- *Shakespeare's Sonnets*, edited by Katherine Duncan-Jones (London: Arden Shakespeare, 2001)
\- *'The Sonnets' and 'A Lover's Complaint'*, edited by John Kerrigan (London: Penguin Books, 1999)
\- *Shakespeare's Sonnets*, edited with an Introduction and Commentary by Martin Seymouth-Smith (London: Heinemann, 1967)
\- Helen Vendler, *The Art of Shakespeare's Sonnets*, (Cambridge, Massachusetts: Harvard University Press, 1999)

Editions of Shakespeare's plays cited
(Introduction by Doug Moston*), Mr. William Shakespeares Comedies, Histories, & Tragedies: A Facsimile of the First Folio* (New York & London: Routledge, 1998)
William Shakespeare: Complete Works (RSC Shakespeare, ed. Jonathan Bate and Eric Rasmussen, 2007)
Antony and Cleopatra (Arden, ed. John Wilders, 1995)
Cymbeline (Oxford, ed. Roger Warren, 1998)
Hamlet (Longman, ed. Bernard Lott, 1975)
\- (Arden, ed. Ann Thompson and Neil Taylor, 2006)
King Henry IV, Part Two (Arden, ed. A.R. Humphreys, 1966)
King Henry VIII (Oxford, ed. Jay L. Halio, 2000)
King Lear (Oxford, ed. Stanley Wells, 2000)
Love's Labour's Lost (Arden, ed. H.R. Woudhuysen, 1998)
Macbeth (Cambridge University Press, ed. A.R. Braunmuller, 1997)
The Merry Wives of Windsor (Penguin, ed. G.R. Hibbard, 1973)
\- (Arden, ed. Giorgio Melchiori, 2000)
A Midsummer Night's Dream (Oxford, ed. Peter Holland, 1998)
Pericles (Arden, ed. Suzanne Gossett, 2004)

Richard III (Oxford, ed. John Jowett, 2000)
Romeo and Juliet (Oxford, ed. Jill L. Levenson, 2000)
The Tempest (Arden, ed. Virginia Mason Vaughan and Alden T. Vaughan and Alden T. Vaughan, 2005)
Titus Andronicus (Arden, ed. Jonathan Bate, 2003)
Twelfth Night (Arden, ed. J.M. Lothian and T.W. Craik, 1975)
The Two Gentlemen of Verona (Arden, ed. William C. Carroll, 2005)
The Two Noble Kinsmen (Arden, ed. Lois Potter, 1997)
The Winter's Tale (Arden, ed. J.H.P. Pafford, 1976)

Secondary sources

Peter Ackroyd, *Shakespeare: The Biography* (London: Chatto & Windus, 2005)

Anon. (with an introduction by A.W. Pollard), *The Queen's Majesty's Entertainment at Woodstock 1575* (Oxford: H. Daniel and H. Hart, 1910)

- (ed. J.H. Cunliffe), *The Queenes Majesties Entertainment at Woodstocke*, P.M.L.A., New Series Vol. XIX (1911), 92-141.

- *A Guide to Kenilworth, containing a brief historical account of the Castle, Priory, and Church* (Merridew & Son; no date or place of publication)

- *A Guide to Kenilworth Castle containing a brief Account of its Ancient History* (Coventry: H. Merridew, no date)

Susan Bassnett, *Elizabeth I: A Feminist Perspective* (Oxford: Berg, 1989)

John Berryman (Edited and introduced by John Haffenden), *Berryman's Shakespeare* (New York: Farrar, Straus and Giroux, 1999)

J.W. Binns, 'Shakespeare's Latin Citations: The Editorial Problem', *Shakespeare Survey* XXXV (1982), 119-28.

- *Intellectual Culture in Elizabethan and Jacobean England: The Latin Writings of the Age* (Leeds: Francis Cairns, 1990)

M.C. Bradbrook, *The Rise of the Common Player: A Study of Actor and Society in Shakespeare's England* (London: Chatto & Windus, 1962)

Leicester Bradner, 'The First English Novel: A Study of George Gascoigne's *Adventures of Master F.J.*', P.M.L.A., Vol. XLV (1930), 543-52.

John Buxton, *Sir Philip Sidney and the English Renaissance* (London: Macmillan, 1965)

J.R. Dasent (ed.), *Acts of the Privy Council of England*, New Series, Vol. VIII (1571-1575). (Nendeln/Liechestein: Kraus, 1974)
- *Acts of the Privy Council of England*, New Series, Vol. IX (1575-1577), (London: H.M.S.O., 1894)

Katherine Duncan-Jones, *Sir Philip Sidney: Courtier Poet* (London: Hamish Hamilton, 1991)
- *Ungentle Shakespeare: Scenes from his Life* (London: Arden Shakespeare, 2001)

Mark Eccles, *Shakespeare in Warwickshire* (Madison: University of Wisconsin Press, 1963)

Roy T. Eriksen, 'George Gascoigne's and Mary Sidney's Versions of Psalm 130', *Cahiers Élisabéthains* No. 36 (October 1989), 1-9.

Elizabeth Goldring, 'Portraiture, Patronage, and the Progresses: Robert Dudley, Earl of Leicester, and the Kenilworth Festivities of 1575' in Jayne Elisabeth Archer, Elizabeth Goldring and Sarah Knight, *The Progresses, Pageants, and Entertainments of Queen Elizabeth I* (Oxford: O.U.P., 2007), 163-88.
- 'The Earl of Leicester's Inventory of Kenilworth Castle, *c*.1578', *English Heritage Historical Review*, 2 (2007), 37-59.

Germaine Greer, *Shakespeare* (Oxford: Oxford University Press, 1986)

Benjamin Griffin, 'The Breaking of the Giants: Historical Drama in Coventry and London', *English Literary Renaissance*, Vol. 29 (1999), 3-21.

Stephen Hamrick, ' "Set in portraiture": George Gascoigne, Queen Elizabeth, and Adapting the Royal Image', *Early Modern Literary Studies* 11.1 (May, 2005) 1.1-30.

Terence Hawkes, *That Shakespeherian Rag: Essays on a Critical Process* (London: Methuen, 1986)

Mary E. Hazard, 'A Magnificent Lord: Leicester, Kenilworth, and Transformations in the Idea of Magnificence', *Cahiers Élisabéthains* No. 31 (April 1987), 11-35

Park Honan, *Shakespeare: A Life* (Oxford: Oxford University Press, 1999

Betty Hill, 'Trinity College Cambridge MS. B. 14. 52, and William Patten', *Transactions of the Cambridge Bibliographical Society*, 4 (1964-68), 192-200.

265

E.A.J. Honigmann, *Shakespeare: the 'lost years'* (Manchester:
   Manchester University Press, 1985)
Elizabeth Jenkins, *Elizabeth and Leicester* (London: Phoenix Press,
   2002)
Ronald C. Johnson, *George Gascoigne* (New York: Twayne, 1972)
Ben Jonson (ed. C.H. Herford Percy and Evelyn Simpson), *Ben Jonson:
   The Sad Shepherd, The Fall of Mortimer, Masques and
   Entertainments*, Vol. VII (Oxford: Oxford University Press, 1952)
Frank Kermode, *Shakespeare's Language* (London: Penguin Books,
   2001)
R.J.P. Kuin, 'The Purloined *Letter*: Evidence and Probability Regarding
   Robert Langham's Authorship', *The Library*, 7 (1985), 115-25.
C.S. Lewis, *English literature in the sixteenth century excluding drama*
   (Oxford: Oxford University Press, 1954)
Richard K. Morris, 'A Plan for Kenilworth Castle at Longleat', *English
   Heritage Historical Review*, 2 (2007), 23-35.
Ilana Nash, ' "A Subject without Subjection": Robert Dudley, Earl of
   Leicester, and *The Princely Pleasures at Kenelworth Castle*,'
   Comitatus, Vol. 25 (1994), 81-102.
Charles Nicholl, *The Lodger: Shakespeare on Silver Street* (London:
   Allen Lane, 2007)
John Nichols, *The Progresses and Public Processions of Queen
   Elizabeth* Vols. I and   II (London: Society of Antiquaries, 1788)
   -     *Progresses and Public Processions of Queen Elizabeth* Vol.
   III (London: John Nichols & Son, 1805)
Brian O'Kill, 'The Printed Works of William Patten', *Transactions of
   the Cambridge Bibliographical Society*, 7 (1977), 28-45.
D.M. Palliser, *The Age of Elizabeth: England under the later Tudors
   1547-1603* (London and NewYork: Longman, 1992)
Don Paterson (Ed., with an introduction), *101 Sonnets from
   Shakespeare to Heaney* (London: Faber and Faber, 1999)
[William Patten], *The Calender of Scripture* [London: 1575]
Irene Potter, *Queen Elizabeth I visits Kenilworth, 1575* (Kenilworth:
   Kenilworth History & Archaelogy Society, 1975)
Roger Prior, 'Gascoigne's *Posies* as a Shakespearean source', *Notes
   and Queries* (December 2000), 444-9.
Charles and Ruth Prouty, 'George Gascoigne, *The Noble Arte of
   Venerie*, and Queen Elizabeth at Kenilworth' in James G.

McManaway, Giles E. Dawson and Edwin E. Willoughby (eds), *Joseph Quincy Adams: Memorial Studies* (Washington: Folger Shakespeare Library, 1948), 639-665.

C.T. Prouty, *George Gascoigne: Elizabethan Courtier, Soldier, and Poet* (New York: Benjamin Blom, 1966)

Derek Renn, *Kenilworth Castle* (English Heritage, 2003)

Anne Righter, *Shakespeare and the Idea of the Play* (Harmondsworth: Penguin Books, 1967)

Jean Robertson, "George Gascoigne and *The Noble Arte of Venerie*", *Modern Language Review*, Vol. 27 (1942), 484-5.

Eleanor Rosenberg, *Leicester: Patron of Letters* (New York: Octagon Books, 1976)

Alexander Schmidt, *Shakespeare Lexicon and Quotation Dictionary* (New York: Dover, 1971)

Michael Schmidt, *Lives of the Poets* (London: Phoenix, 1999)

S. Schoenbaum, *William Shakespeare: A Compact Documentary Life* (Oxford: Oxford University Press, 1987)

Philip Sidney (Edited by Elizabeth Porges Watson), *Defence of Poesie, Astrophil and Stella and other writings* (London: Everyman, 1999)

David Scott, 'William Patten and the Authorship of "Robert Laneham's Letter" (1575', *English Literary Renaissance*, 7 (1977), 297-306.

Walter Scott (Edited with an introduction by J.H. Alexander), *Kenilworth: A Romance* (London: Penguin Books, 1999)

-        *Kenilworth* (London & Glasgow: Collins' Clear-Type Press, n.d.)

T.C. Smout, *A History of the Scottish People 1560-1830* (London: Fontana/Collins, 1979)

Virginia F. Stern, *Gabriel Harvey: A Study of His Life, Marginalia, and Library* (Oxford: Oxford University Press, 1979)

Alan Stewart, *Philip Sidney: A Double Life* (London: Chatto & Windus, 2000)

Gary Taylor, *Reinventing Shakespeare: A Cultural History from the Restoration to the Present* (London: The Hogarth Press, 1990)

Alison Weir, *Elizabeth the Queen* (London: Jonathan Cape, 1998)

Stanley Wells, *Shakespeare: For All Time* (London: Macmillan, 2002)

A. N. Wilson, *A Life of Walter Scott* (London: Pimlico, 2002)

Index

Ackroyd, Peter 173
Admiral's Men 230
Antwerp 176, 232
Apollo 113
Archer, Frederick Scott 13
Arion 67, 68, 69, 70, 173, 216, 225, 226
Ariosto, Lodovico 28, 184-6
Arte of English Poesie, The 162
Arte of Rhetorique, The 159
Arthur, King 38, 57, 232
Arthurian legend 23, 82
Ascham, Roger 159
Awdely, John 117

Bacon, Francis 125
Bacon, Sir Nicholas 27, 106
Badger, John 23, 26, 38, 172, 232
Ballard, J.G. 199
Banks, Iain M. 133
banquet 59, 98, 115, 173, 218
barge 6, 53, 67, 68
Barker, Christopher 75, 190
bear-baiting 58, 200
bears 7, 14, 53, 83, 158, 219, 223, 224, 227
Bedford, Earl of 28, 106, 136, 232
Berryman, John 192
Bible, the 10, 24, 137, 138, 180
Binns, J.W. 252n
Black Prince 102
Blackfriars 62, 225
Bompstead, Christopher 119
Book of Faulconrie, or Hawking 75
Borges, Jorge Luis 155
Boulogne 58
Bradbrook, M. C. 105, 119
Breton, Elizabeth 27,
Breton, Nicholas 161
British Library 76, 152,
Browne, Anthony (Viscount Montague) 81
Bruce, Sir 54, 82
Buchanan, George 163

Burbage, James 171-3, 176, 214, 231
Burbage, Richard 171, 172, 203, 214
Burbage, William 173
Burghley, Lord 24, 60, 85, 89, 91, 106, 108, 116, 120-2, 127, 135-6, 145, 146, 148, 232
Burrow, Colin 197
Buxton, John 161-2, 165

Cambridge 26, 27, 75, 120, 125, 136, 181, 211
Cambridge University 23, 71
Carey, Henry (Lord Hunsdon) 97
Cecil, Thomas 60
Cecil, William See Burghley, Lord
censorship 31, 78, 118, 129, 130, 195, 232
E.K. Chambers 58, 183
Charlewood, John 117
Chartley Park 109
The Chase 5, 8, 9, 19, 22, 46, 47, 66, 73, 74, 78, 79, 95, 153, 240, 242, 253
Chaucer 160, 227
Cheshire 168
Codrus 99 148
Contarenus 112, 114, 149
Copy of a Letter, The 125, 161, 232
Court of Requests 121
Coventry, 5, 13, 23, 35, 36, 56, 58, 59, 84, 166, 219
Coventry players 56-9, 84
Cowdrey Park 81
Cox, Captain 56-8
Croftes, Sir James 146
Cunliffe, J.W. 74
dancing 7, 22, 26, 27, 39, 44, 53, 59, 81, 181
Davies, Sir John 162
deer hunting 46, 53, 73-83
Defoe, Daniel 30, 135
Dethick, Henry 159
Diana 17, 84, 85, 226
Dolce, Lodovico 182

dolphin 60, 66-7, 69, 70-71, 169, 172-3, 213, 216, 219, 222, 224-5
Donizetti, Gaetano 13
Donne, John 165
Dormer, Sir William 81
Drummond, William 157
Dudley, Robert See under Leicester, Earl of
Duncan-Jones, Katherine 62, 97, 158, 191, 206, 212
Dyer, Edward 116

Eccles, Mark 168, 171
Echo 47-52, 103
Elizabeth I
    and the Countess of Essex 109, 232; and the Coventry players 56-9, 84; and the end of the revels 85ff; and Lady of the Lake 40; and the wild man 46-52; and hunting 78-83; arrival at Kenilworth 36ff, 217-8; death 233; in Gascoigne drawing 153-6; relationship with Robert Dudley 19-21, 97, 229, 233

Elsinore 89, 199-201, 204, 212, 216-17, 249
English Heritage 8, 104
Epistulae Morales 69
Eriksen, Roy T. 164
Essex, Countess of 44, 109
Euripedes 181-2

Faerie Queene, The 82
Famous Victories of Henry V, The 177
Feersum Endjinn 133
Field, Richard 62
Ferrers, George 23, 25, 55, 172
Finham Brook 70
Fireworks 18, 19, 33, 39, 40, 41, 45, 50, 59, 60, 67, 87, 93, 145, 196-7, 209, 212-13, 215, 220-1
First Folio 190, 201-3, 205
Furnivall F.J. 65, 105

Gascoigne, George 23, 25-6, 28, 33, 37, 42, 44, 47, 49-50, 68, 74-6, 78, 83, 85-6, 90, 92, 100-1, 114, 116, 118, 129-31, 143, 154, 157, 159, 163, 176, 178-9, 181-2, 188, 196, 198, 208, 211, 215, 218-21, 227, 232, 234
The Adventures of Master F.J 30, 34, 131, 164
Certayne notes of Instruction 131, 158, 164, 191-2
Complaint of Philomene 176
The Drum of Doomsday 74, 131
The fruites of Warre 197
Glass of Government 163, 176, 188, 189, 190, 219
A Hundreth Sundry Flowers 29, 78, 129, 130, 162, 165, 190, 193, 239
Jocasta 28, 30, 38, 154, 157, 163, 182-4, 212, 234
The Noble Arte of Venerie and Hunting 74, 75, 77, 82
The Posies of George Gascoigne, Esquire 129, 130, 158, 176, 232
The princelye pleasures at the Courte at Kenelwoorth 11-12, 25, 45, 50, 55, 59, 62-3, 78-9, 90, 118-19, 121, 128-9, 151, 174, 176
The Steele Glas 83, 100, 155, 176, 196-7, 237, 242, 246, 249, 261
Supposes 28, 30, 184, 187
Whole woorkes 50, 118, 176
POEMS
'Eyther a needelesse or a bootleesse comparison betwene two letters' 27
'Gascoigne's voyage into Holland' 32
'The greene Knights farewell to Fansie' 31, 179, 210, 211
'The lover encouraged by former examples, determineth to make vertue of necessitie' 191
'Phillip Sparrow' 30
'a Sonet written in prayse of the brown beautie' 46, 211, 228

Gascoigne, Sir William 176-8,
Gaudina 112-14, 149
Giocasta 182
Globe theatre 16, 62, 154, 201, 214,
    215, 216, 223, 227
Gloucester 169, 199
Goldring, Elizabeth 229, 234, 256n
Goldyngham, Henry 23-4, 57, 143,
    172, 174, 230
Gorboduc 163, 182-3
Gray's Inn 23, 24, 26, 153, 174, 177-
8, 180-1, 184
Great Mere (see Kenilworth Castle)
Greene, Robert 206
Greenblatt, Stephen 63, 67, 118, 202,
    220-4
Greer, Germaine 233
Grey, Lord 197, 232
Griffin, Benjamin 58, 124
Groats-worth of Wit 206
Guaras, Antonio de 52, 109

Hackney 135
Hamlett, Katherine 206
Harvey, Gabriel 159, 211
Hatfield House 121
Hathaway, Anne 168
Hawkes, Terence 125
Hazlitt, William 75, 83
Hemetes 111, 112, 113, 151, 154, 156
Henry V 6, 168, 176, 177
Henry VIII 6, 41, 58, 151, 168
Herbert, George 165
Hercules 38, 39, 48, 172, 191, 232
hermits 111-16, 151, 153
Hill, Betty 120, 123
Hitchcock, Alfred 199
Hoghton family 168
Honan, Park 64
Hunnis, William 23, 24, 55, 66, 172,
    230
*Hunnies Recreations: conteining foure
godlie discourses* 230
Hyve Full of Honye, A 230

Inchford Brook 70

Inns of Court 29, 180, 181
Iris 84, 86, 87, 89, 214, 226, 228
Isle of Dogs 178
Islington 100

Jenkins, Elizabeth 161
John, King 6, 168
John of Gaunt 6, 102
Johnes, Richard 128, 129
Johnson, Ronald C 189
Johnson, William 172
Jones, Davi 167
Jonson, Ben 57, 58, 157, 178
Jove 84, 224, 226
Juno 84, 85, 87, 89, 95, 226

Kenilworth (novel) 1, 11-17, 68
Kenilworth Castle 5-15, 23, 25, 35,
    37-8, 43, 62, 64-5, 71, 92-3, 105,
    134, 142, 165, 167, 169-72, 190,
    200, 209, 213, 216, 218-19, 228-9,
    233, 236
base (outer) court 39, 40, 53, 56, 57,
    59, 213, 219
battlement 5, 37, 39, 201, 218
Brays 37, 70
Caesar's Tower (Norman Keep) 5, 6,
    8, 39, 41, 43, 47, 235
Clock 47, 56, 101, 217
curtain wall 5, 6, 40
drawbridge 41, 48, 143, 233
garden 8, 22, 66, 91, 207
gatehouse 8, 9, 66, 68
Great Hall 5, 6, 13, 54, 59, 173
Great Mere 2, 5, 6, 8, 18, 22, 36, 39-
    40, 45, 53-4, 66, 73, 87, 98, 169,
    201, 213, 215, 224, 235
inner court 6, 41, 42, 53, 142
inventory 10, 38, 43, 125, 197
Leicester's Building 9, 42, 58, 59, 66,
91
Leicester's Gatehouse (north
    gatehouse) 53, 56, 66, 68
moat 5, 6, 37, 44, 56, 66, 71
parish church 44, 55, 136
Privy Chamber 59

stables 137, 142
Swan Tower 66-7, 71
Tiltyard 5, 39, 56
Kermode, Frank 203-4, 206, 215
Kerrigan, John 197
Kill Bill 203
Kinwelmershe, Francis 181-2
Knollys, Laetitia See Countess of
Essex
Knollyis, Sir Francis 110, 146
Kuin, R.J.P. 123-6, 128, 134, 144-5,
147
Kyd, Thomas 201

Lady of the Lake 40, 48, 53, 54, 66,
67, 68, 82, 98, 228
Lancashire 168-9
Laneham, Robert See Langham,
Robert
Langham, Robert 103-8, 117, 119,
121-6, 128, 132, 135, 137, 139,
140-51, 232
Lanham, John 119, 172
Lee, Sir Henry 111, 114, 149
Leicester, Robert Dudley, Earl of
and Kenilworth Castle 6-8, 10; and
Robert Langham 104-5, 142; and
1575 royal visit 10, 19, 22-3, 33-5; at
Woodstock 111-16; death 233; in
Netherlands 237; relationship with
Elizabeth 20-1, 97, 109; satirised in *A
Lette*r 101-3

Leicester's Commonwealth 21, 125
Leicester's Men 173, 175, 214, 230-1
Letter, A 11-13, 39, 45-6, 49, 51-69,
78, 84-91, 98-109, 117-29, 133-151,
175, 214, 228, 232, 235
Lewis, C.S. 165
Lichfield 110
Liu, Gordon 203
Lord Chamberlain 146, 205
Lott, Bernard 215

Machyn, Henry 60
Madox, Richard 188

Magdalen College 135
Malone, Edmond 171
Marlowe, Christopher 62, 121, 206-7
Martyn, Humphrey 103
Marvell, Andrew 107
masques 38, 40, 47, 50-1, 59, 68, 77-
82, 89, 113, 140, 149, 173, 179,
226, 230, 233
Mercury 75, 84, 86, 136, 214, 226
Meres, Francis 162
mermaid 60, 66-7, 69, 71
Mirrour for Magistrates, 160
Montague House 81
More, Thomas 151
Mulcaster, Richard 23, 26, 42, 144,
172, 230
music 14, 26-7, 42, 44, 53, 61, 67, 95,
181, 200, 218, 225, 226
musicians 53, 66-7, 92, 115, 128
mystery plays 167, 180

Nashe, Thomas 162, 178
Neptune 66, 225
Netherlands 29, 42, 55,164, 233
Nichols, John 12, 35
Norton, Thomas 182
nymphs 40, 67, 84, 226

O'Kill, Brian 123, 125, 134, 137, 141-
2
Oratio in laudem Poëseos 159
Oxford 15, 24, 35, 74, 135, 139, 181,
183, 187, 188, 232
Oxford University 26, 38

Palladis Tamia 162
Paris 19, 64, 74, 232
Pastime of the Progresse 124, 128,
130-2, 234
Paterson, Don 192
Patten, William 23, 24, 120, 122-7,
134-7, 139-46, 148, 151, 157, 171,
173, 225, 231, 235
The Calender of Scripture 24, 120,
123, 137-8, 140

The expedicion into Scotlāde 24, 135, 139, 146
Luctus consolatorius 231
A moorning diti 231
Supplicatio Patteni 140
Perkyn, John 172
Petrarch 30, 49, 163
Phaedra 69
Phoenissae (*The Phoenicean Women*) 182-3
Pigman, G.W. 124, 163
Pinkie campaign 24, 135
Pollard, A.W. 118
Positions 230
Prior, Roger 179
The princelye pleasures at the Courte at Kenelwoorth See under Gascoigne, George
Privy Council 18, 20, 28, 33, 35, 89, 91, 104, 109, 111, 122, 126, 145, 146, 150, 177
progress (royal) 18-19, 35-6, 59, 78, 91-2, 109, 111, 116, 118, 127-8, 146, 150-3, 166, 209, 230, 233-4
promontory 60, 70-1, 73, 168-9, 172, 215-6, 226, 228, 236
Prouty, C.T. 75, 77, 82-3, 154
Prouty, Ruth 77, 82-3
Psalms 24, 138, 163-4, 231
Pugliano, John Pietro 160
Purfoot, Thomas 75
Purlieu Lane 71, 73
Puttenham, George 162

Queenes Majesties Entertainment at Woodstocke, The 118

ragged staff 7, 22, 39, 41, 171, 230
Raimondi, Marcantonio 186
Ralegh, Sir Walter 165
revels 25, 28, 64, 71-2, 118, 128, 170, 181, 188, 220, 222, 226, 229, 235
Ricot 150
Righter, Anne 62, 215
Robertson, Jean 74, 75, 76
Robsart, Amy 11-17, 20-21, 102

Romano, Giulio 186

Sackville, Thomas 182
St Mary at Hill, Billingsgate 135-7
Schmidt, Michael 165
Schoenbaum, S. 168
Scholemaster, The 159
Scott, David 123, 124, 125, 139, 237
Scott, Sir Walter 11-17, 21, 23, 50, 68, 104-5, 123-5, 139
Seneca 69
Shakeshafte, William 168
Shakespeare, Anne 64
Shakespeare, Gilbert 64, 213
Shakespeare, Hamnet 168, 202, 210, 220, 222
Shakespeare, Henry 65, 213
Shakespeare, Joan 64
Shakespeare, John 62, 64, 65, 173, 209
Shakespeare, Judith 168
Shakespeare, Mary 64
Shakespeare, Richard 64
Shakespeare, Thomas 65
Shakespeare, William 7, 8, 12, 16, 17, 60, 61, 62, 63, 64, 65, 66, 67, 69, 70, 71, 72, 73, 74, 76, 97, 98, 108, 119, 162, 163, 165, 167, 168, 169, 170, 171, 172, 173, 174, 175, 176, 177, 179, 180, 185, 186, 187, 188, 190, 191, 192, 193, 195, 198, 199, 200, 201, 202, 203, 204, 205, 206, 207, 208, 209, 210, 211, 212, 213, 214, 215, 216, 217, 218, 219, 220, 221, 222, 223, 224, 225, 226, 227, 228, 229, 230, 235, 236, 237, 238, 239, 240, 242, 243, 244, 246, 248, 249, 250, 251, 252, 253, 264, 265, 266, 268

PLAYS
All's Well That Ends Well 189
Antony and Cleopatra 236
As You Like It 62, 206
Cymbeline 62
Hamlet 89, 153, 200-216, 218, 220-224, 226

272

Henry IV, Part One, 177
Henry IV, Part Two 176-7
Henry VI, Part Two 169
Henry VI, Part Three 168
Julius Caesar 201, 203
King Lear 222-3
Love's Labours Lost 63, 76
Macbeth, 187, 190, 217-20
The Merry Wives of Windsor 220-1
A Midsummer Night's Dream, 60, 63,
   69-73, 97, 170, 174, 179, 192, 224,
   225, 227
Richard II 217
Romeo and Juliet, 179
Taming of the Shrew 179, 184, 185,
   187, 212
The Tempest 223, 225, 226
Titus Andronicus 69, 73
Twelfth Night 69, 194
The Two Gentlemen of Verona 226
The Two Noble Kinsmen 226-8
The Winter's Tale 220
POEMS
Lucrece 62, 211
'The Phoenix and the Turtle' 204
Shakespeare's Sonnets 61, 191, 192,
   195, 198
Sonnet 66 195-8, 208
Sonnet 130 192
Venus and Adonis 17, 62

Shapiro, James 125, 199, 201, 205
Sheffield, Douglas 34, 109
Shepherd's Calendar, The 160
Shoreditch 173, 223
Sidney, Lady Mary 78, 147
Sidney, Mary 163-4
Sidney, Philip 17, 44, 76, 78, 116, 147,
   157, 158, 159, 161, 162, 163, 164,
   166, 213, 215
An Apology for Poetry 159
The Arcadia 164
Astrophil and Stella,163-4,
Defence of Poesie 159

St Bartholomew's Day massacre 19

Songes and Sonettes (Tottel) 160
Southwark, 81, 223
Spenser, Edward 16, 76, 82, 160, 162,
165
Stafford Castle 111
Stamford 177, 178, 232
Stationers' Company 107
Stationers' Register 118
Stewart, Alan 124, 164
Stoke Newington 24, 134-7, 140, 143
Strange's Men 230
Stratford-upon-Avon, 7, 8, 43, 62, 64-
   7, 167-8, 171-3, 199-200, 206, 214,
   221
Strype, John 234
Sudeley Castle 111
Surrey, Earl of 160, 165
Sylvanus 91-5, 172, 232

'Tale of Hemetes the Heremyte' 151,
154-5
Tarantino, Quentin 203
Taylor, Neil 204-5, 209, 213
Theatre, The 174, 231
Thompson, Ann 204-5, 209, 213
Thorpe, Thomas 192-4
'To his coy mistress' 107
Tottel, Richard 160
Tower of London 10, 20, 233
travelling players 167, 181
Trinity College, Cambridge 120, 136
Trinity College, Oxford 187, 188
Tristram, Sir 82
Triton 66-7
Troylus and Cresseid 160
Turberville, George 74-6, 161
Tyndale, William 159

Vénerie de Jacques du Fouilloux, La
74
Vendler, Helen 196
Venice 81, 165-6, 182

Walsingham, Francis 116, 146, 232
Walthamstow 26-7, 44, 151
Wanstead 232

Warwick 5, 7, 13, 19, 35-6, 57, 91,
    136, 142, 146, 172, 230
Warwick, Earl of 7, 20, 91, 136, 142,
146, 230
Wedgnock Park 84-5, 226
Wells, Stanley 199, 214
Whetstone, George 74, 161, 261
Whitgift, Archbishop 120
wild man, 46, 49-51, 53, 170, 221
Willis, Robert 199
Wilson, Robert 172
Wilson, Thomas 122, 126, 159
Wilton, Arthur, Lord Grey of 197,
232
Winchester 135, 145

Windsor 10, 24, 35, 150, 221
Windsor Castle. 10, 221
Woodstock 35, 111, 114, 116, 121,
    149, 151
Worcester 111, 126, 127, 167, 171
Wotton, Edward 160
Woudhuysen, H. R. 76

York 136, 140
Yorke, Rowland 34

Zabeta 86, 94, 100, 130, 140, 149,
172, 229, 231
Zuccaro, Federico 10, 20, 43

Printed in Great Britain
by Amazon